CHARLES NAPIER
FRIEND AND FIGHTER

GENERAL SIR CHARLES NAPIER
From an engraving by G. J. Stodart of a picture by Edwin Williams

CHARLES NAPIER

FRIEND AND FIGHTER

1782–1853

by

ROSAMOND LAWRENCE

★

LONDON

JOHN MURRAY, ALBEMARLE STREET, W.

First published 1952

Printed in Great Britain by Butler & Tanner Ltd., Frome and London
and published by John Murray (Publishers) Ltd.

CONTENTS

ILLUSTRATIONS

PREFACE

MANY can remember the days of Hero Worship, when from the indistinguishable mass certain beings stood like caryatids bearing the world upon their heads. But to youth of to-day such Hero Worship seems unknown, relating only to mass hysteria by the arrival, let us say, of some film star to England—no more, no less. So it may not be without interest to look back on that forgotten emotion, to capture some of the romance and fabulous tales surrounding those heroes in an aura. Is it possible that the contemplation of those super-men, in spite of their eccentricities, did have repercussions on the lives of others?

Impeccable they were not. Far from it. Their eccentricities were sometimes ridiculous ... and yet there is a certain grandeur, a nobility about their actions in direct contradiction to those of that inescapable contemporary figure the Common Man, the Little Man. Compared with his puny vision, his new earth of theory and planning, his dreary rain-coat and squashy hat, I say boldly of those others:

" I see them walking in an Air of Glory."

So to escape from that Common Man who meets us on the pages of our newspapers, who bleats at us from the radio, Sir Charles Napier will do well enough as a symbol of those heroic types.

" A wayward life of adventure," he describes his life, and that indeed it was ! A life that glowed with love and war, and endless disputes, and furious rows with his superiors over the rights of the private soldier, whose champion he became : a life pulsating as embers when blown upon by bellows, till they blaze into flame ! There was a kind of bravura about this old warrior who was given his first commission at twelve ! He inspired wherever he went either admiration or fury.

Was Charles Napier really a hero?

There are divergent views.

But G. M. Trevelyan has said that we are fitting our ancestors into a modern category which did not exist in their day, and that some bias may actually be an aid in understanding their passions.

So the writer of this book, kinswoman to Charles Napier, admits to affectionate bias.

As one would imagine, he himself was an ardent hero-worshipper. Invariably he spoke of the Duke of Wellington as " The Duke ", as though there were no other. His feeling for that great and ill-used soldier Sir John Moore was even stronger, and strongest of all was his admiration for his own parents, Colonel the Honourable George Napier, and Lady Sarah. Indeed, it is in his intimate correspondence with his mother that Charles reveals his own character.

In turn, he became a hero himself. Not only to the schoolboy because of his gallant deeds, wounds, escapes, shipwrecks, his tales of love and war, but as the man who, though *Punch* was responsible, yet was *supposed* to have made the pun " Peccavi— I have Scinde ", the man to whom Wellington appealed to save India, the man of whom Carlyle wrote : " A fiery lynx-eyed man with the spirit of an old knight in him more than in any modern I have ever met." But, greater than all, he was the hero to the private soldier, to whom few had hitherto given a thought. His despatches after the conquest of Sind were the very first to mention their names, and these names were kept from the public. At a complaint in the House of Lords months after, Lord Ripon said he " had forgotten ". " *Forgotten !* " Charles's statue in Trafalgar Square bears witness to the affection he inspired. There it is recorded : " Erected by public subscription, the most numerous contributors being Private Soldiers."

From old letters, and his journal, from living in his Government House at Karachi, and wandering over his battlefields, from talking to Sindis and Baluchis to whom Sir Charles was still a living presence, this book has been written.

As a plant to be successfully transplanted needs its surrounding soil moved with it, the writer has, in transplanting Charles to the present century, brought along Anastasia, his family, his soldiers—yes, and Red Rover, too.

CHAPTER I

ANTECEDENTS

1575–1671

CHARLES JAMES NAPIER was born on the 10th of
August, 1782, at Whitehall. The very word Whitehall
strikes attention. Royal blood it was that ran so rapidly through
his veins, though he himself once described Charles I as a bad
king, a bad soldier and a bad man. But it was Charles II
who had created his son by Louise de Keroualle the Duke of
Richmond and Lennox, allowing him to bear the Royal Arms
with a wreath of roses around the shield instead of the usual bar
sinister.

On his father's side Charles was descended from John Napier,
the inventor of logarithms, whose son had married the sister of
Montrose. Their son had lost all his lands fighting for Charles I.
At the Restoration he claimed them and was offered in exchange
a Dukedom without revenue. He refused, and died destitute.
Those confiscated estates were all the ground covered by the new
town of Edinburgh right up to the tower of Merchistoun, the
ancestral home of the Napiers. The inheritance would have
been great.

But though the Napiers themselves were desperately poor it
seems as though Charles's ancestors and relations were drawn in
with a brilliant and fanciful gilded pencil, as though to excite
our interest. He was the great-great-grandson of Charles II;
the son of the frank and fascinating Lady Sarah Lennox,
who twice refused to marry George III; thus nephew to the
Duke of Richmond and second cousin to Charles James Fox.
Great houses loomed behind him in all their feudal splendour.

Castletown, Leinster House (now the seat of the Dail), Holland House, Goodwood, and so forth.

So in these meagre days it is pleasant to picture the surroundings in which Lady Sarah, Charles's mother, was brought up. She was born to magnificence. Her childhood and girlhood were spent in establishments where distinguished and highly educated men and women met: statesmen, politicians, wits and divines, men and women familiar with crowned heads and the Courts of Europe. It is pleasant to picture the great coaches bearing crests and coats of arms; to wander in imagination down corridors on whose walls hang portraits of ancestors; to picture routs and balls and dinner-parties, with an array of powdered footmen standing behind the chairs . . . and if some feel disposed to sneer at this powder, let us remember that Algernon Cecil writes: "Yet powder, if it has its right, might quite as well be taken for a revolutionary decoration. The ladies who wore it at Versailles on the eve of the Revolution were, after all, enthusiastically reading their Rousseau, and Robespierre had his hair in powder when in due course he sent them to the guillotine."

These great houses had their obligations. There were, of course, bad owners ready to gamble away their inheritance in a night, but there were others also who fulfilled their exacting duties. Charles's own uncle, the twentieth Earl of Kildare, for instance, was the most popular man in all Ireland when he was Lord Chief Justice. Crowds blocked the roads when he drove abroad in his coach and six, and if his wife, Lady Emily, did wear a sack and diamonds of an afternoon, yet the ladies of the household and the gentlemen, too, attended the daily prayers held each morning by the resident chaplain. Life was a life of splendour and state, of etiquette and responsibility, rather than of ostentation and mere pleasure seeking.

Young Charles, like his great ancestor Henry of Navarre, was intolerant of pomp and ostentation, maintaining they belonged to those who feel without them they would have nothing that would impress respect. He was to become, as we shall see, a radical in thought and ways, but nevertheless, from his earliest days, Romance shone about his head like a golden nimbus.

For behind him was not only his mother's royal romance, but the fairy-like tale of her parents' marriage. The young Lord March was brought from school to cancel a gambling debt by marriage with little Lady Sarah Cadogan, still in the nursery. At Richmond House a clergyman was present, and the two young things were told they were to be married. Dumbly the little girl hung her head, but the lad exclaimed in indignant alarm : " Surely they won't marry me to that dowdy ! " But they did. A post-chaise stood ready waiting and the Lord March was hurried away by his tutor for the Grand Tour. He was away three years, and with such disagreeable recollections of his wife that instead of joining her that first evening he went off to the opera. Between the acts he amused himself by studying the company, and spying an exquisite young creature, turned eagerly to the man beside him, demanding to know who she was. " You must be a stranger to London if you don't know the beautiful Lady March, the standing toast of the town ! " was the astonishing reply.

This fairy-like tale ended as all fairy-tales should. They lived happily ever after. How constantly Horace Walpole refers to the passionate and enduring love of the pair. She was said to have been with child no less than twenty-two times, but to the end she retained her beauty, and died of a broken heart within a year of her husband.

It seems inevitable that such a couple should bear distinguished and romantic children. They did.

Lady Caroline eloped with Henry Fox, the son of old Stephen Fox, who founded Chelsea Hospital because " he could not bear to see the old soldiers who had spent their strength in our service beg at our doors ". Lady Caroline became the mother of Charles James Fox.

Lady Emily was the wife of the Duke of Leinster. She took great interest in the new ideas floating about the air. She offered a refuge to Rousseau, and she became the mother of the brilliant young Lord Edward FitzGerald, whose life ended so tragically from lockjaw whilst under sentence of death for treason.

But it is with Lady Sarah Lennox, the mother of our hero, that we are concerned. For a biography to be truthful it should surely describe the steps by which a man climbs—the seed no less than the fruit. Charles almost worshipped his mother all his life. To the writer, at least, the events of her girlhood do suggest a possible reason for the eccentricities of her famous son, his endless rows with authorities, with the Directors of the East India Company, with the Horse Guards. Not so much a pride of birth and his background of important and influential people, which might give a natural poise and good opinion of himself (as he undoubtedly had), but rather the suspicion that the same arts and intrigues of politicians were secretly gnawing at him, just as the arts and intrigues of politicians and councillors had gnawed away at George III's passionate desire to marry that trustful, honest child of fifteen, Lady Sarah Lennox.

Therefore the tale of Lady Sarah must be told before we tell of her famous son.

CHAPTER 2

HIS MOTHER

1744–1782

LADY SARAH had been introduced to Court life at the age of five. Her father, the Duke of Richmond, was one of the Lords of the Bedchamber to George II. The children were often taken by their French governess to see the royal family in Kensington Gardens. On one of these public days the King was promenading in state, attended by his family, on the Broad Terrace in front of the Palace, a kaleidoscope of fashion. The procession of courtiers, equerries, pages and footmen must have looked in the distance like bright confetti. Fashionable by-standers were bowing and curtsying all along the line, as the stout little old gentleman advanced. From their ranks the small Sarah burst like a squib, to the dismay of her governess. Dancing up to the King, she piped : " *Comment vous portez vous, Monsieur le Roi ? Vous avez une grande et belle maison ici, n'est-ce pas ? *" and swept him a profound curtsy.

There was an awful silence. The King stared down at the enticing little creature with the black curls and very pink cheeks, demanding who she was. He was given to fits of irritability and temper, at times shaking his fist at his courtiers. But now this saucy little maid amused him. He demanded she should be brought to the Palace, and Sarah became a constant playmate. Regularly on Monday mornings he counted out his money, and the little girl had to be there. She was fearless and gay, and when he snatched her up and pushed her down into a tall china vase, shutting down the lid, instead of terrified screams, a small voice piped : " *Marlbrouck s'en va t'en guerre . . .*"

When the Duke of Richmond died, his wife shortly following him, Sarah and two of her sisters were sent to Ireland to the elder sister, Lady Emily Kildare. Emily herself was only in her early twenties, but then, had she not attended her first London ball at the age of ten ? She was " married to the person I love best and who is the best and kindest of husbands ", and was glad to look after her three little sisters, whom she loved tenderly. They grew up, riding to hounds, learning the usual accomplishments and deportment, and later taking part in Dublin society : visiting the theatre and opera, the balls and parties, acting themselves in the succession of amateur plays which Mr. Sheridan had made so fashionable. All three had inherited their mother's beauty. Louisa had received several proposals before she was fifteen, and married the Right Honourable Thomas Conolly of Castletown. So in 1759 Sarah's pleasant life in Dublin came to an end. She was transferred to the guardianship of her eldest sister, Lady Caroline Fox, at Holland House in the fields of Kensington. With a chaperon she crossed the Irish channel to be introduced to the great world.

She was fourteen.

Happily the warmth of an affectionate heart awaited here also, for the Lennoxes were united by a strong family affection unusual in those days, and Sarah had the sparkle and fascination of an Irish girl. Lady Caroline, twenty-two years older, was ready to bestow on her the love of a mother. She herself had eloped with her " dear Mr. Fox " and he was devoted to her, as indeed he was to their two sons, Stephen and Charles James, both at Eton. All young people were fond of the indulgent Paymaster, as he of them. A story is told how on one occasion, having promised Charles James to watch the destruction of a wall, and finding to the boy's chagrin it had been pulled down in his absence, this foolishly fond father caused it to be rebuilt so that he should not be disappointed.

So Sarah was quickly " My Dearest Sal ", " My Sweetest Sal ", and was welcomed with open arms just as his other niece, Lady Susan Fox-Strangways, was always welcome at Holland

House. These two girls became inseparable. Apart for a day, they had to correspond at length, a correspondence that was to last for nearly sixty years ! In these early letters Sarah reveals her whole self, and from them we learn her reactions to the King's courtship, which was so soon to set the whole of Society buzzing, and raise Mr. Fox's ambitions to fever pitch.

It was natural that King George II, hearing of Sarah's return to London, should express a wish to meet his little playmate of eight years before.

Lady Caroline took her to Court, and led the young Irish beauty forward to present her. Sarah made her deep curtsy, and when she rose the King began to tease and even romp with her as though she still were a sprightly little child. Sarah shrank back, colouring up, and completely silent. Abruptly the King turned away, exclaiming in a rough rude voice : " Pooh ! She's become quite stupid."

Poor Sarah's discomfiture was so great that it excited general sympathy, and at that moment the young Prince George first saw her. " And between admiration and pity formed an attachment that endured his whole life : that he raved of her even in his madness."

At once he came forward and tried to make amends for his grandfather's offensive manners.

At this old Fox was delighted, and for the next fifteen months was ceaselessly to speak of the young prince's behaviour and its significance. But when Sarah was an old woman she wrote : " I was not near fifteen when my poor head began to be turned by adulation in consequence of my supposed favour. I ought to have been in the nursery, and I shall ever think it was unfair to bring me into the world a child."

Sarah and Susan, bound together by ties of love no less than cousinship, went constantly to the balls and receptions at St. James's Palace after the death of George II, and gleefully Mr. Fox noted in his diary how the King took every opportunity of conversing with Lady Sarah. All impressed upon her she should feel highly flattered. Of course she was. But the

King, though amiable and handsome enough, with his fair skin and blue eyes, was mighty dull for a high-spirited girl. Sarah found better entertainment with her cousins, Stephen and Charles James Fox. Together they rode, and danced, and acted in those innumerable plays in which Sarah took the lead, which Charles was for ever staging, and which in after years he declared had trained him as an orator. Much more diverting, this, than laboured conversation with his Majesty, every eye watching. " Her mind ", writes her guardian, " was still on her dogs, her squirrels, and the childish pursuits and amusements of her age."

The young King had never spoken to her alone till Twelfth Night, at a ball to which only a very few had been invited. Hitherto the halting conversations had been on the ways of kings, and on the parks, and more especially how to connect Holland Park to the Palace, but this night he took her into the Tea-room and turned the conversation upon her life in Ireland.

" Tell me about your sister's household. Does Lady Emily or Lord Kildare govern ? Either a husband or a wife must take the lead."

" I think any husband who allowed his wife to govern would be very foolish," announced this young woman of fourteen ; and then, incredibly, she added : " Everyone says you are governed by your mother."

" And do you not think parents are the best people to govern ? "

" Yes, sometimes. But a German woman is not the best person to govern the King of England."

Her daring takes one's breath away. Is it a wonder that, with such a mother, in years to come her Charles did not mince words when his feelings were aroused ?

And presently the King was asking her to agree to some trifle to which she was opposed.

" No," replied the chit. " It would be telling an untruth."

" But you would not mind telling a white lie ? "

" Yes, I would, sire."

Instead of taking offence the King was afterwards to say that he liked " her so much for her frankness and guilelessness ".

On February 19th, 1761, both Sarah and her beloved cousin, Susan Fox-Strangways, went to Court.   Between the quadrilles and minuets the King, after staring at Sarah, singled out Susan and the following conversation took place.

" You are going into Somersetshire.   When do you return ? " asked the King.

" Not before winter, sir, and I don't know how soon in winter," replied Lady Susan.

" Is there nothing that would bring you back before winter ? " continued the King searchingly.

" I don't know of anything."

" Would you not like to see a coronation ? "

" Yes, sir.   I should hope to see that."

" I hear it is very popular my having put it off.   It would be still better if ladies walked.   Won't it be a much finer sight when there is a Queen ? "

" To be sure, sir."

" I have a great many applications from abroad, but I don't like any of them.   I have had none at home.   I should like that better."   Then he added meaningly : " What do you think of your friend ?   You know whom I mean.   Don't you think her fittest ? "

Lady Susan stammered in confusion : " Think, sir ? "

" There will be no coronation till there is a Queen, and I think your friend is the fittest person for it.   *Tell your friend* I think there is none so fit."

With these words the King rose and crossing to Lady Sarah, who was seated by her chaperon, bade her ask Lady Susan what he had been saying, adding slowly : " Make her tell you all."

Lady Susan lost no time in doing this.   Henry Fox was much elated.   He saw himself governing England through his niece, though he already recognised that Lord Bute was personally and politically averse to the marriage for fear of losing his great influence over the King, and would do all he could to prevent it. But Sarah was lively and very young. To be flattered by the King's attentions, and the importance it gave her amongst the ladies, was vastly agreeable, but that did not mean she wished to have the King for husband ! Indeed, she was far too much occupied with Lord Newbattle even to contemplate such a thing. Now Mr. Fox described the Newbattle affair as " a commerce in vanity, not of love ", and he went so far as to forbid the young man to Holland House, but had the chagrin of knowing the young people were meeting in secret.

Under his parents' direction, Lord Newbattle wrote a letter lamenting that all must be at an end, and Mr. Fox tells us with relief that that day Sarah went to Court. But she arrived much out of humour. Indeed, she had been crying all morning.

At once the King went to her side.

" Have you seen your friend lately ? " he asked her eagerly.

" Yes."

" Did she tell you of my conversation with her ? "

" Yes, sire."

" And what do you think of it ? "

" *Nothing, sire.*"

" Nothing comes of nothing," exclaimed the King, greatly vexed. Sarah looked cross and made no reply.

Even one as infatuated as the King must have resented such bad manners. Sarah was packed off in disgrace to her brother, the Duke of Richmond.

There the meetings with Lord Newbattle began again. " The Jade ", as now her vexed guardian was calling her, was sent on into Somersetshire to the Ilchesters, parents of her beloved Lady Susan Fox-Strangways. They could be trusted to press the King's suit.

Now the irrepressible Sarah liked nothing better than following hounds and one day, returning from Longleat, her horse " put his foot on a stone which broke ". She fell, fracturing her leg.

She was attended to by the local surgeon, who declared her to be " the most agreeable and merry patient he had ever met with ", and the following day the spirited young woman was brought back to Redlinch "upon men's shoulders in a very pretty bed made of branches for this purpose, singing a great part of the way ".

All Sarah's family came thronging to her bedside. Mr. Conolly and dear kind Lady Louisa from Dublin, Lady Kildare, the Duke and Duchess of Richmond, even her schoolboy nephew, Charles James Fox, though as he fancied himself in love with Lady Susan, she, not Sarah, may have been the attraction. Mutually affectionate as all the family of Lennox were, it is more than possible they conspired to point out to this wilful girl the dazzling prospect of becoming Queen. Lord Newbattle had made no enquiry after her it seems, but the King had " trembled in agony, and had not the impropriety of such a proceeding been strongly urged he would instantly have set forth to visit her ".

Lying helpless on her couch, Lady Sarah could reflect on the difference in the character of her two lovers, and the King lost nothing by the comparison. The very man for whom she had refused a throne had made a jest of her sufferings, " while he whose present comfort and happiness she had injured, if not ruined, by that refusal was all heart and sorrow and ready to fly to her assistance ", though he had been prevented as it would have been a breach of royal etiquette. He had begged to know if she were in good hands, and as Lady Sarah only remained at Redlinch for some six weeks, and one reflects on the long periods spent in modern orthopædic hospitals, it seems Mr. Clarke of Bruton must have been a clever surgeon, for " her injury was very well healed in that time ".

Lord Newbattle was no more thought of. Her girlish attachment was completely cured. She had the tenderest heart herself, and the kindness of the King had undoubtedly made a great impression on her, and all the while there was the insidious pressure of all those whom she so dearly loved. Even kind Lady Louisa, who at first had set her face against such a match, now commented : " She won't look cross at the King when she sees him next week."

She returned for the King's birthday ball. Horace Walpole wrote that " it exceeded the splendours of Haroun Al Raschid and the Arabian Nights, when people had nothing to do but scour a lantern and send for a genie for a hamper of diamonds and rubies ". He goes on to describe Sarah in detail, ending up : " she has better white and red than if she were made of pearls and rubies. The King devoted himself to her ", but let us quote again :

" Her place was of course at the head of the dancers' bench nearest his seat (she was not yet dancing because of her broken leg). So the royal chair was moved by degrees more and more to the left and he who sate thereon edged and edged further the same way, and the conversation went on till all dancing was over, and everybody sate in suspense, and it approached one in the morning ere he recollected himself and rose to dismiss the assembly."

The coming match became the talk of Court and London Society. Lady Barrington, a friend of Lady Sarah's, who was famed for her beautiful back, drew her aside one day as they entered the presence chamber together, whispering : " Do, my dear Lady Sarah, let me take the lead, and go in before you this once, for you will never have another opportunity of seeing my beautiful back ! "

For the King's hopes had revived and finally, in an allusion to his first conversation, he murmured : " I hope you will think of it."

Sarah did so.

Then, we are told, " came all the arts and intrigues of reflecting courtiers, politicians and ministers, of favourites and secret influences, then arose all the German Pride and fears of Royal Blood, then envy, hatred and malice reared their secret heads, whilst outwardly they smiled and flattered ".

Sarah was not happy, as the following letter to Susan shows :

" After many pros and cons it is decided I go to-morrow " (presumably to a Drawing-room) " and that I must pluck up my spirits, and if I am asked if I have thought of it . . . or approve

. . . to look —— in the face, and with an earnest but good-humoured countenance say that *I don't know what I ought to think*. If the meaning is explained I must say ' *that I can hardly believe it* ' and so forth ; if instead of that you should be named, I shall say that you were so much confounded and astonished that you did not understand the meaning ; if the answer is ' *I hope you do understand it* ', I shall say ' *that the more I think of it the less I understand it* ' (I hope that won't be too forward). In short, I must shew I wish it to be explained without seeming to expect any other meaning ; what a task it is ! God send that I may be enabled to go through with it.

" I am allowed to mutter a little, provided the words *astonished*, *surprised*, *understand* and *meaning* are heard.

" I am working myself up to consider what depends upon it that I may me *fortifier* against it comes . . . the very thought makes me sick in my stomach already. I shall be proud as the devil . . . but no matter.

" Well to-day is come to nothing, for we were so near your namesake and her mistress (Ly. Susan Stuart and Princess Augusta) that nothing could be said, and they watched us like a cat does a mouse, but looks and smiles were very very gracious ; however I go with the Duchess Thursday, I'll put a postscript in this of it. I beg you won't show this to anybody, so pray burn it, for I can tell you things that I can't other people, you know. Adieu dear Suke.

" PS. My love if I may say so to Ld. and Ly. Ilchester, and my compliments to the rest. Pray desire Ld. Ilchester to send my mare immediately, if he don't want it, for I must ride on it at least once immediately in Richmond Park. Much depends on it.

" PS. I went Thursday, but nothing was said. I won't go jiggiting for ever if I hear nothing I can tell him."

It is painful to think of the nervous state of mind of this frank proud child of fifteen, pushed and coerced on by the people she most loved and trusted, and waiting for the culminating advances from the King which now strangely enough did not come ! Holland House of course was in the greatest suspense. Sarah had no respite allowed her. Meetings were contrived when the King would be unaccompanied by his mother and sister. Sarah was persuaded to make hay in the fields of Holland House. The Lennoxes all shared that same " glow of complexion ", and in her floppy hat, her dark curls clustering beneath its brim, in her laced bodice and kerchief and the full skirt, no doubt she would look the part of rustic better than Marie Antoinette had with her milking-pail. The King used to pull up as he rode down the great Road, dismount and converse with her.

The Court and Society could talk of little else. Mr. Fox was treading on air. Lord Bute he knew to be an enemy, the King's mother also, but surely he could not have guessed at the contents of the letter passing between Lord Bute and the King. Lord Bute was the King's " dearest Friend ". He would inevitably sink " if he did not follow the advice of his Dearest Friend " and so on. . . .

So on July 7th, 1716, Lady Sarah was writing to Lady Susan :

" To begin to astonish you as much as I was, I must tell you that the ——— is going to be married to a Princess of Mecklenburg, and that I am sure of it. There is a Council to-morrow on purpose, the orders for it are urgent and important business. Does not your chollar rise at hearing this ; but you think I daresay that I have been doing some terrible thing to deserve it, for you won't be easily brought to change so totally your opinion of any person ; but I do assure you, which I believe you will, as I know you were more set on it than I was. The thing I am most angry at, is looking so like a fool. . . . Now I charge you, dear Lady Sue, not to mention this to anybody but Lord and Lady Ilchester, and desire them not to speak of it to any mortal, for it will be said we invent storries, and he will hate us all anyway, for one generally hates people that one is in the wrong with, and that one knows one has acted wrong, and it might do a great deal of harm to all the family, and so do me no good. So pray remember this, for a secret among many people is very bad, and I must tell it some."

On July 16th she was writing :

" I went this morning for the first time. He looked frightened when he saw me ; but not withstanding came up with what countenance I don't know, for I was not so gracious as even to look at him. When he spoke our conversation was short : here it is. ' I see riding has begun again, it's glorious weather for it now.' Answer : ' Yes, it is very fine,' add to that a very cross and angry look of my side, and his turning away immediately, and you know the whole.

" The wedding will be private, but the Drawing-room after is the day to come in a fine gown, and unless you have settled it you need not I think hurry yourself to be civil, it's time enough for that. I long to see you tho'. I must go to the first Drawing-room, I shall not trouble them with my company till then ; I wonder if they will name me for train bearer, I wish they would, tho' they abuse me and call me names, for I think it the best way of seeing a Coronation. Don't shew this, but read it to your father and mother, but it's so scrawled I am ashamed even you should see it. I don't believe you can read it but it's quite dark, and I have no time to call for candles. Adieu. Yours S. Lennox."

Poor child !

In August she was writing again :

" DEAR PUSSY,

" I have only time to tell you that I have been invited to be bridesmaid and I have accepted of it. I am sorry to say it is against my sister Caroline's opinion a little ; I beg you will tell me what your opinion is. I think it is not to be looked upon as a favor but as a thing due to my rank and as a matter of course, then why refuse it and make a great talk, to be abused by those who don't know, and perhaps by those who do, for they are always in the right you know, whereas I think accepting it will not be thought by anybody either one way or tother, but looked upon as a matter of course ; those that think at all about it will say perhaps that I want spirit and pride, which is true enough, for I don't dislike it in the least, and I don't like to

15

affect what I don't feel, tho' ever so right . . . Mr. Fox said it depended on my feel about it and Lord Kildare is violently for it, and my sister Kildare rather for it than otherwise. I hope you will too, but you have the happiness of having a proper pride, which I am not endowed with. I was always of opinion that the less fuss or talk there is the better, and to let it drop to the world. But to him and his sisters, I was and always will be as high and grave as possible; for I think the least flirting would ruin my character quite. But this is not his doing, he only sees the list, for others make it. Adieu.

> " Yours,
> " S. Lennox."

What an astonishingly sensible letter for a girl of fifteen !

Henry Holland was writing in his memoirs : " To many a girl H.M.'s behaviour had been very vexatious, but Lady Sarah's temper and affection are happily so flexible and light that the sickness of her squirrel immediately took up all her attention, and when in spite of her nursing it dyed, I believe it gave her more concern than H.M. ever did," and later, writing to his brother Lord Ilchester, he adds :

" The squirrel is dead, and which is worse the pretty horse Beau. Lady Sarah to comfort her has a young hedgehog which breakfasted with us to-day. She bought it yesterday and continues to kiss it much."

It is possible the wily old Fox was eager to minimise Sarah's smart, conscious of the part he had played in the affair. Half angry, half joking, he said to her : " Well, Sal, you are the first vargin in England, and you shall take your place in spite of them all as chief bridesmaid and the King shall behold your pretty face and repent."

Perhaps Sarah was not too grieved that when the Archbishop pronounced these words . . . " As Thou didst send Thy blessing upon Sarah and Abraham to their great comfort " that the King's face darkened, and the congregation shifted in their seats. " During the wedding service on mention of Abraham and Sarah the King could not conceal his confusion," wrote Walpole. But worse was to follow.

All the young bridesmaids were drawn up in a line near her Majesty; Lady Sarah, as premier bridesmaid, at the head of the line and her cousin Lady Susan at the end. " Lady Sarah the chief angel. Nothing ever looked so charming as Lady Sarah. She was very richly dressed. Lord Westmorland, the old Jacobite who had never consented to appear at Court since the Hanovers had succeeded, passing before Lady Sarah fell on his knees and lifted her hand to kiss it. Blushing deeply she exclaimed : ' I am not the Queen, sir ', and in the laughter and talk that followed the incident George Selwyn exclaimed : ' O ! You know he has always loved Pretenders ! ' "

CHAPTER 3

YOUTH

1782–1808

LADY SARAH married the elegant Charles Bunbury, owner of the first Derby winner. He neglected her for his sporting friends, but Sarah held her head high, pretending great happiness though her guardian pityingly called her "The Widow". Eventually she eloped with Lord William Gordon, that strange and erratic charmer. At length her husband divorced her, though still giving his name to Lord William's child. But Sarah had not found what she sought. After only three months she had left Lord William, and gone to live in the park at Goodwood under the disapproving eye of the Duke. By her own wish this young woman who had dazzled London and Paris society with her wit, her warm heart and her beauty, lived in complete obscurity with the little Louisa for eight years! Finally she met the real love of her heart, Colonel Napier, a penniless widower six years younger than herself; penniless because after serving with distinction in the American War he was smitten with fever on the voyage home, and as his condition was considered hopeless his commission had been sold over his unconscious body for the benefit of his infant daughter! Colonel Napier was a remarkable man, friend and pupil of David Hume, and of great physical beauty and strength; but his views were far too radical and outspoken for him ever to be a worldly success, and as a younger son of the late Lord Napier he had inherited nothing. It was not strange that the Duke objected to the marriage, but this time Lady Sarah pleased herself. The marriage was to prove one of those Richmond marriages of

18

COLONEL THE HON. GEORGE NAPIER
From a pastel portrait in the possession of Mrs. Wynne-Roberts

enduring affection, as had been that of Sarah's parents, and Sarah's sisters, and to become as famous even as theirs had been.

Charles was their eldest son. He was only three when the Napiers went to settle at Celbridge, a small town outside Dublin. Poor though they were, their solid house, with its many tall windows looking away to the Wicklow mountains, was quite close to Castletown and Carton, and the boys had the run of the park, the shooting and fishing, and all the comings and goings in the two great houses of the Conollys and the Kildares. Lady Sarah had no carriage, but she had always possessed the gift of adapting herself to any circumstances with humour and dignity. We know she did not envy her sisters in the very least; her heart had recovered its greenness, and the enduring affection of her " Donny " and her brood of lively boys appealed far more than great houses, or the dazzle of English and French courts —though rainy Irish weather was hard to bear !

The three boys had to go to the village school instead of the expensive seminary close by. Occasionally they would burst out ahead of their comrades, scramble on to the backs of the gaunt tall hogs of the village, and go careering down the single street, followed by their yelling schoolmates. These Napiers were "Heretics" of course, grandsons of a Duke, and supporters of the detested Government, but they were always ready to fight the boys of the favoured Protestant school, and to the peasants they seemed one of themselves.

It is unlikely that Charles and his brothers learned much at that village school, beyond the priceless gift of being good mixers. But their own house was crammed with books. We know that Lady Sarah was reading the *Iliad* for her own pleasure at the age of fifteen, and their father, that constant companion, was exceptionally well read. The boys were brought up on Plutarch's *Lives*, the *Iliad* and the *Odyssey*. They learned from the *Iliad* " Glory is never where virtue is not ". They were taught to be proud of their family motto : " *Sans tache* ". It was instilled into them that the mark of a gentleman was to be courteous to servants and kind to animals, to be contemptuous

19

of pomp and show, and to be brave. And what boy could resist a father so strong that he could take a quart pot and crush it flat as a sheet of paper in his hand?

Charles was often ailing, having been dropped in infancy by his nurse, but passionately from the earliest age this child longed for military glory. Tales come down of his courage and determination even at the age of six.

At Castletown there turned up a travelling showman. He must have been a Caliban sort of creature, short but with huge limbs, matted red hair and a terrifying voice. . . . This ogre balanced a ladder on his chin, and bellowed out to a sweep to climb up the ladder and seat himself on top. The boy shrank away terrified, hiding himself in the onlookers. Colonel Napier looked down from his great stature to his diminutive little son. "Will you, Charles?" Charles was silent. Suddenly he looked up at his idol. "Yes!" And amongst delighted cheers the little boy climbed.

Another tale is that Charles, having caught a fish, the half-tamed but very fierce eagle swooped on to his shoulder, eclipsing him with its beating great wings, and snatched the fish from him. When Charles, this meagre little boy of eleven, had caught another fish, he held it high in the air, pointing the spear end of his rod and *daring* the eagle to pounce again. In relating this incident in after years, Sir William writes: "Plutarch would have drawn an omen from such an event."

For William adored Charles, as Charles adored William. They delighted to see in each other the glittering heroes with whom they lived in thought. Hannibal, Hamilcar, Sertorius, Alexander the Great and so on. We smile, but somehow all the doings of this family *did* seem touched by romantic fire! How beautiful they were! How talented! How indomitable!

Their father's sister, Hester Johnson, was one of their favourite aunts. Round her neck she had always worn in a golden locket the heart of the great Montrose, for the latter's brother-in-law had collected it with the other remains after Montrose had been drawn and quartered before his burial in St. Giles' Cathedral at Edinburgh. But more than this. Aunt Johnson had accompanied her husband to India, and their ship, an Indiaman, had been attacked by one of Souffrien's frigates. Aunt Johnson had been urged to go below, but her husband had taken his post at a gun, and she declared : " No wife should quit her husband in danger. Here will I stay and take my chance," and stay she did, with the hand of their five-year-old child clasped in hers. A shot splintered the deck, striking down all three. The child and mother were wounded, and the gold case containing the heart of Montrose broken on her breast. There were other tales, too, of how their handsome aunt, armed with pistol, had once defended her sick husband in the desert, and it was this same Aunt Johnson who poured into little Charles's impressionable mind accounts of fraud and oppression committed by the East India Company. May these tales have had something to do with the suspicions and enmity with which Charles was to regard the Directors of the East India Company in after life ?

At the ripe age of twelve young Charles received a commission in the 33rd Regiment commanded by Lieut.-Colonel Arthur Wellesley, thus beginning his career of sixty years of army life ! One can imagine the pride of this little fellow whose passion from almost babyhood had been the reading of military history.

Soon he was transferred to the 89th, to Netley Camp, where his father was Assistant Quarter-Master, and there under Colonel Napier, whose constant companion he had always been, the little boy became acquainted with military life, its *esprit de corps*, its haunting bugle calls. When the camp broke up for foreign service, Charles was considered too young. He returned to Ireland, exchanged into the 4th Regiment on half pay, but to his great chagrin because of his youth was sent to the large Celbridge school as a day boy. What could he have in common with schoolboys ? We are told he bore himself as though conscious he were an officer, but this was not resented. When it became clear that trouble was coming, this boy of fourteen organised his school-mates into a corps of volunteers, the others willingly accepting him as their leader, even though some were approaching manhood. Now how did it come about that this slight serious lad got together these boys, all Catholics, all opposed to the Government he was upholding, and moreover succeeded in persuading their parents to provide uniforms, drums, flags and fusils? Was it only that he was a born leader, or did they perhaps salute the "Irishry" in him that had ridden the hogs down the village street?

Even at that early age Charles had recognised that "the greatest secret of war is discipline". It happened that two of the small volunteers were insubordinate under arms, and one was Charles's much loved younger brother. Nevertheless, William was seized, tried by a drumhead court martial and sentenced! Not submitting to punishment he was drummed out of the corps. A fight with others followed, wherein William was badly hurt. Charles remained apparently unmoved, but at home in the evening he was undone, offering to his little brother all his greatest treasures. How like him in after life! Stern, and yet compassionate at the same time.

In 1798 the rebellion broke out in earnest, and the Napiers found themselves at the storm centre, for Lady Sarah's nephew, Lord Edward FitzGerald, was the chief leader of the "United Irishmen" and influenced the whole country. In many ways both Lady Sarah and her husband had sympathy with the rebels, but Colonel Napier was a soldier, and she a soldier's wife. Instead of leaving Celbridge he fortified the Hall, armed his five sons, and awaited attack. Later he commanded a band of militia, and through the night he combed the countryside, young Charles of course beside him. The suspense, the darkness, the soft damp Irish airs blowing on his cheek, how these must have thrilled the child—for he was little more. Once they came unexpectedly upon an armed force. Both bodies halted. Colonel Napier gave a test military order lest the dark half-seen shapes might possibly be friends. "At that moment the moon shone out, and Charles Napier, very diminutive for his age, was seen with his small fusil charging bayonets in opposition to Tim Sullivan, the biggest man of the Cork Militia. Tim looked down in astonishment an instant, and then catching his small foe up in his arms kissed him."

Even in the years before, Charles and his brothers had seen the cruelty and horror of civil war. There were informers and subsequent murders by their infuriated countrymen. They had seen labourers in the fields wantonly shot by passing soldiers. On the other hand, houses were nightly attacked in a search for arms. On one occasion Celbridge House was surrounded by several hundred " Defenders " as they were called. Colonel Napier and his wife were away. Old Susan Frost, Charles's nurse, had collected the children in one room and she herself stood at the door armed with pistols. The old man-servant was constantly fired at as he passed from room to room. There was a deep area which acted as protection, but the Defenders got hold of a beam and began battering away at the door. Then old Lauchlin did want to surrender the arms. " No, no ! Never ! Never ! " cried Susan. " Let them take what they can . . ."

With such experiences behind him Charles was already a man in mind when he took up his military duties at seventeen. Used as we are to the lads of to-day chafing at the interruption of their careers by two years' conscription, it is hard to realise that Charles and his brothers considered their soldiering as a vocation. George got his commission at fifteen and writing thirty years later he still remembered the tears in his mother's eyes as she set on his head the shining helmet with its motto : " Death or Glory ".

Looking back over Charles's life it seems to consist of bursts of intense action with intermissions of waiting . . . waiting . . . though perhaps waiting is not the correct word, for ever he was possessed as by some demon who would not let him rest, driving him on to fresh and new efforts of mind, if he could not employ his body. That restless spirit could not have endured the coming years of garrison life had he not foreseen in his secret soul a jewel of military glory, however far off. For what had those days to do with the visions of his childhood where heroes walked " in an air of glory " ?

Already he was troubled at the general conditions of the

private soldier; and the flogging in the army appalled him. There had always been great freedom and affection between himself and his father, and he was desperately home-sick. He writes constantly to his mother. The Peace of Amiens seemed to put an end to his military ambitions. " Sometimes my thought is to sell my commission and purchase one in Germany, if my secret wish cannot be fulfilled, which is to have high command with British soldiers. Rather let me command Esquimaux than be a subaltern of forty years old." Or again :

" Last night I sat up till two o'clock writing on the old subject of grievances and lashing myself into a fury with everything. Abusing the army, pulling off my breeches, cursing creditors and putting out the candle all in a minute, I jumped into bed and lay there blaspheming, praying and perspiring for two hours when sleep came . . . I live in fear of my creditors but that shall not last. I will not be a tailor's slave . . ."

From the description of his clothes he could hardly be that ! He was unable to go to London because he " had no coloured clothes ", and they are expensive to buy. He does get to London but the coloured clothes seem to have been at the expense of his uniform, for Lady Sarah learns " my pantaloons are green and I have only one pair ; my jacket twice turned, a green waistcoat useless, one pair of boots without soles or heels, a green feather and a helmet not worth sixpence ".

It must be remembered that Charles was now a very agreeable-looking young man with a heart like tinder. His connections made it more than ordinarily difficult for him to make both ends meet. Lady Sarah had always been deeply attached to Charles James Fox, and Charles was seeing much of his cousin and presumably being influenced by his politics. Nevertheless brother William and he were also often at Mr. Pitt's house ! William writes : " Mr. Pitt used to come home rather exhausted and seemed to require wine, port, of which he generally drank a bottle, or nearly so, in a rapid succession of glasses, but when he recovered his strength from this stimulant he ceased to drink. . . ." But what shows the easy terms of familiarity on which these boys were, William relates how Lady Hester Stanhope and Charles and James Stanhope on one occasion were blackening the resisting minister's face with burnt cork, when the servant announced that Lord Castlereagh and Lord Liverpool desired to see him on business. "Let them wait in the other room," said Mr. Pitt, and seizing a cushion began attacking his young tormentors. After a ten-minute fight they got him down. "Stop! This will do. I could easily beat you all, but we must not keep these grandees waiting." A basin was brought, Mr. Pitt was washed and towelled, and then William tells us of his surprise to see the two Lords "bending like spaniels" before the man they themselves had been maltreating, and how Mr. Pitt finally stiffly dismissed them "and turning to us with a laugh caught up his cushion and renewed the fight".

This sort of thing was all right for William, so wild with animal spirits and health, but it did not satisfy Charles. Proud and poor, he was chafing at the chain. "I am now anxious to return to Chatham, having no uniform here, and coloured clothes make me ashamed to look a Coldstreamer in the face."

In these letters mother and son speak to each other in a colloquy utterly loving and understanding. When he was twenty-five he was writing from Ashford : "Our men have got the ophthalmia * very badly, and are dying fast also from inflammation of the lungs, caused by coldness of the weather and bad barracks . . . in some cases typhus supervenes. There is no raging fever, cold alone is the cause. Men go off three or four a day ; no officer suffers, they are warmer. You have of course, dear mother, by this time got my lungs into a high state of inflammation, and put out both my eyes : you shall be duly informed when the typhus begins. . . ."

So ran his letters, a mixture of fun and facts, mixed up with

---

* For long this ophthalmia baffled the medical officers—it was then found a soldier had taught the men to hold their eyelids open, while others scraped lime from the barrack ceiling into them. Inflammation was industriously kept up. "Many hundreds of the finest men were lost to the service."

reflections on politics and life in general, and the histories and biographies he was reading; but already the condition of the private soldier was beginning to obsess him : " The soldiers have got pneumonia at Hythe and are dying as fast as we folks at Ashford. Only think of the surgeons taking from one man, in twenty-four hours, one hundred and sixty ounces of blood, and he is recovering. They say bleeding to death is the best way of saving them ! "

Colonel Napier in the meantime had died of consumption, brought by unceasing toil at his desk to provide for his family, after being accustomed to an active and outdoor life.

The sons had always regarded their father as quite exceptional, not only for his integrity, his great stature and strength, but for remarkable gifts also. " None of us is his equal—I have never seen his equal," wrote Charles forty years later. Perhaps they were dazzled by affection. Nevertheless we do know that Sir Joshua Reynolds thought Colonel Napier the model of strength and beauty ; we know too that he was responsible for savings in public expenditure amounting to vast sums (to his own immense disadvantage) and that he had had the perspicacity to single out young Ensign Arthur Wellesley when others thought him a frivolous youngster. " Those who think lightly of that lad are unwise in their generation : he has in him the makings of a great general." And his own last words as he handed his watch to his beloved Sarah are certainly striking :

" Take my watch, Sarah. I am done with time."

In spite of his efforts, he had left the family in straitened circumstances. For the girls indeed there was no provision at all. Lady Sarah, by her marriage, had shown indifference to poverty, but her proud spirit would not brook debt. Celbridge was sold. Charles's precious horses were sold. Her sons rallied round her. Both Charles and George argued against seeking aid from her brother, the Duke of Richmond, and Pitt, remembering how by abolishing all fees Colonel Napier had voluntarily reduced his salary from £20,000 to £600, arranged pensions for Lady Sarah and her daughters.

Charles writes constantly to his mother, so that bowed as she is she can take hold of his strength.

He rejoined the Staff Corps at Shorncliffe Camp, where the three brothers had the good fortune to serve under Sir John Moore. William had been given a cornetcy in the Blues by his uncle, the Duke, but he had been happy to exchange his high pay for the six shillings and sixpence a day, to be with Charles and George in the 52nd under the immediate observation of Sir John at Hythe.

Lady Sarah must have taken pride in her " young animals ", as she called her sons. Did she already see them—" a Brotherhood of Heroes "—as they came to be called ? William so wild and gay with the amazing good looks he had inherited, George so kindly, so wise, and Charles—Charles best of all. Charles who was short, without his brothers' exceptionally fine looks, yet comely too, with those short-sighted brilliant dark eyes of his—yes, Charles, too, had his charm.

" If your ladyship had a dozen sons, you could not do Colonel Mackenzie or me a greater service than by sending them to the 52nd," writes Sir John Moore !

Though he had hitherto shunned the mess for reasons of poverty, Charles had delighted in society since boyhood. " My heart is a cinder, and as heat is said to cure heat, I stand by the fire all day to draw out flame ! " he had once written after describing the quick succession of beauties captivating him. . . . But here at Shorncliffe Camp, Charles was to devote most of his spare time not to these enchanting creatures, but in studying military history, engineering and all kinds of other subjects which, though they did not come strictly within his duty, were to prove invaluable in after life.

His devoted friend was Major Charles Stanhope, Pitt's nephew, little older than himself. It was of these two that Sir John Moore was to exclaim in the fire and swirling smoke of Corunna, " Well done, *my* Majors "—for Charles Napier's urgency was at last to be satisfied.

He left for the fighting in the Peninsular War in August, 1808.

CHAPTER 4

CORUNNA

1808

IN his great *History of the Peninsular War* Sir William wrote :
" The truly great and ill-used Moore was sent into the heart
of Spain by incapable ministers to find not armies, nor enthusiasm, nor energetic government, nor military aid, all of which he
had been promised, but in their stead the greatest military genius
of the world before him, with troops so numerous that their
cavalry alone doubled his whole force. It is known, also, with
what a mastery of war he extricated himself from that raging
storm ; with what a firmness he conducted his retreat ; and
how, turning at Corunna, he ended his glorious life amid the
fires of victory."

Charles, George and William were to serve under their hero :
George as his A.D.C., William with his company of the 43rd,
and Charles, owing to the absence of his Colonel, actually in
command of the 50th. He was twenty-six. He had been given
his majority at twenty-two by Charles James Fox, so one must
admit, radical though he was by temperament, he did find his
influential relations of service at times.

Before Corunna the brothers had taken part in the retreat,
terrible in its path of tragedy over ice and snow and general loss
of discipline. At Corunna itself the 50th met the greatest assault-
ing French column, driving it back with such vigour that Moore
gave instant orders to support and follow up their success. But
Moore fell. The 50th were not supported. There they were
fighting amongst lanes and vineyards and houses. They became
scattered and broken. Young Charles, far in advance, was

hidden by irregularities of ground. Thus " his desperate contention " was unobserved.

Always Charles possessed the faculty of seeing everything in
pictures. Unerringly he seized the salient points, setting them
down in unforgettable phrases so that the " not so quick "
can, too, catch fire. Here is a sample of his writing, a cameo, as
it were, from this battlefield :

" On the 16th of January, 1809, the British Army was opposed
to the French at Corunna. The Imperial troops, being on higher
ground, hung over us like threatening clouds, and about one
o'clock the storm burst. Our line was under arms, motionless,
yet all were anxious for the appearance of Sir John Moore.
There was a feeling that under him we could not be beaten, and
this was so strong at all times as to be a great cause of discontent
during the retreat wherever he was not. Where is the General ?
. . . This agitation augmented as the cries of men stricken by
cannon-shot arose . . . a heavy French column which had
descended the mountain at a run was coming on behind with
great rapidity, and shouting, ' En avant ! tue ! tue ! en avant !
tue ! ' their cannon at the same time plunging from above,
ploughed the ground and tore our ranks. Suddenly I heard
the gallop of horses and turning saw Moore. He came at speed,
and pulled up so sharp and close he seemed to have alighted
from the air, man and horse looking at the approaching foe
with an intentness that seemed to concentrate all feeling in their
eyes. The sudden stop of the animal, a cream-coloured one
with black mane and tail, had cast the latter streaming forward ;
its ears were pushed out like horns, while its eyes flashed fire,
and it snorted loudly with expanded nostrils expressing terror,
astonishment and muscular effort. My first thought was it will
be away like the wind ! but then I looked at the rider and the
horse was forgotten. Thrown on its haunches, the animal came
sliding and dashing the dirt up with its forefeet, thus bending the
General forward almost on to its neck, but his head was thrown
back, and his look more keenly piercing than I ever before saw it.
He glanced to the right and left, and then fixed his eyes intently

on the enemy's advancing column, at the same time grasping the reins with both his hands, and pressing the horse firmly with his knees; his body thus seemed to deal with the animal while his mind was intent on the enemy, and his aspect was one of searching intenseness beyond the power of words to describe; for a while he looked and then galloped to the left without uttering a word."

" A cream-coloured one with black mane and tail, its ears pushed out like horns." The picture of the horse is as vivid as of the man ! How characteristic of Charles ! Foolish some may think it, but horses were an integral part of Charles. One might describe him as " alive " to horses as some people are " alive " to religion. Throughout his letters, his journals, they gallop, they snort, they wrinkle up their noses, they live out their last days at Carton. . . . His horses.

" . . . Again Sir John Moore returned, and was talking to me when a round shot struck the ground between his horse's feet. The horse leaped round, and I also turned mechanically, but Moore forced the animal back and asked if I was hurt. 'No, Sir,' meanwhile a second shot had torn off the leg of a 42nd man who was screaming horribly and rolled about as though to excite agitation and alarm with others. The General said, 'This is nothing, my lads, keep your ranks, take that man away; my good fellow, don't make such a noise, we must bear things better.' He spoke sharply yet it had a good effect; for this man's cries had made an opening in the ranks, and the men shrank from the spot although they had not done so when others had been hit and did not cry out. Again Moore went off, and I saw him no more. It was a little in front of this place he was killed.

" The French pointed out the place to me two months later. There it was he refused to let them take off his sword when it hurt his wound ! that dreadful wound ! Poor fellow. Yet why poor fellow ? . . ."

As he continues Charles is quite frank about his own feelings, and this is interesting when we recall it was only in the first

World War men began tentatively to confess to fear and only in the second that they spoke freely.

Charles tells us that Lord William Bentinck ambled up on his mule " and though the fire was heavy began talking to me as if we were going to breakfast . . . no recollection of what he says remains, for the fire was sharp and my eyes were more busy than my ears. I only remember saying to myself, 'This chap takes it coolly or the devil's in it.' Lord William and his mule sheltered me from shot which I liked well enough, but after having heard officers and men jeer at Colonel —— for thus sheltering himself behind General ——'s horse at Vimiero I went to the exposed side ; yet it gave me the most uncomfortable feel. . . ."

But he was to experience a more " uncomfortable feel " than that !

Reading on, inevitably, we share with this young boy Major his agonising suspense, impatience, and perplexity when no orders come to advance. He walks up and down before the Regiment, for men are falling fast. He orders them to shoulder arms to occupy their minds. The colours, too, are lowered. No orders come. The 42nd advance in line. Still no orders !

" Good God, Montgomery, are we not to advance ? " he cries to a grand old Scotchman who had risen from the ranks.

" I think we ought."

" But no orders have come ! "

" I would not wait . . ." and then the old soldier added slyly, " You cannot be wrong to follow the 42nd ! "

So the young Major gives the word, but forbids firing, still making the men slope and carry arms.

" Major, let us fire," they urge.

" Not yet."

He had advanced without orders, and if he were wrong he would have the men under better control than had they started firing . . . but by and by it is, " Do you see your enemies plain enough to hit them ? "

" By Jasus, we do ! "

" *Then blaze away!* "

The firing was terrible. The howitzers too were pelting them from the hills. Charles was swearing horribly, his face badly burned, his sword-belt and scabbard shot off. The two ensigns carrying the colours fell, but these were snatched up by sergeants. Frenchmen lay about on the ground. " Bayonet them ! Bayonet them ! " screamed the soldiers. " They are pretending." But Charles revolts. " No ! No ! Leave those cowards. There are plenty who bear arms to kill. Come on ! "

Breathless we too follow Charles. We cannot see our flanks ! We had been broken in carrying the village. Charles is running forward, calling out to follow. Three officers and some thirty privates are with him—the shells bursting—the heat—the smoke —the blood—the deafening of our ears . . . and Charles *falls* ! " The Major is killed ! " " Not yet ! " He is up. " Come on ! "

Then an incident at which we sicken even as Charles sickened. Two of the men are killed by the fire of our own men from the village behind. " O God, Major, our own men are killing us. O Christ God I am shot in the back of the head." Then Charles remembers how that father of his had saved a man's life at Charleston by pulling a ball out with his fingers before inflammation swelled the part. Charles tries to do the same. His finger searches. He cannot find the ball. He fears to push his finger farther ! He sickens, lays the poor fellow down, who dies crying our own men had killed him.

" This misery shook us all a good deal, and made me wild so as to cry and stamp with rage, feeling a sort of despair at seeing the soldiers did not come on," he afterwards wrote. " Stanhope was trying to animate them and calling out, ' Good God, where is Napier ? ' When Turner told him I was in front and raging for the men to come on for an attack on the battery, he gave a shout, and called on the men to follow him, but on taking a dozen strides cried out, ' O my God ! ' and fell dead, shot through the heart."

On and on we are torn by Charles's burning words, through briars and thorns of battle. Charles leaves one Harrison with a few others whilst he himself goes to try and find out the whereabouts of the 42nd. There was an obscuring ridge with a hedge on top. Was it possible he was in line with the 42nd, and not in advance? Now flashed through his mind, if fifty men of the 42nd and 50th could be gathered " we could still charge the battery above us; if we failed there was a house near into which we could force our way, and as it was conspicuous from the English position, Moore would send me support ".

Now Charles, staggering on alone, was exposed not only to the French, but also the English, fire. . . . Later he confessed: " Being armed only with a short sabre, useless against a musket, and bayonet, and being quite alone, short-sighted, and without spectacles, I felt very cowardly and anxious."

Smeared in blood as he was, and coming on a French officer badly wounded, the latter, thinking Charles was about to kill him, signalled to others unseen. They blazed away through the roots of a hedge. Their fire passed over his head, but Charles honestly confesses: " Giving up myself for lost the temptation to run back was great, but the thought that our own line might see me made me walk leisurely back. . . ." But when he did arrive it was to find that Harrison and the others were gone! " I felt very miserable then, thinking the 50th had behaved ill; that my not getting the battery had been the cause of the battle being lost, and that Moore would attribute all to me. The battle seemed nearly over. I thought myself the last man alive belonging to our side who had got so far in front, and felt certain of death, and that my general would think I had hidden myself, and would not believe me to have done my best."

One feels the misery and despair, the dreadful sense of failure in those words. The rocket had shot up so triumphantly just to fall a dead stick.

Wretchedly, and still under heavy fire, he tries to rejoin his regiment and comes on a wounded private. " O praise God, Major! my dear Major. God help you, my darling. One of your own 50th." "Can you walk with my help ?" "Oh no, Major, I am too badly wounded. . . . O Christ God my jewel, my own dear Major, you won't leave me. . . ."

The man was screaming in his agony, and the dreadful cries rasped Charles's nerves, always so compassionate, and added to his own fears. As he stooped, trying to raise the poor wretch, he himself was hit in the ankle and rendered helpless. The private's cries were then on terrible, " and fell bitterly as reproaches for my want of courage and fortitude . . . yet what could be done by a man hardly able to walk and in great pain, with other duties to perform ? I felt it horrible to leave him, but selfishness and pain got the better of me." So with the help of his sword Charles limped on with much suffering, clothed in misery, till he came up to four privates who told him they were cut off, and indeed even as they spoke two parties of the enemy were advancing on them.

"Follow me !" cried Charles immediately, and forgetting all about his wound sprang up with a great shout. But his leg failed him. He stumbled, was stabbed in the back, and fell heavily forward on his face. Trying to rise he saw the man who had stabbed him making a second thrust. Charles's four companions had all been bayoneted, their cries now ringing in his ears. He himself was being clubbed in the back with the muskets of men who had come up behind. Charles, keeping hold of his own musket, defended himself with the body of the Italian who had first attacked him, but he was growing fainter, and at that moment a man " seized the musket with his left hand, whirled his brass-hilted sabre over my head, which was bare, for my cocked hat had fallen off. . . . Fire sparkled from my eyes : I fell on my knees blinded, without quite losing my senses, and holding still on to my musket. Recovering in a moment I regained my legs and saw a handsome young French drummer holding the arm of the dark Italian who was in the act of repeating his blow. Quarter was then given, but they tore my pantaloons in tearing my watch and purse from my pocket, and a little locket of hair which hung round my neck ; they snatched at everything, but while this went on two of them were wounded, and the drummer Guibert ordered the dark man who had sabred me to take me to the rear. When we began to move, I resting on him because hardly able to walk, I saw him look back over his shoulder to see if Guibert were gone; and so did I for his rascally face made me suspect him. . . . Guibert's back was turned towards us, he was walking off, and the Italian again drew his sword which he had sheathed. ' This rascal is going to kill me. Brave Frenchmen don't kill prisoners.' Guibert ran back, swore furiously at the Italian, shoved him away almost down, and putting his arms round my waist supported me himself : thus the generous Frenchman saved me twice."

Meanwhile, as he supported the almost fainting Charles, they met an old Irishman of the 50th. The latter halted, cocked his piece and levelled it at Guibert. Charles threw up the man's musket. "For God's sake don't fire ! I am a prisoner, badly wounded, and can't help you surrender." "For why would I surrender ? " "Because there are at least twenty men upon you." "Well, if I must surrender there ! " said he, dashing down his firelock across their legs and making them jump. "There's my firelock for yez." Then coming up to Charles, he shoved away Guibert and others, sending them reeling. " Stand away, ye bloody spalpeens : I'll carry him myself, bad luck to the whole of yez."

Bleeding, in extreme pain, robbed, his trousers torn and in great anger, so was our Charles brought before General Renaud. What a change from the young eagle of the morning !

General Renaud asked him his rank and how he came to be taken. " Taken because my regiment would not come on," exclaimed Charles in great anger . . . but afterwards he blamed himself for most bitter injustice " in abuse of the glorious old 50th for they had gone farther than any other corps in the army ". His thought had been that the regiment had given way, not knowing that Lord William Bentinck had ordered them back contrary to Sir John Moore's orders.

The General had a surgeon to dress his wound, but Charles's

leg was so swollen his boot could not be got off without cutting. This Charles refused to allow, hoping in his heart to escape.

The French on the whole were kindly enough. When Charles and Hennessey were about to pass a large gap in a wall French soldiers called out : " Don't cross there, or you will be shot." The officer instructed them to stoop, and the incorrigible Hennessey whispered, " Be Jasus ! They're afraid."

Charles, whose one idea was to be seen by his own people, stood erect, and it is pleasant to record that the officer also walked erect. When the French guard crawled forward on hands and knees, Charles urged this man to do the same. " Crawl you too, I cannot run away." His characteristic care for an enemy much tickled the French. The incident was after reported to General Renaud, who passed it on to the two Marshals, Soult and Ney.

On the hill Charles was in such shocking pain he was laid down on some straw near a fire. It was getting dark, and a French officer passing by, seeing his condition, paused. " War ! War ! War ! My God will this horrid work never cease ? Poor young man." He stood there awhile melting in pity, tears running down his cheeks. Before turning away he gave Charles a drink. But the man on whose straw Charles had been laid, coming up, kicked him savagely, and dragged him off it by the neck. " God damn you," shouted Charles, and the other Frenchman took his part.

Later he was dragged away into the shattered ruins of a building and thrown into filth with which it was filled. His tormentors began to laugh, whereupon Charles raged like a bear, becoming so violent and abusive it seemed as though in retaliation they would kill him. By this time his misery was extreme, his pain beyond bearing, so that even before the enemy he could not keep from groaning aloud. Again some kindly officers came to the rescue, offering him broth and wine, and finally carrying him to Hennessey. It was impossible for Charles to lie down, so the faithful Irishman held him upright in his arms. Later came an officer from the General with Charles's sword, desiring him to wear it, for he had used it well. He managed to dip a stick in his own blood, and scrawling his name and rank on a scrap of paper sent it with his sword to Marshal Soult with a request to speak to him.

The officer did not return.

Before Hennessey left he unbuckled Charles's silver spurs.

" The spalpeens would murder for them," he muttered.

" When you escape give them to my sister," whispered Charles, but secretly he thought that Hennessey guessed him to be dying, and naturally enough had decided he might as well have the spurs as the enemy.

Now Charles was alone again, his trousers were rent, he had no drawers, no waistcoat, he had been unable to touch the broth offered to him, and high up on that dark Portuguese hillside it was searchingly cold this January night. Charles, lying in extreme pain, was unaware that Sir John Moore was dead. He thought his General was angry and that the regiment was dragged in disgrace. Where was the glory of war now?

Hours of day, and then a second night to begin. Men came and went, flickering in and out of Charles's consciousness, as they made up the fire, offering him with rough kindliness broth he could not touch. Rolling themselves in their greatcoats they slept there on the ground, and then went away again even as his wandering meaningless thoughts came and went. . . .

Why did George not come with a flag of truce? . . . the regiment was disgraced . . . Moore was angry . . . he would not let his A.D.C. come . . . but George would never abandon him . . . so George must be dead . . . that was it . . .

So Charles's wild thoughts disintegrated, took shape and passed one into another . . . whilst even then his distracted brother was searching the battlefield with a torch, turning over stiffened corpse after corpse, just as the brother of Charles Stanhope was also doing. George had seen Sir John Moore killed, he had seen both Charles and Charles Stanhope leading the charge, he had seen the one shot down, and heard of the other " Major Napier is killed ", but where, oh where was Charles's body? Miserably he searched on in dressing stations and hospital.

It was not till after the afternoon of the second day that Charles managed to drag himself out of the demolished house. There he found help and persuaded the man to get him to the latter's regiment. To walk was agony. And what must Charles have felt hobbling through Elvina amidst, as he afterwards wrote : " All the bodies of my poor 50th soldiers scattered about." We know Wellington's emotion after the Battle of Waterloo, but he was a veteran, and he was a victor. This was Charles's first battle, and it was defeat, and it was captivity. Who can gauge the bitterness, the mortification in the heart of this draggled eagle ?

Amongst the dead there were many wounded crying and calling for help and food. Past these Charles must go. Charles, so sensitive to the cry of pain, that even as a little child of three on hearing the melancholy caw of a crow he had stretched out his arms weeping—" Whatamatta poor bird. Whatta matter ? " —wept and would not be comforted. He was taken to Soult's quarters, and on into the kitchen. Soult's A.D.C. treated him with every kindness and offered him money. This Charles refused, and in spite of his weakness he up and spoke how he had been robbed, all meeting him having enquired : " *Estéil pillé ?* " " *Oh pour ça oui joliment pillé.*"

Hennessey had his spurs, but all else had been taken, including the little locket of hair which he had worn round his neck. What romantic creatures these Napiers were. Whose hair was that ? And the spurs. They had been given to him by his sister Emily when he got his majority, he exclaiming : " Now I am your knight." Did he know of the ladies of Rajasthan and their " bracelet brothers " ?

Charles himself had a broken leg, a sabre cut on his head, a bayonet thrust in his back, ribs broken by cannon shot, and contusions from butt end of musket, but the cries of the wounded were still weighing heavily on him, and Marshal Soult promised immediate help should be sent to the village. Charles himself was given a bed in the Marshal's own quarters, but the pain from his broken ribs, and we may guess his thoughts, prevented sleep. The following morning he was ordered to Corunna. He was hoisted on to a horse, and attended by a dragoon entered the town with the troops. A Spaniard jostled purposely it seems his wounded leg three times, and Charles in extreme torture recovered his old self sufficiently to hit the fellow on the head with all the force he could muster, shouting great oaths, to the huge delight of the French, for it was not only the British Army that despised the Spaniards.

It had been on the night of the fourteenth that the transport and battleships had at last arrived for the evacuation. Moore, fearing a sudden change of wind, had embarked his sick, nearly all his guns, and all his cavalry, though it was only a thousand horses that could be taken. The rest were shot down there on the beach.

"Now if there is no bungling I hope we shall be away in a few hours."

Instead Corunna.

And now on January 17th Charles, still ignorant of his Chief's death, still miserably hoping against hope for a flag of truce to exchange him for some French officer, was watching the assembled ships in the bay below his feet. The night before, in black darkness, while their commander lay dying in great pain yet asking after his officers, and trusting that England would be satisfied, and that his country would do him justice, the remnants of regiments and corps had boarded the vessels. Their discipline had been restored, but so terrible had they looked in their blood and filth and tatters, starved, bare-footed and hollow-eyed, we are told that the men of the town crossed themselves as they passed.

Practically the whole army was on board, but the watching Charles could not guess at the full disaster that had overtaken England. He did not know that the total loss from the previous October was nearly twelve thousand men, and five thousand horses, and all baggage. He could not know that even this remnant of an army, battened higgledy-piggledy down in the holds of the transports, was to return to fill the hospitals of England with typhus.

Charles knew nothing of this. But from his heights he saw the ships in the harbour below weigh anchor and move inexorably away.

The British had gone.

For three months he was to be a prisoner of war. His family mourned him as dead, except for Lady Sarah who remained obstinate. "Where is his body then?" she repeated. Finally the Government were persuaded to send a frigate to make enquiries. The tale has often been told how Baron Clouet, Ney's A.D.C., who had been consistently kind to Charles, on receiving the flag of truce hurried away to tell Ney. "Let him see his friends, and tell them he is well, and well treated," replied the Marshal. Clouet hesitated, looking earnestly at his Chief. "He has an old mother, a widow, and blind." "Has he? Let him go then and tell her himself he is alive."

Now exchange of prisoners was not permitted at this time, and Ney by his generous action ran the risk of getting himself into grave trouble, but for some reason or other—(William suggests Charles being a cousin of Charles James Fox)—Napoleon actually approved of his Marshal's action. Small wonder Ney became sacred to the Napier family for all time.

It was peculiarly unfortunate that the exchange offered for Charles the Commander was merely two midshipmen! This naturally angered the French and held up Charles's release. It was not till March 20th, 1810, that his captivity ended. It was his father's birthday, a happy omen, for all his life Charles paid considerable attention to such coincidences whether good or bad. Arriving in England he scribbled on a scrap of paper these lines from Hudibras :

> "I have been in battle slain,
> And I live to fight again."

and sent them to his beloved mother who had refused to believe him dead.

George, Louise, and Emily, the giver of the spurs, came down to Exeter to meet him. There was their darling Charles on the top of the coach looking for all the world in his stained and faded red coat like some Chelsea pensioner, except that his beard and whiskers were black, not white.

CHAPTER 5

PENINSULAR WAR

1808–1812

FOR many years the battered little spur which Hennessey contrived to unfasten from Charles's boot when the latter was propped up by the fireplace of the ruined house at Elvina, was in the possession of his descendants.

And this is its history.

Outside the ruins Hennessey was seized, and together with a few Spanish and English prisoners marched off to the Pyrenees. Escaping, he made his way to Oporto, selling one of the spurs for food. The other remained hidden in his armpit. He reached Oporto just as Marshal Soult attacked. Hennessey, of course, joined the patriot force, and as he confided to Charles, " was mighty spiteful against the French ! " Again the Irishman was taken prisoner, but again he still contrived to keep the remaining spur. In his own words he " made an offer at the sentry ", beating out his brains with his own musket, and making off with it. And still he kept the spur ! The Buffs came up. Joyfully Hennessey threw his lot in with them and fought the French at Talavera.

It was at Talavera he came across George Napier. He showed him the spur, but surrender it he would not. All through that campaign Hennessey served. When he reached England, instead of setting off to see wife and child, or rejoining his regiment, this man of one idea travelled more than two hundred miles to find Emily Napier. And to her he gave the spur.

In the meantime he and Charles had met. Neither alluded to the spur, Charles for obvious reasons, but he got Hennessey promotion to corporal, and leave to go to Cork to visit his wife. Hennessey carried with him a letter to a friend of Charles's, the Collector of Customs. Before seeing his wife, the man, as though drawn on a string, went to Aldridge, who told him that meanwhile Charles had gone back to the Peninsula as a volunteer !

" Ogh ! Murder. Is he gone back ? And the regiment not with him. By my soul I'll niver stop behind but off I'll be too."

" Well, Hennessey, you must do as you please, but go and see your wife and child : come to me in the morning, and tell me what I can do for your family if you do not come back."

" Och, good luck to the wife and child. I'll not go near them *are fut*, but off this minute."

So even in those early days of his life Charles roused the intense affection of the common soldier. Touching letters, too, have been published from one Ensign Leslie to his brother testifying to the affection of those less humble . . . " he is indeed my steady friend . . ." writes Leslie, " I may say nurse when I am sick and my guardian when I am well. ' Well, Leslie, how are you ? What have you been about since last I saw you ? . . . My God, I'll work you up. You must not mind though ; it's all for your good. Do you want for anything ? Be sure you say if you do ! ' All the time I was ill he used to sit with me for hours and make me laugh whether I would or no. Ill I certainly was. I thought I would make a die of it."

Leslie had carried the regimental colours in the retreat before Corunna. Two years later he in his turn looked after Charles when convalescing, and in recognition of his devotion he was asked to stay with Lady Sarah at her house in Cadogan Place, and was moreover given a sword worn by her husband. His pride and delight were great. Poor young man, he was eventually shot through the heart at Vittoria, his Mary, whom he was shortly to marry, only learning of it through the *Gazette*.

This of course was in 1813, but harking back to 1810, what must Lady Sarah have felt when her three bright ones, with their fine free ways, recovered from their wounds only to disappear once again into the thunder clouds of the Peninsula ?

43

As Hennessey had been told, Charles had joined the Light Division as a volunteer in January. "Two short years! and lo! here I am again; but Moore! Stanhope! Stanhope! Every turn of the road brings you before my eyes." In the Coa action he had two horses shot under him. All three brothers took part in the fighting during the retreat to Busaco. Just before the battle they learned of the death of their gentle sister Caroline. As we know, the family were unusually attached to each other. Silently each went to his post with God knows what swelling thoughts in his heart. Pretty Caroline, Lady Sarah alone and blind, the coming battle!

Charles was beside Lord Wellington. The fire became so intense all dismounted. Charles, the only officer in a red coat, refused.

"No! This is the uniform of my regiment, and in it I will stand and fall this day."

No doubt this would be considered foolish bravado to-day, and Charles paid for his gallantry by the wound which was to trouble him all his life, and even at times to cause fear of madness.

"Who was that?" enquired Wellington, as the litter was borne past him. And Charles, his eye injured, his jawbone shattered, his nose broken, half fainting from pouring blood, managed to take off his hat, and wave it, muttering: "I could not die at a better moment."

Glittering words . . . perhaps merely tinsel to the modern eye.

"Poor Napier. After all his wounds he is gone at last."

He heard those words, and afterwards confessed they made him uneasy as on the field of battle they are "sometimes over-quick in burying, so with a light twist I intimated 'alive but not merry'".

His litter was carried to a convent, and lying there apparently dying he heard officers near by discussing of all extraordinary things in the middle of a battle the remarkable beauty of his father and mother! We are now so resigned to the utility common man with his drab raincoat, we forget that once beauty was an end in itself, and that physical beauty in man as well as

WILLIAM NAPIER
From a miniature by Miss Jones

woman was esteemed in the most unlikely circumstances, as the following tale will illustrate.

At the battle of Cazal Noval, in which Charles was to be yet further wounded, a certain young captain of the Grenadier company of the Royal Scots came on an officer stretched out speechless beneath an olive tree. He was deathly pale. Guessing the man to be seriously wounded, he ran up to him and in his own words was " deeply impressed with the classical outline and beautiful expression on his countenance ". Now this was William, who had inherited his father's good looks—Charles's brother. But the young captain had no notion who he was, and in the midst of firing and excitement did not notice his uniform. He gave the stricken man brandy and cold tea, and then murmuring, " Heaven protect you," ran off to join his company. To quote him again : " In after life I often spoke of this wounded officer as the handsomest man I had ever beheld."

It was sixteen years later the captain, now Colonel Sir John Morillyon, was at a dinner. As the men were about to join the ladies, and while I was " standing near the fireplace with my arm resting on the mantelpiece, the men were speaking about ' handsome men ', and I said of all the handsome men I had ever seen . . . there was none to be compared with *the one*. . . ."

" Napier sprang from his chair, put his arms round me and exclaimed : ' My dear Wilson, was that you ? That glass of tea and brandy saved my life.' And a few tears trickled from his bright and animated eyes. . . ."

Well, whether Charles really heard the officers discussing his parents' beauty or not, the following morning found him on a horse, his frightful, frightening wound still undressed. At Coimbra he hoped for attention, but the rascally army doctor —afterwards believed mad, let it be said—hearing a rumour that the enemy was approaching, not only left Charles's wounds undressed but escaped on Charles's horses ! They were recovered by Charles's servant, who also bandaged his master's face as well as his unskilled fingers could. So Charles rode on in the dust, tormented by flies, under a blazing sun, several days to Lisbon. The 50th Regiment passed him on their way to join the army. Seeing their old officer in such plight they gave him three cheers. He had need of them, poor Charles, and one guesses how his heart sprang to them.

At Lisbon there was George badly wounded too. For both trailed weary weeks in hospital, months indeed for Charles ! But the fourth day after the battle he was writing : " I am wounded, dear Mother : the ball passed along the cheek-bone and lodged in the upper jaw, from which it was extricated with much pain to me . . . you never saw so ugly a thief as I am. . . ."

And a day or two later : " Your letter has given me pain and pleasure. The latter to find you bear so nobly the trial you have gone through. . . . Our Caroline is gone, my Mother, but every day teaches us there is little to lose in losing life . . . and much to be gained.

" Lord March has just come in and tells me you have had your eyes done and can see a little. Oh, my beloved Mother, is this blessed news true ? Great God, grant it to be so . . . my anxiety is too great to write. I am afraid.

" As to my sufferings there were none after pulling out the ball : so that matter is settled. Perhaps the use of my choppers will never be regained, but only painful at dinner : so at grace I put up a prayer for the fellow who shot me."

So he writes to his mother with his own peculiar mixture of seriousness and jokes, and all manner of tenderness. As William once said : " From the sublime to the ridiculous is part of his idiosyncrasy : an exuberant humour rioting like a merry devil in a nun, always possessed him, and in adverse circumstances most strongly."

So as his sufferings became worse we find this sort of thing written to his mother. He had invited some friends to dinner and asked his man if it were ready.

" ' Quite, sir.'

" ' What is there ? '

" ' There's no soup.'

46

" ' Anything else ? '

" ' There's no sosingers.'

" ' What next ? '

" ' There's no visibles (vegetables).'

" ' Go on.'

" ' There's no nothing.'

" ' Hum ! a good negative dinner. You must borrow.'

" ' There's no time.'

" ' Buy.'

" ' There's no money.'

" ' Credit."

" ' There's no tick.'

" ' Are there no rations ? '

" ' Yes, sir, I ate the beef."

" Three times has this letter been commenced in a most serious manner," says Charles, " and on most serious subjects, but nonsense will come, and devil take me if I can stop for the life of me."

He also tells of Black Charles his cousin. It was Black Charles who had tried to persuade him to dismount, and had helped to carry him off the field. " I like Harry Fox and Charles Napier the better for not staying with me, and would not have thanked them if they had : I should have attributed it to dislike of returning into fire. . . .

" Black Charles is a queer fellow as ever crossed me, and as honest a one. He is going to Cadiz. We shall see him no more : this is a copy of his letter to the First Lord of the Admiralty :

" ' Sir, my leave of absence is just out. I don't think it worth remaining here, for I expect you will give me a ship as I am almost tired of campaigning, which is a damned rum concern. C.N.'

" He is the delight of my life," writes Charles, " and should live with me, and be trusted with any enterprise. If I were a great man . . . Lord Wellington lately said to him :

" ' I could easily beat the French, but England has no other army, and it would cost me ten thousand men : so we must have prudence, and fight when they must lose men, and we not.' Be comfortable therefore, dear Mother, no more Talaveras will shake you with fear. . . ."

December : " My jaws are crooked, and the doctors say will always be so. My lip is very uneasy and will always be so. My cheek is better and the swelling may go. My mouth opens stiffly. My eye still stares, yet is stronger, more easily shuts and sees further : it is said the sight may be lost, but it is not dim, and if it goes why Hannibal had only one eye : I have a mind to pluck it out."

In January : " My wound will always be inconvenient, having broken the gristle of my snout inside . . . my jawbone is broken to smithereens."

February : " What havoc I make with ancient dames, or rather they with me. There are two Englishwomen here . . . the elect of my heart is eighty-five. . . . My surgeon, a shrewd little Scotsman, calls me a fool for thinking of joining. ' Imposseeble.' ' Redecklous.' ' Wait. . . . No patience. But go if you like. . . . Ye'll lose you neb though.' This doctor says that Lord Wellington should be hanged for the loss of men at Talavera and no successes can wash him clean. Now I'm not for hanging but making him Duke of Portugal if he succeeds. . . ."

Charles's surgeon had said he could not join. ' Imposseeble.' ' Redecklous.' ' Ye'll lose you neb.' But in March the Light Division was leading in pursuit of Ney, and Charles was away ! With his wound still open, he rode day and night for ninety-two miles on his half-bred Arab.

" My poor horse had two pounds of Indian corn on which he performed this severe journey in twenty-two hours, including the three hours' halt," is his own comment. On his effort to reach the army he found Portugal had been made a desert.

Ahead of him he could hear the roar of battle at Redinha, and as the wounded men came in he anxiously asked if his brothers were still alive. It was on March 14th he met a litter of branches covered by a blanket. " What wounded officer is that ? "

" Captain Napier of the 52nd, a broken limb." Another litter followed. " Who is that ? " " Captain Napier, 43rd, mortally wounded."

Charles looked at them. He spoke a few words, remounted the famished, fatigued Blanco. He rode on to the fight ahead.

But things were not so bad as they had seemed. Ten days later Charles is writing to his mother : " Says I to Blanco, ' Suppose we walk over the mountains, old boy, and see the other boys.' " He admits, her George is in constant pain and cannot sleep without opium, and William will be on duty in two months " but he ought not to for six. . . . Are we cats that we live and bear such wounds ? But now having told you, dear Mother, exactly the facts as usual, adieu. This is enough after a ride of forty miles over the most rugged mountains in Portugal. Poor Blanco almost gives up the ghost."

Conditions indeed were terrible. The country was devastated. Gaunt silhouettes of walls, gaping roofs, dead bodies of human beings, of mules and goats and bullocks, to mark where villages had stood. There was no one to buy from, nothing to buy, and nothing to eat. In the sky circling birds of prey, and vultures on the ground tugging out the bowels from the carcasses of men and beasts, or squatting too gorged to flop away. The sights, smells and sounds Charles witnessed day after day must have sickened one so sensitive. A brightness and a darkness, a dazzle of sun, dust, blackened ruins and bunches of flies. A cold wind from the snow. What a lamentable record of what man does to man. Where was the glory now ?

He apologises for " no civil letter for you, dear Mother . . ." his letters are " fleed, bugged, centipeded, beetled, lizarded and ear-wigged ; cleanliness is only known to me by name. Moreover, a fuzz-bush makes a bad table for writing on and a worse chair when breeches are nearly worn out with glory. Writing is not agreeable : only to tell you how George and William are. . . . Neither poor Blanco nor I are troubled with much bile now," he admits, but he does not add that for nearly three whole days he has had nothing to eat at all, though he does

49

exclaim, " England, how little you know of war ! " He mentions that a splinter of bone is sticking out of his jaw, and that sleeping out on cold nights and severe riding made his wound bleed through the nose, but he is equally concerned for Blanco. " Blanco is starving, and curls his nose into a thousand wrinkles cursing Bonaparte . . . there my biscuit has run away on maggots' legs . . . though not a bad soldier, hang me if I can relish maggots."

Thus he made light of his own sufferings, though that hard biscuit must have been torture to his shattered jaw when, as so often, there was no time to soak it. He even showed no impatience when Lady Sarah expressed great amazement at his carelessness in not writing and concerning himself with " the great public question of the regency ". It was natural she should take particular interest in the mad old king. Charles gives her his reasons for calling it a trifling quibble of politicians. With tragedy and ruin about him, starvation and plunder, the loss of many comrades, again he must have thought: " England, how little you know of war," but he betrays no impatience.

As his brother William once wrote : " No wounds, nor sufferings, no inconvenience of time and place, no privations or inclemency of weather ever interrupted his efforts to relieve her anxieties, and assure her that she was always first in his thoughts."

By her own waywardness Lady Sarah had not become the wife of George III, but her husband and her sons crowned her Queen for all time.

CHAPTER 6

BERMUDA

1812–1813

"REMEMBER now, dearest Mother, that fight more, or no more fight, a hundred thousand men are in the pickling tub with William and myself, it was our turn to escape and we did so."

So Charles wrote after the battle of Fuentes Onero.

He regarded his wounds as a kind of insurance against death.

And later :

"Almieda is blown up. The whole army is disgraced. Lord Wellington must feel it deeply. To have all his operations for securing the town against a large army succeed, to see that army defeated and retired, and then to have the generals under him let the garrison out. It is enough to break his heart ! England will begin to see that our generals are ——"

Charles was now in his twenty-ninth year. He had changed since the days of Corunna. It was indeed unlikely that one of his temperament should witness the unparalleled misery of that 300-mile retreat of the British Army and remain unchanged. Across the mountains in howling gales, alternately frozen and drenched, the army, a demoralised rabble, famished, wounded and with broken boots and bleeding feet, became completely out of hand. On New Year's Day when they reached Villafranca "every soldier took what he liked, everything was plundered, carried away, and trampled under foot ; the casks of wine were broken open so that half their contents were spilt over the floor, and the general fury and unruliness of these hordes of men was such that those officers who attempted to maintain order had to make haste to fight their way out of the crowds, if only to save their lives " (Schaumann, *On the Road with Wellington*).

What a memory for Charles, whose pride of life was centred in the army ! What a memory, only redeemed by the splendour and glory of the fighting divisions which were covering that retreat !

Yes. Charles had changed. Everyone remarked on it. How could it be otherwise ?

Though never possessing the startling good looks of his brothers, yet he had been personable enough, and had taken a healthy interest in appearance and dress. Now he cared less than nothing for either appearance or personal comfort. Indeed, he seemed to go out of his way to deny himself both, and this trait was to grow on him, handing out ammunition as it were to his enemies, and to caricaturists in later life. In the light of modern thought one wonders, though he had jested to Lady Sarah that his facial wounds were as good as medals, whether secretly he did mind that disfigured countenance, that staring eye and crooked jaws.

And he was still a major.

Like most of us Charles was shackled by his own temperament. His particular fetter was a sense of grievance, and this sense of grievance, sometimes justified but sometimes not, was to grow on him as it grew on his brother William, bringing both much unnecessary unhappiness.

The present grievance was understandable. He was not favoured by the Horse Guards. Ever since Corunna, the Commander-in-Chief, Sir David Dundas, generally known as Old Pivot, refused to give him promotion for his conduct. Moreover, he also denied promotion to George who, had Sir John Moore not been killed, would have brought home his despatches, and so gained promotion as a matter of course. Charles attributed this to the jealousy of Sir John Moore, but Sir John Fortescue offers another possible explanation. " Why the old man should have been so hard on them it is not easy to say. But having begun his military career by walking to Woolwich from

Edinburgh to join the artillery as a fire worker, and having laboriously worked his way up to the highest post of all, he may have thought that the Napiers, with all their grand relations, might well be kept waiting for a little."

That "the Commander-in-Chief entertains the highest opinion of your meritorious service" by no means satisfied Charles. "The stiff old brush," he storms in a letter to his mother. "Writing in such a fury hurts my wounds." He threatens he will appeal to the Prince Regent. He did. This, combined with Lady Sarah's own influence, obtained for him the command of the 102nd by the Duke of York, who had again become Commander-in-Chief. They had just come back from Botany Bay with a bad record. Charles learns "that the state of that corps requires that you should join it without delay".

They were not to go to the Peninsula as Charles had hoped, but to Bermuda.

"I would almost quit the army than go to garrison Bermuda," declared William fiercely.

But for once Charles dissented from dear brother. "To get a regiment that is in bad order is agreeable. My fear was a good one, where no character could be gained, and some could be lost," was his opinion. And indeed, in spite of murder, a record of mutiny and drunkenness in the 102nd just returned from Botany Bay, Charles, following the teaching of Sir John Moore at Shorncliffe Camp, eventually brought this regiment to such a high pitch of efficiency that he was to command it against the Americans in 1813.

The purpose of this book is to trace a continuous line of development in Charles's character, the care and appreciation of the men of the British Army. This was later to manifest itself in many ways for the betterment of the private; his patient and constant attendance at all court martials, his insistence on proper food, proper clothing, and above all on better barracks, were all the outcome of this line of thought. So now, setting out for the Bermudas, his indignation is great at Plymouth to find "the idle official rascals had thought it quite unnecessary" to get the soldiers bedding. " Five hundred soldiers on a voyage which may last two months with only the deck to lie on is shameful."

The voyage was indeed prolonged by bad weather and threatened shipwreck. Poor Charles was very miserable with seasickness as always. And in spite of his cock-sure attitude to his appointment he found to be mewed up in a small island, cut off from the great happenings in Europe, hard to bear. He was out of harmony with the people, with the wetness and warm langours of the island. Many things displeased him. " The smell of cedars is overpowered by the smell of rum ! " Lady Sarah learns that the men are allowed ten pounds of flour, but the commanding officer hands them only eight, the remainder being sold. Now bread fetched a shilling, sometimes two shillings, a pound. " What becomes of this large sum is unknown to me, but it would be easy to pocket £900 or £1,000 without detection." Fuel had hitherto been bought by contract. Charles insists on his quartermaster buying good clean wood, ensuring his men getting good bread. He gets known as Baker Napier.

He drills his men incessantly. " But to what end ? I only do it to keep them from drink and myself from rust."

For he is appalled at the constant drunkenness of his regiment. " It is beyond endurance," he exclaims. " I feel myself failing in self-command as to temper."

He had once written to his mother : " You know my antipathy to flogging. You know that it is unconquerable. It began from hatred of the sight, and a disgust, not yet gone, though habit reconciles one to horrible sights. I am convinced it could be dispensed with." But now sadly, sternly he writes to her : " The lash will be used, for drink is killing them, and discipline subverted. . . ." " Poor fellows, for all their sins they are fine fellows, and their blood should be kept for better use than being drawn with a cat-o'-nine-tails. . . ."

Yes, this man who had boasted " a young one should never see a bloody back " has himself to see that they do. But we feel sure he would never exercise that right of a commanding officer to flog again a back when still only half healed.

Who knows but that it was Hennessey of the spurs who had brought home to him the atrocious flogging that took place in the army in those days. It is worth recounting the incident, for though it occurred before Charles had joined the regiment he gives such a full account it must have impressed him deeply.

Hennessey had pretended he had rheumatism and lost the power of his legs, so could not walk. It was clear the man was malingering, and he was sentenced to 500 lashes. This he bore without a groan, and still maintaining he could not walk he had to be carried to hospital. After his back was healed he was tried, again sentenced, and received another 500 lashes. At the end of each 25 he was offered pardon if he would confess and return to duty. He would not. Unbelievably he was again tried, and again condemned, but this time to 600 lashes. But Charles shall finish the story himself.

" A church stood 500 yards away from the place of punishment. Colonel Walker said : ' Hennessey, if you will run to that church and back I will forgive you.' ' No,' he said, he could not stand. He had lost the power of his legs. After receiving 500 lashes he exclaimed : ' Colonel, take me down. Jasus, boys I can't stand it. I'll run to the church.' He was untied and did run to the church and back."

Charles adds that Hennessey had borne 1,500 lashes from sheer obstinacy, for he had never been ill a day. Nevertheless, it is clear that the punishment appalled him. Just as his great teacher Sir John Moore had maintained discipline without the cat-o'-nine-tails, so Charles had hoped to do. But the climate, the salt diet, the monotony of the life, were too much for the men.

All this, and his various theories such as " that the voice of a commander should seldom be heard in anger . . . only a touch up is invigorating, only let it come out at once and like the devil, hail, rain, thunder, lightning ", or that the men were less likely to succumb to the two curses of the island, yellow fever and consumption, when he took them for marches in extreme heat, instead of avoiding exercise : that his regiment had fewer men in hospital than any other—all these things came tumbling out to his mother. From the rich treasury of his life he did not add that his men were individuals and addressed as such, but we have the authority of one Captain Robertson of the Royal Artillery for saying : " He was himself drill master and master also of every detail : with exception of beating a drum there was no part of a soldier's duty, from the sentinel to the sergeant-major's, which he could not teach, and do as smartly as his smartest non-commissioned officer. Nor was his knowledge restricted to his own arm ; he was conversant with engineer's duties, and with those of artillery, whose practice he generally attended."

Yes, of such things, mixed up with reflections on the campaigns of Alexander the Great, and Hannibal, the proper equipment of cavalry, soldiers' marriages, baggage, the mode of learning foreign languages, Charles wrote. It will be remembered that his mother had had similar outpourings on every kind of subject, from political events, social gossip and philosophy to her cousin, Lady Susan Fox-Strangways. But she was an old lady now. One suspects that Charles's theories and moralisings, original as they were—" My friend Stewart is dead : I wonder how he likes it ? "—did not interest her so much these days as the little tit-bits of news such as they ate whale-meat on the island and it tasted like veal ; or how Charles, to keep his mind off yellow fever and consumption, had flung himself into garden-ing. " It is a kind of madness * with me : gardening from morning to night should be my occupation if there were anyone to command the regiment ; it won't let me think of anything else."

Now that she would appreciate ! How it would recall her early married life when as a bride of sixteen she had spent day after day alone at Barton vehemently planting trees and garden-ing whilst Sir Charles Bunbury was gallivanting with his sporting

---

* This " madness " seemed hereditary, for the writer received from one of Sir Charles's granddaughters a letter written at the age of eighty-eight in January : " I hate these cold winds. They won't let me garden. I do resent it so."

LADY SARAH NAPIER
From a pastel portrait in the possession of Mrs. Wynne-Roberts

friends. But better even than the gardening bits must have been her son's protestations of undying affection.

"I would sooner take another shot through the head to be near you . . . my broken jaw does not give me half the pain the living so far from you"; or, "dearest, blessed Mother, to return to you is the first wish of my heart. When the American war is over I must go home or mad. . . ." "To come home for the rest of my life and drive old Blanco in a buggy. . . ." And here it may be said, extravagant as this may seem, Charles was not obsessed by his mother in the modern sense of the word. She did not dominate his actions or possess him. There is a letter in which he exclaims : "God be praised, dear Mother, that you are not quartermaster general. If you were, how the dragoons would fly with expresses ! 'What is in that bundle before you, dragoon ?' 'Orders, your honour.' 'What have you behind, dragoon ?' 'Counter orders, sir.' Well, as a dutiful son I must answer you, but I am inclined to quiz you. I won't go to Brighton and I will go to London. I was born on the bank of the Thames and partake of the quality of the water, never good until fermented and stirred up ; then, when all other water becomes bad it freshens from contrast. So far from thinking with you my reforming efforts are useless. I hold them to be of consequence."

Yes, these letters seem to have been an extension of Charles's character as it were. To clear his mind he had to write down what he thought of life, of death, of duty, just as in later years when Commander-in-Chief in India he wrote almost daily to his brother William : "I never think my military ideas proof till they are seen by you."

These letters to his mother were to continue during the operations against the Americans which were soon to commence. In May, 1813, Sir Sydney Beckwith arrived in Bermuda. He divided his force into two brigades, appointing Charles to the larger. Charles writes to his mother : "My self-confidence makes me wish for the Chief Command, yet am I fearful of estimating my powers too high, and much I dislike sacking and burning of towns. It is bad employment for British troops. . . ."

Did his memory turn to that scarecrow army crossing the mountains of Galicia ? Did he fear his own cherished and disciplined troops might too get out of hand ? For he was to write : "I will with my own hand kill any perpetrator of brutality under my command." He need not have feared. After the terrible atrocities that were to take place at the storming of Little Hampton committed by the foreign rabble of which the expeditionary force was largely composed, proudly Charles wrote of the regular troops : "Never have I seen soldiers like the Marine Artillery. They had it in their power to join in the sack, and refused. Should my life extend to antediluvian years their conduct will never be forgotten by me."

For himself he had said : "A pair of breeches must be plundered, for mine are worn out, and better it will be to take a pair than shock the Yankee dames by presenting myself as a *sansculotte*."

Plundering and ruining the peasantry by driving their few cattle he found hateful. If only the American Government would repay these poor creatures by levying the whole loss as a tax, he says, his care would go. There speaks Charles. His sympathies always ranged with the weak against the strong. Operations were unsatisfactory. Charles explains it thus : "Had either Sir John Warren, Sir Sydney Beckwith or Admiral Cockburn acted singly and without consultation we should not have done such foolish things. . . . There were three commanders. Cockburn thinks himself a Wellington, Beckwith is sure the Navy never produced such an Admiral as himself . . . between them we got beaten at Craney."

So Charles decides that a General in a blue coat and an Admiral in a red is a mistake, a conviction that remained with him throughout life.

His letters continue to his mother.

She hears of him from Nova Scotia. Their tents are pitched on a hillside where the thermometer registers 38°. The week before they had come from the stifling atmosphere of the ship with the thermometer stuck at 96°, and for the previous months in Bermuda it had never fallen below 80°. " No wonder," jokes Charles, " in the morning it is a concert to hear 1,600 mens' teeth chatter together, and it screws up my wounded cheek wickedly, yet as soldiers cannot choose climate, and though they don't live long now, methinks there is enough iron in me to knock off twenty years still, if a lead don't shorten the date. . . ."

He was only thirty-two, wounded several times and weakened by fever. His heart was away in the Peninsula, far from these abortive landings and muddles. Wonder and admiration for the foe he fought was to him essential. Long past was his hatred against Napoleon changed to admiration. He had written in his journal : " If war is to be made, make it with energy. Cato the elder said war should nourish war. Cato was a wise and energetic man. Cæsar agreed with him and Cæsar was a cleverer man. Bonaparte, greater than either, does the same."

So Charles contrived an exchange back into his old regiment which was fighting in the Pyrenees.

And when he reached England Napoleon was in Elba.

The war was over.

On half pay he joined the Staff College at Farnham.

Books. Books. Books. Books of all kinds. Since the coach had rumbled down the village street of Celbridge, bringing the Colonel and Lady Sarah and little Charles squeezed in, he had been surrounded by books, he had buried himself in history. At Farnham he is studying Alexander the Great's policy, digesting it for his own future use if ever the chance may come. He is writing of Hamilcar. He pores over the use of Cavalry, as he had in those langourous days in Bermuda. He goes into the utmost detail. Light dragoons and heavy dragoons, the latter to have heavier men, not heavier baggage. No trappings. " The horse must not be killed by useless weight. A dragoon should have no kit but a cloak, a pair of shoes, two flannel shirts, and a piece of soap." So was born his famous dictum which was one day to revolutionise campaigning in India.

All this intensive study was interrupted by the astounding escape of Napoleon. Of course Charles got himself to Paris. He took part in combat, but like William was denied their supreme ambition of meeting Napoleon. According to William the British Army shared their own admiration for Napoleon. William writes that the army thought of him not as a foe standing alone, but a soldier to be hailed by every other soldier who had gained great glory by fighting against him ! This rather astonishing assertion does seem to be borne out by an incident which William recounts in his life of Charles.

William himself was in Paris. His post was at the piquets guarding the barrier of St. Denis. He was asked by the Captain if he was to salute when Louis XVIII entered. " I have no orders on that head, and I give none," said William. The King came up ; the crowds pressed forward. There were shouts of " *Vive !* " but often " *l'Empereur* " whispered after.

The British had had no orders. They brought down their muskets and with their hands resting on the muzzles stared at the King. He was taken aback, visibly angered, and *mousquetaires* rode hurriedly up, brandishing swords, shouting, gesticulating. The British soldiers remained motionless, their heads bent. The *mousquetaries* closed threateningly upon them. Up went all heads, and streams of tobacco juice squirted out over those glistening cuirasses. A shout of delight rose from the crowd, and women, well-dressed women, were kissing those scornful British soldiers.

CHAPTER 7

CEPHALONIA

1822–1830

"IF reform comes the glory of England will be brighter than the battles of the last twenty years have made it. The freedom of England being rendered complete, Louis XVIII and his brood will be lost, for our example will be followed by all England," writes Charles who, back at Farnham, is immersed in politics. "Grievances will be righted, and a reform will be affected, though to resist it Castlereagh would risk civil war I believe," but he quickly adds if civil war should come Lady Sarah must not fear, for "with three sons soldiers, one a sailor, and another a lawyer, it will be hard if you don't swim for these are the finest trades in such cases".

It is difficult to avoid the thought that history repeats itself like the recurring pattern on a wallpaper, for it gives an uncomfortably familiar feeling to read the words he was to write later.

"I cannot get rid of the consciousness that the conduct of England, or rather the English government, has been disgraceful. We are starved at home and lose our character abroad: we injure, we insult and gain nothing. . . . At home our people hunger and our best men fly to America. Shall we never have a fair representation of the people, and a parliament that will chastise the present government?"

Charles, back at Farnham, was still on half pay, pestering the authorities for employment without success. Holding the theories that he did on the game laws, taxation, the treatment of Roman Catholics in Ireland, no wonder that he was not popular at the Horse Guards! Soft soap cannot affect abuses.

Something more abrasive is required.   Charles had it in plenty. So, although admittedly Charles Napier was very well on active service—his success with his men, his six wounds and the eulogies of the Duke of Wellington could not be denied—but suited for a home military post?   No !   thought the Horse Guards.

So after two more years chafing Charles writes once again to the Commander-in-Chief.

Thus he cut a new notch in his life . . . his years in the Ionian Isles.

Sir Thomas Maitland was Governor of the Islands.   A curious person indeed.   We read how on one occasion when the Senate were assembled waiting for him, he strolled into the middle of the room in shirt, slippers and red nightcap.   His hands clasped behind his back he halted in the middle of the room, stared round at the Senators and exclaimed to the Secretary, " Damn them.   Tell them all to go to hell," and grunting to himself, turned and left the room.

This was the man who gave Charles his chance, after he had spent purposeless months as Inspecting Field Officer, negotiating with Ali Pasha, the champion of Greek independence.   Charles's opinion of " Old Tom " was not high, although he afterwards came to modify it.   Hard drinking, coarse, yet " Old Tom " was not without talent, and he had displayed shrewdness in appointing Charles as Military Secretary of Cephalonia.   Charles was delighted.   It was as though he had stepped straight into a world of light.   He was released from that dark dominion of war, with its misery, its blood and filth as well as its glory.   He was in this flooding light with worthwhile things to do on every side which he was convinced he was the one man to tackle.   His letters sparkle with the beauty of the Grecian Islands, the seas, the wild flowers, the people themselves.   " The merry Greeks are worth all other nations put together.   I like their fun.   I like their good humour, their Paddy ways.   They are very like Irishmen.   As to cleanliness they cannot brag. . . ."

Charles rolled up his sleeves, so to speak, and flung himself delightedly into changing this turbulent island into a model of what it should be. Peacock and cerulean seas, tiny scarlet anemones glowing amongst the stones, and grey-green aromatic herbs, branching pink asphodel and almond, and snow lingering on the tall Black Mountains all through the scorching summers were all very well. But then lawless chiefs ruled the island, intimidating the judges : clans from the isolated mountain valleys made wars ; agriculture was almost at a standstill, communications were practically non-existent. Rape, murder and child slavery flourished in that lovely island.

Exactly the field for Charles, and he knew it.

" My predecessor is going home half dead from the labour, but to me it is health, spirit, everything," he exults.

He rose at four, worked till noon except for a light breakfast. Then he bathed and rode out to superintend the public works he had immediately started. Roads, barracks, prisons, hospitals, markets, schools, lighthouses . . . all these were to come, and did.

" I take no rest, and give nobody else any . . . a too easy chair is the rack for me."

At the beginning he writes : " My kingdom is of sixty thousand people, and martial law exists. That is the court of justices are closed, and I can send anyone to death without trial or appeal. That is a fearful power in the hands of one man ; but feeling no inclination to be unjust or cruel it does not annoy me . . . I even like it. . . . Now tell me, dearest Mother, all your goings on. Every moment left for thinking of you is so applied, and with regret that my otherwise pleasant life is passed far from you."

Civil courts were established, and at the end of only three months martial law had ended. " The natives will regret the end of martial law, for as I settle four or five suits daily and they have no advocate to pay, whereas in the civil courts these would have taken months, even years, and rogues to be paid all the time."

The prisons and the dungeons horrify him. He tells Lady Sarah of one where thirteen men were almost suffocated. Seven

63

he took out immediately, vowing it was better to hang them than have them as he had seen.

Now no longer chained to his desk he gets two hours of riding for one of writing. Out of doors in this wonderful light, he thinks, " is well, and I am well when there is time to ascertain, but that is so seldom I may have been ill without knowing it. No one is sick when they have enough to do, and now I am going to begin a great work."

By corvée he had already carried a road over a precipice to unite two fruitful districts, but " The Great Work " was far more ambitious. A lofty range of mountains bisected the island, and Charles was to build a road which would be blasted and hewn out of rock. Though these mountains of Cephalonia do not rise over 5,300 feet, when the " road " was completed it was compared to Napoleon's over Mont Cenis, for the perfection of its gradients, and Charles himself was to write years later :

" Many a poor mule will say a good word for me at the last day when they remember the old road," and the only fault he could pretend to find with that young Captain John Kennedy of the Royal Engineers, who became his closest friend till life's end, was over those gradients. " John Kennedy, a constant slope for 25 miles will not do. You have but one fault ; you would keep a horse on the drag for 25 miles, and for that you will have to walk up a red-hot slope with bare feet . . ." but on every other subject but gradients : " If ever man or woman differ from John Kennedy they are wrong."

There had been jubilation throughout the island at the proposal of the road, till it was discovered that not only the peasantry, but the rich, and even the priests themselves would have to work with their own hands, or pay for one day in the week. But Charles stands out not only for his own passionate industry, but for the way he stimulated others to work. When the islanders saw that it was he and John Kennedy who led the way in all places of difficulty, clutching on to overhanging rocks and precariously jutting bushes to save themselves from dropping into blue space, their attitude was changed. One guesses how

Charles was enjoying it all, just as in the deserts of Sind in later years he snatched the spade from an astonished private to show him how to dig.

So the happy fruitful days passed in quick succession. Roads, a market place, a mole, lighthouses, schools, hospitals, and barracks, not forgetting the pyramidal base for Sir Thomas Maitland's statue. "This is very interesting because it pleases the people who consider the statue itself a great effort of genius : their pride is great, and my dislike of old Tom will not lead me to make war on his statue. This life is pleasant for me, very much so : but my constant desire is to see you again. . . . There is nothing so good for everybody as having something to do ; it diverts the mind and preserves health ; therefore read and amuse yourself, my dearest Mother, amusement is even better than business for old people. Read novels, laugh, cry, scold, eat, drink. . . ."

In addition to all this public work Charles was watching the struggle for Greek independence, helping with advice and encouragement. "The Greeks are more like the Irish than any other people. So like, even to the oppression they suffer, that as I could not do good to Ireland, the next pleasure was to serve men groaning under a similar tyranny." He and Lord Byron became great allies over this common cause.

Amongst all else Charles had to prepare for the entrance of the whole Suliot nation with their women, their arms, their treasures : "There are more than fourteen hundred, and above half are Palikars, old warriors. They wear the beautiful Albanian dress and their faces are the colour of a tea urn ; they are well made, not large, and are ignorant of every trade, but making war as robbers make war, and have a chief for each tribe. They came starving, and dying of sea-sickness, of want, of fatigue, having been crowded in little boats under a broiling sun : my first step was to get the women and children ashore, and at last all were landed and were fed. They are to be placed in a fortress which is so large that they will have fields and vineyards within, and be four hundred feet above the sea on a steep rock. No Palikar deigned to carry baggage ; their poor wives had to do that, and said such was the custom, and for their husbands to break that custom would be foolish. Many of the women carried the arms of their dead husbands and brothers ; but there had been more women killed than men, the latter having by sallies escaped the shells which fell into Suli. Their arms are magnificent, and great presents they have offered to conciliate my good will, which, however, they have got on cheaper terms. They have also begged me to receive a history of their recent war, written so that the world might know they acted bravely and honestly. It is easy to deal with them, so obedient and well conducted are they. . . . The Turks behaved infamously about their treaty, and would have broken it and destroyed the Suliots but for our men-of-war who secured the hostages on board. What is to become of these people ? My wish is to form the men into a regiment. The labour of getting food for them has been very oppressive to me, and eight or ten have died of fatigue before they could be sheltered. Their appearance at my conference with the chiefs who stood with their hardy looking warriors in the rear, was picturesque. They have given me three thousand dollars to pay for their expenses, and as it has been done for one thousand they will be agreeably surprised."

One can picture how Lady Sarah, so far away, must have waited on Charles's letters ! For years the deep understanding that existed between Charles and his mother had been nurtured by correspondence. Vivid descriptions of things that interested them both, like the making of a garden, the beauty of the islands, as well as projects of his public works, his political plans, his thoughts, and, too, his irrepressible jokes, were all written to her in that lively sloping hand of his.

" Old Tom " had been ordered to Italy for his health and Sir Frederick Adam was acting as Chief at Corfu. A small-minded man, he was forced to bolster up his self-esteem with ostentation. The stark simplicity of Charles's rule in Cephalonia, and even more the success of the precipitous roads carried out at half the expense of the flat roads of Corfu, must have mortified Sir

Frederick. Knowing the opinion Sir Thomas Maitland held of his Military Resident, Sir Frederick did not dare to crack his whip over Charles. He flicked it. In one letter Charles describes such a flick : " Sir Frederick Adam, for want of larger faults, has fallen to work on my moustachios ! An official order has come to shave. This order was obeyed to a hair."

Yes. Every hair was carefully collected, tied up, and sent with his compliments to Sir Frederick at Government House, Corfu.

" One can only laugh at the gambols of an ass," Charles tells his mother.

But he had made an enemy.

And now Charles's biographer is confronted with a difficulty. A situation arose for which no completely satisfactory explanation can be offered.

In spite of great susceptibility to a pretty face, Charles had always been very chivalrous and clean-living. Amongst the bitter things which his detractors came to say of him in later years there was never any hint of scandal. We know that Charles himself had blamed Byron for drawing so much attention to the Maid of Athens, so having " caused the poor girls to get so many admirers amongst our travellers ever to get married to their own countrymen. I think our people behave ill in paying so much attention : they should either marry or be off."

But now Charles himself loved a beautiful Greek, Anastasia, and though she was to become the mother of the two daughters he idolised, no regular marriage seems to have taken place. Anastasia, like all Greeks, was a fervid patriot, and it is possible that loving Charles, yet she resented in her wild heart that an Englishman should rule over her countrymen. " Always have the Ionians been averse to the nation ruling over them whether these were English, Venetians, Turkish or Russians," once wrote Charles. " Having had no kindness from the world, and much ill-usage, they are not steady but bound and leap like a newly-launched ship."

A tale has come down that it was Anastasia's obstinate refusal of marriage, that it was she who refused to give their daughters a name. It has even been said that she maintained so perfect a love as theirs might be spoiled by a formal bond. This sounds nice, but it must be admitted that Anastasia had a violent temper, though it did not last long. When Charles was leaving for England, she refused to accompany him, but insisted nevertheless he must take the little girls with him. This was impossible, he thought, whereupon Anastasia put the children in a boat unaccompanied, and pushed them out to sea. They were rescued by a fisherman who brought them back to Charles at the last moment.

In the years to come these children were to accompany their father everywhere. His journals are full of their doings, their sayings, and in course of time of the doings and sayings of their children also. It was for the sake of earning money for Anastasia's daughters, indeed, that he eventually went out to India when a sick and ageing man.

Did Lady Sarah know of Anastasia ? He had once written : " I tell you, dearest Mother, but I could not tell it to others." He had always poured out to " my beloved Mother " his aspirations, his questionings on the meaning of life, of death, his jokes, his rages, but it must be remembered that now Lady Sarah was old, and almost blind. His letters would have to be read aloud. One assumes she did not know, but the question must remain unanswered.

The absolute silence that has been maintained about this episode in Charles's life in the many books that have been written of him is rather strange, for at that time it was not unusual for officers serving abroad to take unto themselves the daughters of the country. There was a tale there had been some form of marriage between Charles and Anastasia in the Greek church, but many years later an old relative thought that this had been merely to prevent talk at the time. The present writer was told by one of Sir Charles's granddaughters : " Only after we were grown up, and were married, did we gather that something had been carefully hidden from us." Nevertheless her mother had not hesitated to call her fifth child after Anastasia, as can be seen from this, to modern eyes, astonishing list of child-birth :

NAME	PLACE OF BIRTH	DATE OF BIRTH
Charles Napier	Karachi	8 July 1845
Montagu	,,	11 Oct. 1846
Katherine Emily . . .	,,	8 Nov. 1847
Robert Archibald . . .	London	12 May 1849
William *Anastasius* . . .	Simla	10 Sept. 1850
Henry Edward	,,	3 Oct. 1851
George Napier (*died* 1950) .	Blackheath	29 Nov. 1852
John Pitt	Paris	31 Dec. 1853
Richard Napier	Curzon St., London	4 Feb. 1855
Emily	Clifton	1 Aug. 1857
Susan Sarah	,,	18 Aug. 1858
Louisa Augusta . . .	(?)	29 Jan. 1860
Arthur Montagu . . .	(?)	15 Mar. 1861
Caroline Amelia (*died* 1950) .	London	21 Sept. 1862
Edith Katherine (*died* 1949) .	London	26 April 1865

Looking at the portrait of this old lady of eighty-eight, painted when a young married woman, looking then at her features lovely still in her old age, thinking of her amazing vitality and sense of fun, this writer remembers not only that this was the great granddaughter of the famous Lady Sarah Lennox, but also that she was the granddaughter of Anastasia the Greek so loved by Charles.

It may be of some interest to quote a letter from another of Anastasia's granddaughters, this time a spirited old lady of merely eighty-four. She writes : " Yes, I am afraid my wild and beautiful grandmother did not want to be tied by marriage or anything else. She adored her beautiful country. And when my grandfather left it she refused to accompany him. It is quite true she stuck the two small girls in a boat, and sent them out to sea, so that my grandfather had to take them with him, as a fisherman returned them to him at the very last moment. The mother he left in Greece, and begged a brother officer to take care of her. She was not legally married to Sir Charles.

One of our dear old great-aunts told me this had been said at the time to make less talk. I think my grandfather was devoted to her. I have never heard that they quarrelled. She was a beautiful wild creature, and a devoted patriot. Her country came always first. I think you will understand and forgive, as we are both evidently proud and broad-minded about that wild, fascinating grandmother. I am sure you will bring out her virtues, and not her faults. She had a violent temper, which never lasted long, so she would most likely have rescued the little girls if the fishermen had not found them. I have inherited her passionate temper, and so too have some of my sisters."

Charles was now in his forty-first year. A warm friendship had sprung up between him and Lord Byron. It was not only their mutual ardour for the Greek cause, but also their mutual love of a joke. When Byron lay dying Charles was uppermost in his mind. He had given him a letter for the Secretary of the Greek Committee in London. "Colonel Napier will present to you this. Of his military character it were superfluous for me to speak; of his personal I can say from my own knowledge, as well as from all rumour and private report, that it is excellent as his military. He is our man to lead a regular force, or to organise a national one for the Greeks. Ask the army. Ask anyone."

When he had spent nearly four years in the islands Charles wrote to his mother: "Here I am finishing my fourth year in the Ionian Islands: sharp work for a man's constitution thus to lay in liver for the close of life."

This is the first whisper of that voice which was later to mutter so ominously, and eventually to destroy him; and he goes on: "I want to hear how you are, dearest Mother. You are old and I am far from you. In war this would be necessary; in peace it is stupidity and weakness . . . I have stopped a massacre of the Jews here, all prepared for the love of Jesus! The Greeks have in consequence called me King of the Jews, and say the latter gave me twelve thousand dollars for protection.

Would it were true." So he switches from affection to fun and then to anger. . . . "The Turks at Constantinople insult our flag and seize our merchant ships because they are built by Greeks! And Lord Strangford, the ambassador, advises our merchants not to go to Constantinople in such ships. England is thus insulted on the sea by Turks, who have not a hundred sailors in the world! A few days ago a Turkish ship took five Greeks out of one of our boats and hanged them. . . . If this business falls into our ambassador's hands, everyone knows how it will end . . ."

June 26th, 1823 : "As I am always thinking of you, dear Mother, my pen goes whenever a boat leaves the island. My liver hurts me : an effect of torment like the geese of Paris who are worried to make their livers swell. . . ."

But leave did come in November. "This saves me much worry, which to a man whose liver, nerves and temper have been enduring irritation for a year is of some importance. I want rest badly."

This is not surprising. He had carried out his amazing reforms and schemes under the greatest difficulty. And it must be remembered that all the while he was pushing forward the interests of the island he was deeply occupied with Grecian affairs. He had written to Lord Byron :

"As to myself, I would willingly go to Greece, but will only go there if I can live on my income, which ceases if I am struck out of the army list by the King : therefore I can do nothing till it is ascertained whether this would happen or would not happen. . . . If by going on half pay I can serve the Greeks without further loss, whatever small stock of military knowledge I could offer your lordship in such an enterprise should then be at your disposal."

The Government, when asked to let Charles take a command in Greece, refused. In 1825 the Greek deputies offered to place him at the head of their army, but could not make it financially possible for him to resign his commission.

Whilst in England Charles busied himself with an elaborate

memoir on Cephalonia and all its works, with maps and sketches, pointing out the best sites for barracks, and the means of keeping the soldiers in health. He busied himself too in studying the Poor Law, and meeting reformers of prison, preparing himself thus for further reforms in Cephalonia.

In the meantime Sir Thomas Maitland had died, and when Charles got back to Cephalonia Adam was Lord High Commissioner. Charles was back amongst his own people. They were overjoyed to see him. He was delighted with his building at Luxuri and the progress of his prison, but angered to find that all his road money had been dribbled away with nothing to show for it. " It is surprising that the plain way of going to work is so little attended to. My plan was to have as few things as possible but to keep them going by vigilant laborious superintendence. In my absence the work has been doubled and dispersed, while the superintendence has been reduced . . . the prisons have one hundred and twenty culprits ; with me they never exceeded seventy. Forty men are on guard : with me eighteen sufficed. . . ."

Lady Sarah heard the growlings of the coming clash between him and the High Commissioner, but no doubt she was entertained by Charles's bishop.

" To bless us," Charles tells her, " we have got a bishop appointed . . . an excellent pious man who formerly lived by sheep-stealing, which he now calls his pastoral life," and then he goes on to describe a new acquaintance, in which he is perhaps quite unconsciously amusing. This was Dr. Wolff, the missionary, who afterwards became famous for his wanderings in Persia, Bokhara, and Afghanistan. Passing through the Ionian Isles he was shipwrecked, and arrived at Cephalonia in an open boat. Dr. Wolff's own narrative tells us that after his arrival Charles made his appearance on the shore " with convulsive eyes and shoulders, with fire-flashing glances, and a pleasant countenance ".

This jerking of his elbows into his side, and the twitching of his features, were the result of those desperate wounds of his.

Dr. Wolff continues : " The first thing that extraordinary man said was : ' I know your sister-in-law, Lady Catherine Long, very well. She is one of the prettiest women I ever saw.' Charles then added : ' Now, Wolff, I know you too, very well. I know that you are going about preaching that the world is coming to an end in 1845. It serves them right.' "

He was addressing the shipwrecked man through iron bars of the lazaretto where all newcomers were confined before being allowed on shore, and Charles continued with the utmost friendliness : " You are not allowed to land, but I and my friend Kennedy and Dr. Muir will often come to see you. I shall send you victuals, and you can do just what you like. You must remain here twenty-six days, for we don't wish to catch the plague, though it's all humbug. But we must submit to humbug. I shall come to-morrow with the Jews and Greeks to whom you may preach. You may tell them that there is no difference between Jew and Greek, for they are both rogues alike."

The following day Charles did bring a number of Jews and Greeks. " Now here I am come to stand by you," he announced pleasantly, " if you cannot convert them they shall get a d——d licking."

The doctor rebuked him for swearing, whereupon the Resident said humbly : " I deserve the reproof, for I swear like a trooper."

When the twenty-six days had elapsed Wolff became Charles's honoured guest at the beautiful Government House by the water's edge.

" I never saw a man who set a better example by having family prayers in his home," declared Wolff.

As his guest was a converted Jew, Charles summoned all the Jews to come and hear him preach. He said he would give a Bible to each who could read. " Can you read ? " demanded the Resident. " Yes." Charles put a Bible into the man's hands. " Read ! " But the man could not read. " I have a good mind to give you a d——d licking . . . the soundest licking you ever got . . ." shouted Charles.

Nevertheless, when Dr. Wolff left the island he had conceived

an extraordinary admiration for his host. In his narrative he
speaks of Charles as " the greatest man whom not only England
but all nations have for centuries had ". He believed that
Charles had " divine mission ", which under the circumstances
does seem a little surprising !

On January 1st, 1820, Charles writes : " A happy New Year
to you, beloved Mother ; all happiness to you. I cannot let the
day pass without telling you how much I love you." He tells
her he is making a garden in a convent, for dearly she loved
making a garden. " The vegetables are all given away, not sold,
and spare seeds alike. The nuns are all becoming gardeners,
earnestly watching the soldier who, by the way, is a very handsome
young man. Whether they are attracted by beans or beauty is
not known, but it is supposed by beans, as the ladies average
about ninety years each."

With such nonsense he beguiled his mother : " What a great
relief nonsense is to a man who has been working hard," he once
wrote. " I have a quantum of wit in me beyond the ordinary
run of men, and if it had no vent my death would ensue from
undelivered jokes." But with his nonsense too he recounts to
Lady Sarah the horrible storming of Missalonghi, and his introduction of a settlement of Maltese agriculturists from whom he
expects great things.

And on August 26th of that year Lady Sarah died.

Not one word in Charles's journal.

Silence.

Years before Charles had written : " Children and parents,
dear Mother, should be friends, and speak openly to each other.
Never had I a petty dispute with you or heard others have one,
without thanking God for giving me a Mother, not a tyrant."

When he was thirty-four he had written : " Beloved Mother,
I cannot pass over my birthday without reflecting that for thirty-
four years no benefit has accrued to me of body or mind, which
cannot be in some way traced to you."

He had always been a victim to what soldiers call the " mother
sickness ". She was the theatre of his actions. He confided to

her what he would confide to no one else. William wrote:
" Like Sertorious, he would have abandoned the greatest enter-
prises for his mother's sake." And in his letters how often we
come across such sentences as these : " Dearest blessed Mother,
to return to you is the first wish of my heart . . ." or " I would
give the world to be with you. May I have the delight of being
with you next New Year's day . . . anything so as to be with
you . . . and pitch my sword where it ought to be . . . to the
devil. . . ."

Their lives had been entwined together, and yet no one could
say Charles was tied to his mother's apron strings in the usually
accepted sense, and Lady Sarah herself had admitted in his babyhood : " I am not one who knows how to nurse and fuss over a
little child."

Probably no young and pretty woman could have filled the
place of Lady Sarah, his confidante, his friend, the pivot of his
life.

What was Lady Sarah's secret ? She had refused an offer of
marriage from George III. She was the confidante of Charles
James Fox as well as his cousin. She was kissed by Louis XV,
not only on her left cheek as her rank entitled, but also on her
right. When a Seigneur demurred : " *En verité c'est trop, sire,*"
swift came the retort : " *Je ne sais si c'est trop, mais je sais que
ça me plaît.*" She was a brilliant success at the French Court,
bewitching even de Lauzun. She was divorced by Sir Charles
Bunbury, but he continued on friendly terms, permitting the
little daughter of Lord William Gordon to bear his own name.
All might be explained by her unusual fascination and beauty,
but it does not account for the way her second husband idolised
her. " Loving you as I do, Sarah, I'm quite sure I'll never
repent marrying you." And repent he never did.

And when her husband lay dying Lady Sarah was to write to
her cousin Lady Susan Fox-Strangways, September 10th, 1804 :
" I am one who will keep the King's marriage day with unfeigned
joy and gratitude to heaven that I am not in her majesty's place.
It was the happiest day for me, in as much I like my dear sick

husband better than a King : I like my sons better than the Royal sons, thinking them better animals and more likely to give me comfort in my old age."

On the death of his mother, Charles came to England without Anastasia, without the children.

In April of the following year he married Elizabeth Kelly, a widow of over sixty, with grown-up children, and almost grown-up grandchildren. She was poor, she was an invalid, and Charles by this marriage found himself a father-in-law to an intimate friend of his own, two years older than himself !

With his susceptibility to a pretty woman, together with his intense love of children, this step is hard to explain, and no one of his many biographers has attempted to do so. It must be remembered, however, that they have also maintained complete silence over Anastasia, either from ignorance of her existence, or from prudery. Now Anastasia was a passionate patriot, a fighting patriot. She had refused to leave Greece. There had been the dreadful incident of the little girls pushed out to sea. Someone had to look after these children of his. With the yawning gap left in his life by the death of Lady Sarah it would be natural for Charles to turn to some older person. Possibly he confided his dilemma almost immediately to Mrs. Kelly, for the Kellys were old friends of his, as is now disclosed by correspondence bequeathed to the present writer.

Agnes Kelly, a daughter, had married Samuel Laing, who afterwards became the well-known writer and traveller. Samuel Laing and Charles had served at Hythe together, and in 1808, when the former was on a transport expecting to sail at any moment, he had sent to Charles a draft for £300 which he " expects to be honoured by his brothers for the use of those nearest and dearest to me ". At the same time he writes to Mrs. Kelly to consult Charles " on every occasion ", repeating that he trusts " Napier in this delicate and depressing situation ".

Both young men fought in the Peninsula, and when Laing returned he married his fiancée Agnes Kelly. The friendship between Charles and Samuel continued, so that it was natural enough that Charles should now turn to his old friends in his grief. Captain Kelly does not seem to have been of much account, and had died six months earlier. Agnes Kelly was also dead. Her sister Mary appears to have been looking after the Laing family, whilst Eliza remained at home with her mother. Charles can have lost no time in confiding his troubles to Mrs. Kelly, for in February, from an outraged letter from Samuel to Mary, it is clear that Charles has proposed to her mother ! Samuel is beside himself. His letter, haranguing Mary, is worth quoting.

" Mrs. Kelly, now turned of three score, is surely entitled to judge herself of the suitable and the ridiculous in any step which she chooses to take in life. I have merely to take care that my children are not mixed up in intimacy with any connection, however near, who is considered by the world to have acted unsuitably or ridiculously. That the world will so judge of a woman past sixty years of age with children and grandchildren grown up marrying not a man of her own age, but a man in the flower of life, young enough to be her son, is unquestionable, and it is equally unquestionable that it is my duty as a parent to take care that my children have no [illegible] connecting them with what the world, perhaps very unjustly, finds unsuitable."

He continues pompously :

" I do not think it was right in you, dear Mary, not to communicate this matter to me, so soon as you were acquainted with and commented upon it. I know it is a subject on which we could not speak without feeling very awkward and confused, but it is a matter which affected my children entering into the world, in as much as the estimation in which their grandmother is held in the world affects them. Elizabeth thinks that this letter is the first intimation you yourself have received of the matter ; if it is, my dear Mary, I must as a parent say that the mother of grown-up daughters, and almost grown-up grandchildren, who is going to change her condition, even if everything is suitable, has no other consultation or announcement of her intention with them than is contained in this letter, shows such an ill-regulated mind, and such a disregard of a correct view

77

of what is due to them, that I do not think it right my daughter
and son should imbibe their principles of action, either from
precept or example, and I will certainly not allow my daughter
to be in communication with her grandmother in any way."

Perhaps Mary was intimidated by her brother-in-law, who was
also her employer ; for at first she had written off to Charles in
her ungrammatical fashion : " How is it possible not to see some
of your kindness to my mother, and not to feel grateful, she
expects says to be happier with you than she has been for the
last thirty years . . . I am so little able to speak or write about
this, but if you do make her happy may God bless you in
future and forgive you the unhappiness you have caused her
children. . . ."

Yet now, both she and her sister become bitter and censorious,
and siding with Samuel.

No doubt it was natural that both women should be upset at
their mother, whose " health and convenience has been the
governing principal " (poor Mary's spelling !) " of our lives ",
being carried away to some outlandish island " far from the
respect of love of many friends " and the pills and potions of a
certain Mr. Bishop. Then it must be remembered that the lot
of the old maid at that time was dreary enough. The two sisters
may well have thought their mother had been greedy in securing
two husbands, when they had none. There is no reason to
doubt their genuine care for her, but when the following slips
out from Mary, it jars : " It is very likely that seeing my mother
with so many luxuries might make it more painful to put up
with bare necessities." That at all events is honest. She
hastily adds that she would rather see her sister " work her bread
than be indebted " to Charles, and adds waspishly : " I warn
you, Colonel Napier, that I may be led to say and do more than
you or my mother may like. There has been no unkindness, and
therefore can be no increase. I say so boldly because on this
point I could as boldly lay my heart open to God . . . I asked
Mr. Bishop if my mother was in a state to be spoken to on
business ; he was doubtful, and therefore I did not mention Mr.

Laing's letter . . . I am not called on to speak to her and not at all more likely to kill her considering the small quantity of feeling you give no credit for perhaps it is necessary to remind you of this . . . you may think I threaten, remember, Colonel Napier, you do the same yourself if you can fight I can talk, we may be both unequally unwilling to hurt my mother's feelings. I believe we had both better take the share that falls in the business quietly, you the ridicule, and me the shame. . . ."

" You the ridicule."

That must have stung Charles. But he bore with the sisters very gently, very kindly for their mother's sake. " If ", he writes, " a breach rises between you and your mother, it will be upon yourselves for no ill-temper shall be drawn from me upon the subject. I shall not show her your letter, nor the extract from Laing, or speak to her in any way, and I hope that you will not, for I think it might kill her. . . . I have just lost a mother. It is an *awful event*. Take my advice, dear Mary, you and Laing, and let a year pass ere you make serious resolves which may not be in your power to revoke should the hour arrive, when you would much wish to do so."

For to one so attached to his own family as was Charles, it must have been peculiarly painful to feel that he had innocently come between mother and daughter. Certainly he did his best. But across Mary's reply to this letter of his, his quill has driven : "I did not answer Mary's second letter. Her feelings appear to be as bad as her English and her spelling."

The break was now complete. The marriage took place in April. The Napier family received Elizabeth Kelly with " the affection due to my wife and her own character," writes Charles. " She will live loved and respected as she *well deserves*."

But Samuel Laing only learned of the marriage by " public report ".

Charles took off his wife to Cephalonia. There is no account of what the lady thought of the Island, or of the two dark-eyed little daughters of Anastasia she was to mother. It is unlikely that children bred of Charles and Anastasia would be without character or easy to manage ! But both Susan and Emily in after life were to speak of their step-mother with real affection.

This strange marriage was a complete success.

As Charles had foretold, the warmth and sunshine benefited Mrs. Napier's health. Doubtless his affection, his merry teasing ways and even the care of the two little girls also played their part. Two and a half years later Mrs. Napier is looking forward to a reconciliation with her own daughters, hoping to meet them in Tours, where they are staying with the grandchildren. She writes reassuringly : " Colonel Napier is much too anxious for my comfort and peace of mind, and is so liberal and kind-hearted to recriminate in any way whatever that might give pain to any of us. He has fully made up his mind to meet in perfect cordiality. Have no fear. Peace is our aim and desire."

Mary's reply is not available. What can she have written to cause the old lady to exclaim piteously : " I cannot think you meant to write so unkindly to your mother " ?

Laing's reaction was even more extraordinary. He demanded money from Charles, maintaining it would be unfair to cause him the expense of removing his children from Tours to avoid meeting their grandmother ! He also wrote to his mother-in-law, beginning his letter " Dear Madam ". He reminded her that " from the period of my marriage into your family up to the period of your present marriage you received various remittances from me, amounting now, with the interest upon them, to a very considerable sum of money. As long as you were connected with my family, and while you had no means or prospects of repaying them, it would have been folly to have considered these advances as debts."

He sent a duplicate of this letter to Charles, saying he can only suppose from some extraordinary concealment Charles has suffered his wife to remain under pecuniary obligations which are debts of honour as well as being legal debts. He claimed a lump sum of three thousand pounds, suggests the buying of an annuity for the family, and expects the setting up of a " separate establishment " for Eliza.

Not unnaturally, Charles repudiates both debts of honour and in law. Angry letters followed. Charles got Lord Napier, the head of the family, as having " a cooler head " to reply, but by and by he became so exasperated by Laing's demands he is tempted to challenge him. It is a sordid and distasteful affair. It is easy to imagine Charles's angry misery at the inevitable distress caused to his wife whom he had come to love so dearly. Finally he returns Laing's letters unopened. The first dozen are tied up in a packet. They lie before the writer. On the outer cover Charles has written : " This villain's letters must be kept, or after death he will traduce my character." And in that dashing flowing handwriting, faint and brown though it be, one feels the burning indignation.

Mrs. Napier is taken seriously ill, and Charles hurries off with her to England in his anxiety, the little girls left behind for the time being.

" My wife has had a dreadful overturn," he writes. " I try not to think of it. Bacon is right. A man is more fit for public life without wife or child. Yet when death comes there is perhaps more comfort in love than glory. . . ."

Then comes a truly characteristic touch. Without any pause at all, without any sense of incongruity, he adds : " Poor old Blanco died in the Bay of Biscay, dropping suddenly. My poor old Beast."

Blanco being his favourite Peninsular charger, comrade for sixteen years.

Mrs. Napier did not die. For the next three years Charles continued his journal, and letters to his brothers and sisters exist ; but the lively descriptions of people, the conditions of his life and work in Cephalonia with which he had kept Lady Sarah so amused, are no more. The sparkle and laughing freshness of those early days have vanished as the breath of spring. His days instead are clouded over by frustration. Sir Frederick had resolved that all administration was to be directed in future from headquarters at Corfu.

Doubtless Charles was prejudiced, but we too are conscious

of the ridiculous situations in which we find ourselves with over-much control.

" Two men died of plague," writes Charles, " and long after they were buried came an order directing a peculiar treatment for cure. Answer dead. Some weeks later came full instructions for burying them. Answer. Bodies of victims are not kept as curiosities, they are buried at once. . . ."

Then, too, Sir Frederick had passed an act through the Ionian Parliament for taking the roads and other public works out of Charles's hands, boasting he " would tie up Napier's hands ". He had decreed that convent properties and religious gifts and legacies should be handed over to head-quarters. Sir Thomas Maitland had set his face against this, and now the anger of the Cephalonians mounted high that they should be taxed for the benefit of Corfu.

There Sir Frederick had built himself three palaces within gunshot of each other. True one was eventually handed over to be a lunatic asylum, but proved not suitable.

" It was not constructed for so many," was Charles's dry comment.

He had " saved money for fools to squander ", he added.

Charles had touched at Corfu when carrying his wife home. Sir Frederick Adam received them both, and accompanied them down to the ship with these rather surprising words : " Stay as long as you please, Napier, but remember that the longer you stay, the worse for us."

Yet before Charles was due to return Sir Frederick Adam was to say of him : " His tyranny is such that we could not allow him to reserve his office. . . ." Though in the same breath he acknowledges : " If the good he has done in Cephalonia were put in balance against the evils, the good would infinitely counter-balance them."

Strange is the heart of man.

Charles himself admits the corvée was unpopular at first, but not after.

" My conviction was that four days in a month was not too

82

much for men who can in three months earn full sustenance for a year. The Resident worked, the engineers worked, British sergeants worked, and soldiers worked. Who then could laugh or condemn work? No one did. Having worked for Government, they now work for themselves; and the women of several districts praise the corvée, saying: ' Our men do not leave all the digging to us, and we have time at home to spin.' "

No doubt the feudal chiefs remained hostile, but it cannot be denied that the greater part of the islanders were devoted to Charles. There are many stories illustrating this, but perhaps the most touching is that when he left Cephalonia for ever the peasants voluntarily cultivated a small bit of land he had left uncared for. Year by year they never failed to send him the value of the crops without disclosing their names. For Charles was not to return to Cephalonia. There in London he was faced with charges of oppression.

Charles thought on his miles of mountain roads . . . so derided till they succeeded . . . his spacious streets and covered markets; the mile and a half long mole running right out to the lazaretto through whose bars Wolff had peered, the barracks, the Courts of Justice, of Police and Treasury. He thought on his Maltese Colonists at Pronos, the girls' school, the opening of ports, the teaching of terraces to the people so that the whole rocky isle had become a vast vineyard, the hospitals, the barracks . . . all, all had been of absorbing interest—except perhaps the convents! " The only things that bore me are the church and convent affairs," he had confided to his mother long before, " excepting a beautiful nun of sixteen who dislikes being one very much, and I have blowed up her old devil of an aunt, the abbess, for making her one. Nay more! I told the girl's friends that if she would run away with a handsome young Greek, I would, as head of the church, stand between them and all harm."

They offered Charles the port of Zante, the " Golden Island ", capital of the Ionians, thus of more importance than Cephalonia.

Often had he described the beauty of Zante to Lady Sarah —but for him Cephalonia was ever shining in a light more bright, more lovely; Cephalonia had his heart in thrall—till death.

In any case his character must be vindicated.

Zante?

NO !

Sixty years later a Greek lady was to say: " They still speak of Napier as a god in Cephalonia."

CHAPTER 8

THE NORTHERN COMMAND

1839

CHARLES now found his bed shorter than he was able to stretch himself in. For, unbelievable as it seems, this able man was to endure no less than ten years of unemployment on half pay. Even reflecting that every year has three hundred and sixty-five days, every day twenty-four hours, every hour sixty minutes, every minute sixty seconds, we can only faintly guess what this meant to one of his fiery temperament. " I take no rest for myself, and give nobody else any," he had written to his mother from Cephalonia. Ten years out of harness ! " To-morrow, and to-morrow and to-morrow." One pictures him eagerly waiting for harness to fall on his shoulders as the horses of the old London Fire Brigade used to stand waiting, their harness suspended above them, ready to drop on their shoulders, so that they could leap forward at the alarm. Ten years !

To the miseries of inaction was added the problem of supporting an invalid wife and the two little daughters of Anastasia. Moreover, rightly or wrongly, he was smarting under a sense of injustice, feeling that his services were neglected whilst men who had served under him were rewarded. Since his quarrel with Adam he was ready to quarrel with everyone. " I have no home, my purse is nearly empty ; verily all this furnishes food for thought."

From Berkshire, to Hampshire, and then on to Bath, he moved restlessly. The state of the country worried him. " If my wife were young I would go to New South Wales, to get out of the way, and rear young kangaroos to play with Susan and Emily," he writes. He gets cholera in the epidemic that was sweeping the country, and then in 1832 becomes almost distraught, for Elizabeth his wife died.

In his private journal he gave vent to a terrible outburst which to us in this more controlled age might seem almost unbalanced. The unkindness of her children, of which he had been the unwitting cause, and which so easily might have come between them, doubtless added to the poignancy of his grief.

For the time being he is undone.

He moved off to Normandy, with the two little girls again left on his hands. What can he do? It may have been about now that Susan and Emily meet a dark gentleman they had never seen before, and learn he is their uncle. They only saw him once. Well, Charles plans their education, plans amazingly advanced for the day.

"I will teach my girls only useful things. French, for example, because it will be of real use, and it would be painful for them not to know what so many fools know. But my object will be to teach only one thing at a time . . . you remember my father always said the advantage of Scotch education was that it taught but one thing at a time. By useful I mean:

1. Religion as a foundation; to this I trust for steadiness.
2. Accounts, to teach the value of money and how to regulate a house.
3. Work, that spare hours may not be lost if rich: and if poor, that they may make their own things.
4. Cooking, to a certain extent, that they may not be at a loss if a revolution throws them on their own resources, and also to guard against servants' waste.
5. That they may not be dumb in a foreign land which would kill them.

"These things I can teach them, if I live until they are fourteen: then they shall learn anything to which their tastes incline.

"They begin to make out French when they like. Walking in the street a French lady made an observation not intelligible to me, but Susan whispered, 'Papa, I know what that lady said.' 'What two pretty children those are.' Then after a while, added : 'I think that a very pretty woman,' she being very like an ourang-outang."

Could such prosaic details of education be all that remained from those shining hours of light, of love and laughter, in their Isle of Cythera with its almonds, anemones and asphodel floating in the azure seas ? Or did that part of his life with the mother of these two little girls still exist in isolation and intensity, some-how, somewhere for all time ?

And now what was this extraordinary man like at this period ? He had a loud strong voice, very vehement, not from passion but intense earnestness. He was short and wiry. He had a slight stoop such as is seen in those who are constantly in the saddle. His step was alert, and Rice Holmes in his life writes : " His aspect was noble and commanding, and when he smiled, of winning sweetness. Wavy locks of iron grey clustering above a broad massive forehead, a nose curved like the eagle's beak, dark eyes gazing with piercing intensity through spectacles that seem inseparable from his face . . . in that look, though ambition had grown weary with waiting . . . was the certain promise of heroic deed."

In 1834 there was a suggestion that Charles should be Governor of certain parts of Australia. He made conditions which he considered were essential, and which afterwards proved to be so. Impulsively, he married the elderly widow of Captain Alcock, R.N., to be a mother to little Susan and Emily, and a companion to himself in the Colony, only to learn that though his nomination was ready, his terms would not be complied with !

Curiously enough, even as a boy he had written to his mother : " Now never to marry any but a widow has been a vow of mine . . . a widow I am bent upon." Well, he was to marry two. How brightly life had started at Celbridge in primary colours : breathing and eating with the heroes from Plutarch's *Lives*, their glittering examples to hand down to future generations ! But since boyhood life had become more and more complicated, and now in his secret journals, and his esoteric correspondence with his brother William, we guess that Charles is confused and not happy.

He is still unemployed, and his barren years go trailing after him as he seems pushed step by step into obscurity.

William is now taking an active part as a reformer. Charles is seeking to uphold the rights of the common folk against the private interests of a single person who would appropriate these general rights to his private profit—but he is not a " republican ". " Republicans are contrary to Nature. God has created us of different sizes, both morally and physically. He has also ordained that we should walk upon our feet, and under the direction of our heads. Now a republican form of government seems as if we were all to agree to be cut to an equal length, and that all who had heads and feet left should walk on the one or the other according as the fashion should be decided by a general vote passed every four years ! Now, this I do not like. I am very fond of my feet ; I buy good worsted stockings, and good boots for them ; I keep them warm and dry with great care ; but I have no idea of their pretending to wear my hat, and making my head do their work."

Feverishly he strove to occupy himself in writing. A dialogue on the Poor Laws, an essay on Military Law, translations of Comte A. de Vigny's *Servitude et Grandeur Militaires*, and so on. He and his brother George received the rank of the Knight Commander of the Bath, and Charles asking if he has a right to " supports " declares " one must be a French drummer for poor Guibert's sake. . . ." But it is work, *work* ! not honours for which his soul cries out. " You and I and George ", he writes to William, " are broken off like worms chopped by the spade ; we twist about, heads and tails separated, not knowing where to look for each other. . . ."

At last this most unhappy period of his life came to an end. England was approaching the hungry forties and there was fear of general rising in the manufacturing centres. Charles, known alike for his military gifts and his sympathy with the workers, was appointed to the Northern Command. He entered on his command at Nottingham in April, 1839, saying after his ten years, " Here I am like a bull turned out after being kept in a dark stable."

He had once written : " My delight would be a shaved head, a vertical sun, and a fiery horse, and no hat. . . . The retreat through Galicia iced me, and I am not yet thawed," and with the label of Conqueror of Sind tied round his neck, too many envisage him only as a skinny, fire-eating old man, riddled with bullets, galloping *ventre à terre* across desert under burning skies ! Yet with equal truth he could be pictured as Cephalonia's able administrator, or in the rawness, the grime and squalor and hungry misery of the North of England. For the part he played preventing rioting of the Chartists was just as true an expression of his character.

He had always been suspicious of Industrialism. " Manu-facturers produce corrupt morals, bad health, uncertain wages and dependence on foreign market," he declared in his sweeping way. And radical as he was, when he came up north the tight-fistedness, the hardness and greed for " brass " were bound to enrage a warm-hearted, generous nature such as his.

" At this moment the best hand-loomer can only earn 5s. a week, the price of food being that this will not give him bread without firing, clothes or lodging. Hence a good workman must starve. And with this fact our rulers are called statesmen ! "

It was William who had taken the place of his mother now in correspondence, and William had prepared him for the conditions he would find. William had written the year before : " The noise of the machinery was deafening, the heat intolerable, the smells disgusting, and the haggard faces, distorted forms of the women and children employed were heart-sickening. None of the children and very few of the women dared to look at us as we passed through the room. Misery of mind and body, pain and fear and hopelessness were in every countenance. It is a hellish system. . . . And yet one gentleman who was with us having a wife and half a dozen children of his own about him, on my remarking on the diseased looks of the children told me . . . that tables had been made out which proved these squalid creatures to be more healthy than any other class of working people."

To any soldier it must seem incredible that Charles had Northumberland, Durham, Cumberland, Westmorland, Lancashire, Yorkshire, Derbyshire, Nottinghamshire, Flintshire and Denbigh to control with four thousand men scattered in twenty-six detachments, every magistrate being anxious to ensure protection for his own area ! This is not to imply, however, that the whole of northern England was in a state of unrest. But at Halifax Charles had found forty-two troopers quartered in twenty-six billets. " Fifty resolute Chartists might disarm and destroy the whole in ten minutes," he observed grimly, " and believe me, gentlemen, that a mob who has gained such a momentary triumph is of all mobs the most furious and dangerous to the inhabitants."

On May 1st he writes : " My command is better in hand. At first all was darkness. I grovel about like a mole. . . . Will there be a civil war ? My opinion is there will only be a row at Manchester which will be put down."

"God send me through this work as a gentleman ought to go through with it," is his constant thought.

And that there was no serious disturbance was probably due to the respect held by the Chartists for his combined determination and humanity.

He goes to the Chartist meetings secretly in mufti. With his real sense of comradeship and understanding of the common man he boils with indignation. The words pour like molten metal from his pen in letters to William, and in his journal : " Chartism cannot be stopped, God forbid that it should."

" Hell may be paved with good intentions, but it is hung with Manchester cottons."

So intense and vivid is the illusion he casts upon us, we too feel, we too see the misery about him.

Though denouncing the agitator he yet had no criticism of the poor. It was the " rich " who would not fairly pay their workmen who stirred his indignation. "God forgive me, but sometimes they tempt me to wish they and their mills were burned together." Thus he thunders.

But just as in 1798 Colonel Napier's sympathies had lain a great deal with the Irish Republicans, but being a soldier and a servant of the Government he had considered it his duty to fortify his own and his neighbours' houses, and to hold the small town of Celbridge, combing the country night after night in search of insurgents, so now his son forty years later did not forget *his* duty as a soldier, and the family motto " *Sans Tache* " of which his father had taught them all to be so proud.

Having obtained a secret introduction to the Chartist leaders he told them in forthright fashion : "I understand you are to have a great meeting on Kersall Moor with a view to laying your grievances before parliament : you are quite right to do so, and I will take care that neither soldier nor policeman shall be within sight to disturb you. But meet peaceably, for if there is the least disturbance I shall be amongst you, and at the sacrifice of my life, if necessary, do my duty. Now go, and do yours."

His journal breathes indignation, pity and abuse. The Poor Law calls forth his anger. "The poor here have resolved to die rather than go into the Union Houses. . . . Many of those who were willing to go were refused. I know of an old man who being starving was told, ' Oh you can't have anything to-day, come again Thursday ! ' ' But I have gone without food for two days, and shall be dead before Thursday ! ' ' Oh, we can't help that, you must weather the storm as others do,' and he would have died had not the mayor fed him."

For this Mayor of Nottingham Charles is full of praise : " My excellent friend William Rowarth worth a host. . . . In Nottingham he and the gentry got up a meeting, and in a few days £4,000 was collected in spite of the Poor Law people who said we were encouraging idleness." And of Wright the banker he declares : "There is one family here that would save a city from God's wrath . . . a better fellow never rolled in riches as he does I believe.

"I like Nottingham. The poor people are so good. Thank God we have had no row, and not a drop of blood has been spilled. The gentlemen here are so good as to give me credit for this, which I am not sure of deserving, save from my great desire to prevent mischief."

That year Charles's younger brother Henry was writing thus :

"Charles works too much. He is often not in bed till one or two, and always up at five or a little after, and is eternally writing at an average about fourteen to sixteen hours a day. He has a cough, complains of short breath and weakness, and is allowing his own zeal to carry him too far for his own health. I doubt his being able to go on thus. The fatigue of reading and writing is very great, for I see that, as corporal punishment has diminished, court martials have increased, and he reads every word. His purse, too, is pretty well picked by these visits of inspection for he receives a travelling allowance that will not cover the bare posting when forced to take four horses and his aide-de-camp, all things included he cannot get out of an inn much under two pounds a day, although he burns tallow candles, and left the best hotel in Manchester because they objected to give them to him."

Meanwhile Charles fumed at the usual indifference of White-hall to the well-being and comfort of his soldiers. Not only was barrack accommodation inadequate, it was also filthy. Food was bad. Billeting he objected to because of the danger of seduction. Yet troubled though he was over the conditions of the private he had no wish to pamper the men in any way as the following letter will show. It was addressed to an officer who had written complaining of the barracks in which he and his men were housed :

"Never", writes Charles, "put into a list of real grievances things which are imaginary. 'One half of your accommodation is stone floored !' My dear Sir. I have been living for nine months in a lodging with stone floors, and my wife and daughters bear them very well. Soldiers must not be so delicate ; my own room is just seven feet by ten and stone floored."

This from the man so susceptible to cold in his wounded jaw, he had once written : " Shadrach, and the other fellows, I can't spell their names, but the three salamanders could not stand the fiery furnace better than me.   The kindest thing anyone could say to me is, ' Go to the Devil.' "   Now in the raw and rainy cold of the north he said he " did very well in his seven-foot stone-floored room ".

But secretly did his thoughts hark back to the lizards baking on rocks in Cephalonia ?

Surely.   For this Charles was always in pictures, delighting in them for their own sake.   To shut his eyes a moment to pallor and the grime of industry, and see and hear instead the brown and merry Greeks !   To remember how often he had looked down from some height on to a floor of peacock and wine-coloured seas, where the islands lay basking and drenched in sunlight, each ringed about with dazzling white foam ! . . . these Grecian islands where he had been on such happy terms with himself !

He recalls, too, in his journal the wild glorious days of the Peninsular.   " We were three active chaps then.   I was 28, George 26 and William 25.   And now !   *Och hone.*   57, 55, 54. I command half England, George rules the Cape, and we are both Knights Commander of the Bath.   William is a Companion and finished his history this month.   This is not bad, but what good is it ?   A few years we are gone, forgotten.   Yet is it pain to go to those who are gone before ? "

These are the words of a man who feels his work finished, but through the gloomy reflections quickly the old fun sparkles again.

" Sept. 27th.   Anniversary of Busaco in which I was shot through the stem, and George through the stern; that was burning the family candle at both ends."

In June, 1839, he went up to London to be invested.   The contrast was too great.   The hardness of men's hearts and the starvation in those northern towns rose between him and the glittering fripperies of the Court.   For through those spectacles of his which always seemed a part of his features Charles himself had seen a young and pretty woman in the drenching rain on Christmas night, one child in her arms, another at her breast, and she about to be delivered in the street. She had come into the town that morning, wet, famished, friendless, seeking her husband all day who was trying to find work. Now in her extremity she sought admission to the Poor-house, and Charles himself was to hear her refused, and moreover abused for being what she owned to be. He himself heard the quiet words she asked : " Tell me what to do, either good or bad," and he himself was to write : " Devil a bit would the Poor-house folk take her in. . . ."

With memories such as these darkening his mind, no wonder this man, who all his life had shown supreme tenderness for the weak and oppressed, found the showy brilliance of the Court trifling, childish, distasteful. Writing of it one sees he turns from it, feels himself detached, belonging to a former generation ; his comrades are " worn, meagre, grey-haired, stooping old men ", but characteristically enough he must end on a humorous note, sardonic though it be :

" There was our pretty young Queen, receiving our homage, and our old shrivelled bodies and grey heads were bowed before her throne, intimating our resolution to stand by it as we had stood when it was less amiably filled. I wondered what she thought of us old soldiers ! We must have appeared to her like wild beasts, and I daresay she looked at us as she looks at the animals in the Zoological Gardens. Lord Hill is old, and has lost his teeth ; poor Sir John Jones looked like a ghost ; and Sir Alexander Dickson is evidently breaking. Thinking how these men had directed the British thunders of war, I saw that death was the master ; the brilliance of the Court vanished, and the grim spectre stared me in the face : his empire is creeping over all. Yes, we are in the larder for worms, and apparently very indifferent venison ! "

Most of us have shared these sentiments at yearly reunions. Could we sum them up so neatly ?

CHAPTER 9

INDIA

1841

METTERNICH once said of Napoleon : " He provokes us
to take measures of security by putting about rumours,"
and in years to come Charles was accused by Dalhousie and
others of magnifying dangers to advertise his own skill in dealing
with them. But now the way in which he had discharged his
duties in holding the rioters in check without bloodshed must
have eased the tension which had existed between him and his
superiors for so long, for in April, 1841, he was offered a post
on the staff of the Indian Army. Hitherto he had been considered at the Horse Guards as quarrelsome and intractable and
an alarmist. But it could not be denied he had said : " My wish
is to prevent an outbreak, not to provoke one," and he had carried
this out successfully.

Charles was worn, grievously out of health, and in his
sixtieth year. It seemed that this opportunity had come too late.
He hesitated about accepting the offer. He felt he had lived his
life. (How strange to think he was yet to begin that for which
he is now best remembered.)

The value he set on his brother William's judgment was great.
For years now it was William who had filled the place of Lady
Sarah. " Go, if you feel a call for such a service," said William.

And Charles confesses : " My spirits were very low until my
mind was fixed for India, then they rose." Worn and ill though
he was, perhaps he caught a glimpse of that possible military
glory so long desired, so long denied, just as the afterglow may
light some high spot before it too fades into night. But another

95

reason is given in this extract from a letter to Lieut.-Colonel Whingates, C.B., R.A., commanding at Carlisle, and written with his old pungency.

"Many thanks for your kind wishes. I am very rational, my wishes are only to barter a great lack of sovereigns in this country, for a lac of rupees in that. I am too old for glory now. If I was as active a man as I was when I smashed that fiery —— [illegible] I might do some good. If a man cannot catch glory when his knees are supple he had better not try when they grow stiff ! All I want is to catch all the rupees for my girls : and then die like a gentleman. I suppose if I survive 6 years I shall do this."

He had tried to insure his life, but no office would accept him. As he truly said long after, the reason for which he was refused was the very reason for which he was anxious to insure himself ! He added : "When I look back to the desperation which made me come to India at sixty years . . . I feel how strong is my love for my girls. Had I died then, not a farthing was left for them. My passage to Suez was paid beforehand perforce, and my pockets were empty. . . . At Bombay the purser received my last money, a bill for £500 in payment of the voyage from Suez, and returned two pounds." Just as his father had worked himself to death to provide for his family, so Charles was prepared to do the same for Susan and Emily.

But now his mind was made up; there is no denying that Charles's spirits rose in leaps and bounds. The years dropped off his shoulders. At last, at last, he was to get the desire of his heart. The bonfire had been smouldering all the time it seems, and now it broke out strong and vigorous.

He set out for India, accompanied by his wife and two little girls. Behind his shoulders the chills, the rain, the disappointment and disapprovals of England. Here Charles stands revealed in the glittering sunlight of the East. Is it to illuminate more brightly the brilliant qualities—and defects—of his character ?

Charles assumed command at Poona at the end of December,

1841. He always loved a hot sun and brilliant skies. After the winter in those dour manufacturing towns of England, wet and cold, aggravating his rheumatism and the pain of his facial wound, Poona must have seemed particularly pleasant with its sparkling hot sun, cool nights and the green still lingering on its Seven Hills after the monsoon rains. But gloom was brooding like a thunder cloud over all India from the late and appalling disasters of the Afghan war and the blow English prestige had suffered. Women and children brutally murdered in frightful conditions of frost and snow, and a whole army wiped out with the exception of Dr. Brydon, who reached the British force at Jellalabad, and the few hundred prisoners as hostages whose chance of ultimate survival appeared slight indeed.

On January 2nd, 1842, Charles is writing in his journal: " Macnaghten has been assassinated at a conference with the insurgents ; falsely called rebels, for what right had Lord Auckland to depose Dhost Mahomed ? It was a scheme of self-seeking merchants that caused the war, and we have caught a tartar."

He continues that the situation in Sind is causing anxiety, and that he would probably be sent there, fifteen hundred miles away from his family, " to head 20,000 men in a difficult war against natives defending one of the most difficult countries in the world ; and to add to this the worse part of the affair, a bad cause. I am not acquainted with the troops to be commanded or the people against whom we war, yet the eyes of the world will be upon me, for the whole world sees and talks of our Afghan failure which it will be for me to repair. To try my hand with an army is a longing not to be described, yet it is mixed with shame for the vanity which gives me such confidence : it will come and I cannot help it, but as to my body it is not so. Oh ! for forty as at Cephalonia where I laughed at eighteen hours' hard work on foot under a burning sun : now at sixty how far will my carcass carry me ? No great distance ! Well, to try is glorious." In July he was ordered to take command of Upper and Lower Sind. Lord Ellenborough, the Governor-

General, told him all the politicians were to be placed under his orders. "Down comes Lord Ellenborough to abolish at one slap the whole of the political agents. This is very hard on Major Outram," but it undoubtedly gave Charles much satisfaction all the same. "I never quarrel with such people if they behave well," he writes, rather provocatively one feels, "and I think them useful in their place: but that place is not as councillors to a general officer: he should have none other but his pillow and his courage."

Critical as always he wrote: "What a Government! What a system. I go to command in Sind with no orders, no instructions! How many men are in Sind? How many soldiers to command? No one knows. I am, if sharp enough, to find that out when I am there."

His words, if forcible, are right, for Fortescue writes: "This bitterness was perfectly justifiable. The Government of India, whether civil or military, was at that time and until the abolition of the East India Company as rotten as could be."

Charles finally sailed from Bombay for Karachi on September 3rd, "Old Oliver's day, the day he won Dunbar and Worcester," he notes cheerfully, and then adds:

"Charles! Charles Napier! Take heed of your ambition for military glory; you have scotched the snake, but this high command will, unless you are careful, give it all its vigour again. Get thee behind me, Satan."

It was near the end of the monsoon, but outside the harbour the sea was still in uproar. Hardly had the *Zenobia* left harbour when several cases of the worst type of spasmodic cholera appeared amongst the men and the numbers increased. Let Charles tell his tale.

"Rain came down, and the decks became scarcely bearable from heat and stench; for to clean them was not possible, and as men died they were rolled up and instantly cast overboard. The darkness of the night, the pouring rain, the roaring of the waves, the noise of the engine and the wheels, the dreadful groans of the dying all in horrid convulsions; the lamentations of

98

men and women who were losing wives, husbands and children ; the solemnity of the Burial Service read by the glimmer of a solitary lanthorn held up to the book, presented an altogether dreadful scene.   No man knew whose turn would be next. . . .

" . . . The 5th, 6th, 7th night and day were passed in this dreadful manner ; and in these four days of wretchedness we threw fifty bodies into the waters.   The decks were covered with filth, the sick packed close together, no room for the living until the dead were thrown away, the survivors nearly broken down with fatigue of nursing, the doctor Cullum exhausted, the engineer dead."

Even worse was to come, for now the sailors were also attacked and they took to drinking.   Fortunately on the eighth day the disease became less virulent, patients dying in ten or twelve hours instead of three, and many even began to recover.   Those that died, however, still turned blue.

" Towards evening on the 9th there were no new cases and we reached Kurrachee at night.   It was dark and both mates were drunk, and we got out of our right channel. . . .   Then we cast anchor where we should be high and dry at low water, but where the rough sea running would have beaten us to death.   The decks were still covered with sick, most of them convulsed, all utterly helpless to the number of eighty, and again therefore we heaved anchor. . . ."   Most of the crew were now drunk and it was only by the seamanship of the captain and the support Charles gave him in keeping discipline that the ship was saved.

" Ten more died, including a friend of Charles and also a very pretty woman.   We had saved her on board but when she landed a second attack killed her.   Her poor husband was distracted . . . had only been married a few days.   A sergeant, just made major, also died, having left his wife and children behind him ; that bolt shot close to me : if I had it would quickly have disposed of me, being weak from not touching food for four days, prostrate and helpless from sea sickness. . . .   So ends the sad story of the *Zenobia* where we lost out of 299 soldiers fifty-four in four days, and sixty-four before the eighth.   The sea captain

(Newman) by firm and skilful seamanship, saved the vessel: his conduct was admirable."

It is difficult to picture Karachi as it must have looked to Charles in 1842. Just a hamlet of mud houses in a desert of rock and salty sand whose white glare was painful to the eyes! But there were two Queen's regiments there and artillery, and how gladly he must have heard the calling and sounding of bugles all day, and seen the whole place alive and twinkling with soldiers in their red coats, tight white trousers and black shakos. What a change from the tragedies of the cholera ship!

And already Charles saw a vision, not what Karachi was, a miserable hamlet . . . but Karachi as it would be.

The episode of the cholera had been an inauspicious send-off for Charles's Sindi Campaign, and now came another. Reviewing the garrison at Kiamari he decided to try a few rockets he had brought up from Bombay. No one knew much about them. One blew up, stripping Charles's trousers and tearing a long deep ugly wound in his calf.

" What an unlucky devil I am! Two thousand soldiers were standing around . . . and I alone hit!"

But he had always been what we should now call " Accident prone". Scarcely a year passed without some incident more or less serious! Himself, he wrote: " Got a devil of a tumble yesterday which makes me glad because I could not do better without having my yearly accident without being really hurt. To run twelve months without some *petit chose pour passer le temps* is not for me."

Present-day psychologists would probably put this down to the conflict in his own nature. That intense sympathy with every form of suffering, and his love of domestic life for ever warring with the passion for military deeds, and fame and glory!

Be that as it may here was Charles again with an ugly wound. It was stitched up, but refused to heal. A few days later he was steaming up the Indus in the *Comet* to his future.

CHAPTER 10

THE "COMET"

1841

THE alluvial country of Sind in which Charles was to spend the next few years of his life in violent activity is roughly the size of England and Wales. On the east is the pitiless Rajputana desert, with its sculptured dunes, its cactus, its scrub and camel bush pale against the deeper value of the sky; on the west the stark Baluchi hills; and on the north the sandy wastes and marshes of Bahawalpur. Down through Sind like an artery runs the Indus, that royal river 2,000 miles long from source to mouth, rushing at times through a rocky defile such as the Sukkur Gorge, or broadening and sweeping into a majestic and tranquil stream past small villages and shrines, past the tall " maypoles " of Pirs with the votive rags flickering all down their ropes, past cultivated patches, to flow ultimately through those marshes crowded with water fowl, by many mouths into the Arabian Sea.

Those who are familiar with travel on the Indus will recall the easy gliding days, like some tranquil interlude in life. Particularly this must have seemed so to Charles. As he rested on board with his bandaged leg, those quiet days were separating him from the charnel house of the *Zenobia*, and from the inexorable approach of the Future, and all that it might mean.

As the *Comet* steamed up the river, the waters reflecting the colourless brilliance of the sky, the faraway steep-scarped banks topped with dusty tamarisk; as the sound of the Shaduf floated groaning and creaking across the water as the camel turned its wheel, of what was Charles thinking? Did he see the great golden Sindhi boats with their high poops and rudders dreaming down the glassy stream ? Did he see the crocodile, loglike on a sand spit ? Did he hear the melancholy cry of the man forward, swinging the lead ? *Sarrhe panch FUT !* . . . *Arrhe FUT !* . . . and then the sudden commotion as the steamer ran aground on some hidden sand-bank ? And in the early morning when the wind blew cool, and a V of flamingos winged overhead flushed rosily by the rising sun whilst the banks of the river warmed to gold, did he see them ? Probably not. The Future could not be stayed any more than the gliding stream as it slapped away at the sides of the boat. The Kabul disaster must be avenged. The eyes of England were on him, Charles Napier. These were his thoughts.

Sixty years old, often troubled by his Peninsular wounds, yet the blood now coursing through his veins was as the blood of a young man. His mind was in yeasty turmoil, the old fighting spirit well alight. Ambition, longing for military glory struggling with his innate feeling for humanity, his love of justice, his pity for suffering ! His life-long interest in soldiers and all their doings, his acquaintance with the glorious heroes of old, his knowledge that Alexander the Great had himself gone this way more than two thousand years ago, carrying with him the famous copy of the *Iliad*, keeping it with his sword under his pillow at night, all these thoughts must have struggled for predominance in Charles, as the simultaneous voices in a fugue struggle for predominance, emerging and retreating to emerge and go their own way, and yet are contained in a single whole.

And this conflict was to find expression in his secret journal. " My ambition is not for a butcher's bill. The fear of exciting such bloody work is always in my mind. My wish is to spare them."

Yet, " the great receipt for quieting a country is a good thrashing first, and great kindness afterwards : the wildest chiefs are then tamed ".

Did he remember how he had written to his mother in the early days of disillusionment in the army. " To me military life is like dancing up a long room with a mirror at the end, against which we cut our faces, and so the deception ends. It is thus gaily men follow their trade of blood thinking it glittery, but to me it appears without brightness and reflections, a dirty red."

Well, what colour did he see it now?

It might be as well to look back over the preceding years to see why Sind had come to play so important a part in the affairs of Great Britain, why Charles felt he was on the threshold of great events.

It was not till 1831 that the British had first attempted to edge into Sind. Alexander Burnes was deputed to explore the Indus.

" The evil is done. You have seen our country," exclaimed a native.

And so indeed it was.

But there were other reasons why the expansion of the British to include Sind was almost inevitable. To begin with there was much friction on that border between Cutch (then the British limit strongly held by British troops) and Sind. The Afghans, who had invaded and plundered Sind in 1760, and still claimed suzerainty, objected to British action on the Cutch border.

Then Ranjit Singh, ruler of the Punjab, fixed greedy eyes on Sind, anxious to reach the sea. But for fear of the British he could easily have overrun Sind.

The French, too, were hankering after a footing. They had already tried to get into relations with Ranjit Singh; and in the 1830's Louis Philippe had sent presents to him, and decorations to French officers in his service.

These fears and the shadow cast ahead by the Russian Bear in Afghanistan were all present, but probably the chief motive in that age of industrial development was the opening up with the Indus of trade with Central Asia, the Punjab, and Kashmir.

Reflecting on these Powers standing round Sind like dogs eyeing a bone, one cannot help recalling the fate of Poland through the ages.

For some sixty years past the country had been ruthlessly ruled by usurping Baluchi princes of the Talpur tribes. The country was divided into three : Khaipur in the north, Mirpur in the east, and Hyderabad in Lower Sind. The descendants of these original princes were called Amirs, or Ameers as it was spelt in those days. Their rule was oppressive, the country given over to the preservation of game, the people taken from their cultivation to act as beaters for the sport-loving Amirs, their little properties heavily taxed. Nevertheless it would be a mistake to suppose that life under these Amirs was worse than any other under native rule. . . . Even at the beginning of the twentieth century there could be found amongst Indian Civilians some who considered the lives of Indians on the whole were brighter in a Native State than under British rule; that the average Indian prefers a gamble even if it be of life, a chance of riches from poverty depending on a whim, a lucky meeting, the eye of favouritism, an " auspicious occasion ". He prefers an occasional bellyful of indiscriminate charity, to the even justice, the equal opportunity afforded by the British where each man gets his deserts, where justice is for all, and where there is no favouritism.

But Charles, ignorant of India, would not know that.

When Afghanistan was invaded in 1835 Lord Auckland could not march through the Punjab as then the Sikhs would have gone to war, so he had to take the long devious road by the south through northern Sind to Kandahar. This invasion was an indefensible act, and unwillingly enough the Amirs had signed a treaty forced upon them, agreeing that certain forts should be occupied. Probably still more unwillingly they had guaranteed navigation of the Indus to be free to all who lived upon its banks. This must have been particularly galling, for the chief source of revenue had been from toll of river traffic.

All this, of course, had taken place before Charles had arrived in India. The Amirs had been coerced into signing treaties owing to their intrigues, and by this time they were regarding Britain " as a pestilence in their land ". Tolls on their trading boats were to be abolished, and Rustam, the Amir of Khairpur, had for the time being to surrender the Fortress of Bukkur. Though the Amirs were to be recognised as rulers, yet quarrels amongst them were to be referred to Colonel Pottinger, the Resident, and all the foreign policy was to be under British control. Moreover, the Amirs were to pay £30,000 a year towards the expense of the British force stationed in their own country !

This is not pleasant reading. The Resident himself was dissatisfied.

" It seems to me," he wrote, " that it would be better at once to take possession of Sind by force, than leave it nominally with the Amirs, and yet deal with it as our own. The one line is explicit and dignified, and cannot be misunderstood ; the other I conceive to be unbecoming to our power, and it must lead to constant heart burnings and bickerings, if not to a rupture of all friendly relations."

His post was taken over by Major James Outram. Karachi and other places were temporarily occupied, and Lord Auckland, the Governor-General, was succeeded by Lord Ellenborough, and at this point Charles came out to India at " the tail of the Afghan storm " as he himself describes it.

Lord Ellenborough felt he himself had no concern whatsoever with the rights and wrongs of his predecessor's policy. He accepted the situation as he found it. British interests must be safeguarded in Sind. Charles's views coincided exactly with this view, still further reinforced by his passionate desire to help the oppressed Sindis, and always with the conviction that he, Charles, was the man to do it.

From Karachi he had sent on before him an official letter declaring in no uncertain way that the Amirs were not adhering to the terms of their treaty, and peremptorily ordering them to do so in future.

On September 15th the steamer *Comet* arrived at the little village of Kotri. The news of the coming great man had reached the Amirs already. Charles was met by one hundred men bringing him gifts, Eastern fashion, as Melchior, Balthazar and Caspar had done. There were silver trays heaped with flowers, fruit and vegetables. There were ten sheep, and at the house of the political agent, awaiting Charles was a vermilion palanquin lined in vermilion cloth with emerald velvet cushions, as he was still unable to ride. For his retinue there were many camels with rich Sindi trappings, high peaked crimson saddles, and padded with cushions of all colours. There were fifty irregular Sindi horsemen, their wiry little horses scuffling and whinneying, those unshod hooves raising clouds of dust which must have hung luminous in the sunshine, so that stalking camels with lifted noses, and the crowds of armed and unarmed peasantry around, must have appeared and disappeared like golden phantoms.

Now Charles had an eye for the picturesque as any can see from his journals. He is almost Hellenic in those clear-cut cameos that he gives us. After all, he had been brought up on Homer, and the similes must have been familiar to him from boyhood. We feel sure that all this colour, display and detail must have delighted him. Sir Robert Peel, we know, rated him as a writer far above William the historian, " Not I only, but all of those of the Government are immensely struck by their mastery, clearness of expression, and feel with me he is as good with his pen as he has long proved himself with his sword."

So we may feel sure that all this colour, display and detail delighted him and painted the brightest pictures possible in his mind. Noisily the procession approached Hyderabad, that strange city with its fantastic wind-catchers crowded higgledy-piggledy on every flat roof. Mounted Sirdars with their retinue now came cantering out to meet him, some with spears, all with sabres, glinting in the sunshine. Through the swirling dust, flashes of orange, rose and scarlet of lungis, of silken scarves from Tatta, the high cylindrical Sindi hats in gold cloth . . . all the gaudy raggle-taggle crowd shoulder to shoulder, flowing like some brilliant stream, washing round the base of the great Hyderabad Fort, pouring on towards the Palaces of the Amirs !

And then his own men, his own British soldiers in their scarlet coats, white trousers and black shakos. This after those grey years of inaction, those grey days in northern England ! Charles's heart must have swelled. This was surely a fit opening for what he felt in his bones must surely come !

The Amirs rose and helped him from his palanquin. By and by they were all trying on his great spectacles, which puzzled them. Repeatedly they asked him if he were happy and comfortable, as indeed is still the custom in Sind. "Is all well with you ? Are you happy ? Is your belly comfortable ? "

Charles, notorious for his carelessness in dress, was on this occasion in full uniform with decorations, and very hot he must have been . . . but even so the contrast between the obsequious Orientals gorgeous in their gold embroidered coats and jewelled turbans, and the old warrior jerking his elbows into his sides as was his wont, and fixing them with eyes as bold and unwinking as their own hunting hawks, must have been extreme.

They offered him six thousand pounds.

It has been pointed out that this was a *Nuzzur*, that is, an official gift of money, which was, of course, meant to go into the State Treasury if accepted, but which was really intended to be politely declined.

But Charles was ignorant of Indian ways. He thought he was offered money for himself. Now his wife, and the precious little Susan and Emily were still down in Bombay. They were wholly dependent on his pay . . . and he lived in his times. . . . But his hero the Duke had declared that the only loot he had ever taken was four red ivory counters with P.B. enrolled upon them, which he had snatched up from the card table at Versailles when Pauline Buonaparte had fled so hastily after Waterloo.*

So proudly Charles refused the money.

" Possibly," he noted in that revealing journal of his, " this may be the last dependent reception they may give as princes to a British general."

Ominous words.

* In the writer's possession.

That old argument. Should evil be done that right may come? Now further complicating it is the undeniable fact that Charles's eyes are, despite himself, fixed on "military glory". He had that happy faculty which Gladstone later was to have, of persuading himself that everything he did was marked out for him by the Deity. Labouchere, the editor of *Truth*, and a follower of Gladstone himself, said, it may be remembered : " I don't mind the old man keeping an ace or two up his sleeve, but I do object to him saying that the Deity put it there."

The following day again the *Comet* was forging its way upstream through the silt-laden waters. The surrounding country was desolate and sandy, interspersed with jungle. Charles in his sunhelmet, staring through his great spectacles, decided then that the Amirs would never rule the country as it should be ruled.

" These poor foolish Amirs ! " he mused. They destroyed villages and cultivation so as to keep these *shikargarrh* (game preserves) for their own use. They refused wood for the four armed steamers of the British, and by tolls they destroyed the welfare of their people " who are frequently seen to pick the grains from the dung of the officers' horses, to eat ".

" *Mene ! Mene ! tekel upharsin !* " writes Charles in his journal. " How is all this to end ? We have no right to seize Sind, yet we shall do so, and a very advantageous useful humane piece of rascality it will be."

It was on October 5th that the *Comet* reached Sukkur on the right bank of the Indus. Immediately opposite the houses of Rohri climb up to the sky like tall golden cliffs pierced here and there by tiny windows which look for all the world like sandmartins' nests in a bank. Close by the fortified island of Bukkur, which the Governor General had occupied with British troops, and then set a little further down the river is the Sikh monastery of Sadh Bela whose bells one can still hear floating across the water morning and evening, just as Charles must have heard them more than a hundred years ago.

" *Ta*-ta, *Ta*-ta, *Ta*-ta, Tata . . ."

Yours
C Napier

CHAPTER II

SUKKUR

1842–1843

THE cold weather had now begun; the wind which bent and
swayed the tall pampas grasses was blowing from the north.
Charles, who loved a burning sun, must have found the passionate
climate invigorating, for though the nights were cold, as soon
as the sun rose, a scarlet ball showing between the stout trunks of
the date palms, night mists dispersed, and the twinkling dew-
drops on every tamarisk tree dried as by magic, while the camp
followers, numb and shrouded in their orange and red and pea-
green blankets and head shawls, would emerge to thaw in the
quickly increasing warmth, as they squatted on their hunkers
lighting camp fires.

How clearly one pictures Charles . . . always an exaggeratedly
early riser, galloping his Arab charger Red Rover before sun-up.
Along the river-bank he went, buttoned up in his blue coat with
poshteen worn over it, to shut out the early chill.   On he goes
at hand-gallop, in a cloud of dust, iron-grey hair and whiskers
astream, his beak of a nose and fingers numb, past some mud
wall with the dusty palms crowded behind it, past a tomb, past
a country cart whose solid wheels and ungreased axles torture
the air, past a Persian wheel with its plodding camel.   A stripey
tree-rat glued to the tree-trunk glances over its shoulder in
bright-eyed alarm; a woman with a pitcher on her head, and her
bangles winking in the level rays of the sun, turns to stare after
the snorting Red Rover and his rider. . . .   On they go. . . .

In the light of all that has happened during the past hundred
years, the Sind campaign has been dwarfed into insignificance.

Indeed but for the pen of Sir William Napier and the quarrel with Sir James Outram it would scarcely be remembered. So it would be tedious to enter into the negotiations with the Amirs that were now taking place. Suffice it to say that on November 11th, 1842, Lord Ellenborough had drafted a new treaty assuming the guilt of the Amirs, and directing Charles, the man on the spot, to prove this assumption. Already Lord Ellenborough, thinking poorly of Outram's political ability, had given Charles over-ruling powers.

Now Outram felt that certain proof of the Amirs' guilt was too difficult, therefore he advised Charles to ignore this, and merely take note of sundry minor breaches of the treaty which had been signed. This our Charles would not do. Many have said he was eager to prove the Amirs' guilt, but it is just to say that he did make most exhaustive enquiries to get at the truth, and one of many entries in his journal is that already quoted. " My ambition is not for a butcher's bill. The fear of creating such bloody work is always in my mind : my wish is to save them, and I am likely to succeed."

At this time he thought highly of Outram. It will be remembered that he had described him as the Bayard of India in the following speech.

" Gentlemen, I have already told you that there are to be only two toasts this evening. One, that of a lady . . . the Queen . . . you have already responded to. The other shall be for a gentleman. But before proceeding further I must tell you a story. In the sixteenth century there was in the French army a knight renowned for deeds of gallantry in war, and wisdom in council . . . indeed so deservedly famous was he, that by general acclamation he was called the knight ' *sans peur et sans reproche* '. The name of this knight, you may all know, was the Chevalier Bayard. Gentlemen, I give you the Bayard of India, *sans peur et sans reproche*, Major James Outram of the Bombay army."

Yet, alas, this was the same Outram of the sad and bitter tale to follow in which intercepted letters, rancour, the strain of war in a fearful climate, Indian intrigue, and finally the fierce vituperation of William Napier in defence of his brother, all were to play their part. An ignoble quarrel between two noble men, but at this time Charles was only beginning to differ from Outram's policy of appeasement, as we should now describe it.

The old General was not only occupied with intricate mediation with the Amirs, but he was immersed in immense correspondence as always. This astonishing man found time even to superintend the further education of Susan and Emmy, fast growing up in Bombay. Papers in arithmetic were sent to him to correct. He insisted on their walking at least a mile every day, and they were forbidden to wear the long frilled drawers of the period. In addition, Charles was intent on disciplining his troops, and checking extravagance. He had always been popular and a good trainer of the young since those far-off Bermuda days when he had trained both officers and men to " high efficiency ". True he raged now at the sight of the wounded soldiers with the second column " thrown down like dogs after the retreat from Afghanistan. Neither the Staff Officer, nor their own officers, took any care of them. Those gentlemen had a bit of my mind, and not all yet."

There is a proverb, " Huge winds blow on high hills ", and Charles raged too when he learned of the British destruction of Aurangzeb's beautiful Bazaar in Kabul. He raged at the indifference and callous neglect of Indian soldiers by the East India Company. Did he think on those tales told him in boyhood by his Aunt Johnson? Forthwith he ordered warm clothing for the shivering drivers of artillery wagons in the hills. Lord Ellenborough had put the political department in those forceful hands of his, and by God! now he would spend lavishly with one hand, whilst ruthlessly retrenching with the other, so saving the country large sums of money annually exactly as his father had done in Ireland years before.

Yes, Charles could storm, and his oaths were volcanic, but it was more often that his officers were delighting in his wit, his fun, his lurid stories.

It was at this time he issued that famous order which has been quoted for its characteristic humour. "Gentlemen as well as beggars may, if they like, ride to the devil when they get on horseback; but neither gentlemen nor beggars have any right to send other people there, which will be the case if furious riding be allowed in camp or bazaar."

His young officers took this well, must indeed have found it piquant, for it was not as though their own Chief did not ride like the devil himself. The wilder the horse's spirit the better he was pleased, and the only pace known was a hand-gallop. Nevertheless Charles, always scrupulously considerate, would never gallop in the bazaar.

Every day the sun of northern Sind glittered on the tall cliff-like houses of Rohri, and on the flat roofs of the opposite town of Sukkur. Every day the fortress of Bukkur, occupied by the English, rang out bugle calls, and the shriller cry of trumpets, and sound and stir of army life mingled oddly with the light Ta-Ta, Ta-ta, TaTaTa . . . from the island monastery in the stream. Negotiations, mediations, manifestos passed between Charles and the Amirs. As the waves of an incoming tide seem to retreat as well as advance and yet move inexorably on to the flood, so it was that events were moving towards war.

For just as Lord Ellenborough had thought poorly of Outram's political ability, considering his own choice of Charles Napier far more suitable to deal with the Amirs, Charles was now thinking so himself!

"Outram provokes me," he writes. "He pities these rascals who are such atrocious tyrants that it is virtuous to roll them over like ninepins."

It will be remembered he had once acknowledged to his journal that he could not do with people who differed from himself. "I confess not to like those who differ in their opinion from me. I may love and respect them, but I do not like them as companions: it is very tiresome to have every-thing one asserts argued: my temper won't bear it."

Yes. The Amirs were the source of trouble. Whatever excuses Outram might make "Evil was to be found in high places ". So thought Charles, scouring the country on Red Rover. Everywhere he recognised the hand of the Amirs pressing on the people. Wives murdered on the slightest pretext, crushing taxation, infanticide (this was denied by Outram but afterwards supported by Sir Richard Burton). A man kept in a cage for years ! . . . Then the animal suffering he saw all round him must have added fuel to Charles's indignation. Though his own horses were the most precious to him, yet Charles was linked in sympathy to every animal just as his mother Lady Sarah had been. Years before he had written : " We are a hot, violent crew, fond of hunting, fighting, fishing, and shooting . . . yet all gave up when young because we found no pleasure in killing little animals. . . ." So the sight of pi-dogs, hairless and pink with mange, their ribs starting like hoops through their skins, the poor over-burdened camels, the droves of little donkeys pattering along with tied-in gait because of the too tight breeching strap, and their dreadful sores stirring with maggots, must have exacerbated him to frenzy.

It was in these days of waiting we can see the trend of Charles's thought. He rides on a camel to Shikapur, some thirty miles away. The motion is pleasant enough, but he is noting that though the soil is rich, owing to the annual inundation of the Indus, yet all is waste. Woods, wild boars, game of all kinds, abundance of water, " everything but justice. The Ameers rob by taxes, the hill tribes by matchlocks : the cultivators can only earn their living close round their villages where a shout calls them in a minute for defence within a square mud fort with towers at the corners. The robber rules. With God's help, ere I am six months older he shall have a wipe, as a beginning for a new era in Scinde. I am gathering up my reins, my feet are in the stirrups, and my hand is on my sword, and if I do not put these chaps to right with vigour and without rigour great is my mistake."

One can but recognise that Charles was now obsessed by the idea of turning the " Unhappy Valley ", as Sind was known, into a paradise of his own as Cephalonia had been. The sins of the

Amirs absorbed him utterly whilst Outram was for glossing them over. Charles, in his headlong fashion, was convinced the destruction of the Amirs would be the future basis of law and order.

And yet . . . and yet . . . recording his negotiations with them, this strange contradictory man is writing :

" I almost wished they proudly defied us and fought, for they are so weak, so humble, that punishing them goes against the grain : but these feelings must not affect deeds : we are acting, substantially, justly, and for the good of the mass, while these Talpurs are like their own crocodiles."

It was in the middle of December that he delivered his ultimatum.

He was ill. He was old. He was loaded with responsibilities. He was wasted and weakened by diarrhœa, separated from his wife and Susan and Emmy, and now his nephew John Napier, who was on his staff, and whom he loved most dearly, lay at death's door.

" This is a hard trial for an old man of sixty. Yet what signifies these troubles ? I feel a spring in me that defies all difficulties."

At Rohri he communes with himself on the eve of assuming the offensive.

For all his life, in spite of his droll ways, Charles was subject to fits of melancholy, and religious reflections that would have surprised his brother officers, used as they were to his fun and grotesque stories, his oaths darting through his sentences like sparks amongst stubble. He could soliloquise even in the face of battle, and just before opening the offensive we read in his journal the following :

" Ten thousand men are encamped here at Elore, a town built by Alexander the Great. My tent overlooks this most beautiful encampment. The various sounds, the multitude of followers, I suppose twenty thousand, the various costumes and languages, and the many religions produce a strange scene that makes men think. Why is all this ? Why am I, a miserable little wretch, supreme here ?   At my word all this mass obeys . . . multitudes superior to me in bodily and mental gifts !   A little wretched experience in the art of killing, of disobedience to God, is all the superiority that I their commander can boast of !   My God ! How humbled I feel when I think!   How I exult when I behold I have worked my way to this great command, and am grateful at leading it, yet I despise myself for being so gratified.   Yes ! In the depths of my soul I despise myself.   Not for feeling unworthy to lead, for I am conscious of knowing how to lead, and my moral and physical courage are equal to the task : but I despise my worldliness.   Am I not past sixty?   A few years must kill me : a few days may !   And yet I am so weak as to care for these things !   No, I do not.   I pray to do what is right and to have strength to say, Get thee behind me, Satan !   Alas, I have not that strength.   There was but one Being that could say that !   All that I can do is to feel that I cannot say it ! the weakness of man and the pride of war are too powerful for me, or I should not be here; he who takes command loves it ! "

"Well, this comfort remains . . . with a wish for war and having the power of bringing it on, I have avoided it studiously !   These Ameers deserve everything, but I have not sought to draw down on them : so ends my soliloquy.   I must go to work, but will first walk out to see all the camp fires sparkling on their long long line.   What a magnificent sight !   If we had but an enemy in our front ! "

The last sentence is significant.

His battlefields in the Peninsula : his battles in Sind yet to come . . . yes, and his own nature a battlefield, too, so long as life should last.

MIANI AND HYDERABAD

1843

WITHOUT entering into tedious detail, it is necessary to point out the custom amongst the Amirs of Upper and Lower Sind, that one should rule over the others with the title of " Rais " and with the symbol of the " Turban ". Rustam, the present holder of the Turban, was a blameless and courteous old man, but who was to succeed him ? His eldest son, or Ali Murad, his half-brother, forty years younger ? Now Ali Murad was ambitious, handsome, astute. Suspecting the British would soon be masters he had decided to throw in his lot with them, and Charles, deceived by his plausibility, had promised the " Turban " to him on the death of the aged Rustam.

But on New Year's Day, 1843, Rustam complained that Ali Murad had forced him to resign the Turban and the office of Rais, together with the extensive lands which had been assigned to him many years before.

There was instant panic amongst the younger Amirs at the collapse of their old Chief, they detesting Ali Murad. They fled forthwith to their fortress called Imam Garh, which lay lost far away in the great desert. And now followed that episode which Wellington was to describe as " one of the most curious military feats he had ever heard of ".

Charles's reason for the " curious military feat " was that this fortress, never seen by European eye, was believed by the Amirs to be inaccessible. The old general felt the Amirs could carry on petty warfare, harassing the British, and retire to this fortress hidden in the desert for safety. " Whilst this feeling exists," he argued, " they will always think themselves independent and safe ; but I think Emaum Ghur may be reached, and they be taught that they have no refuge from our power, no resource but good behaviour. Scinde will then be quiet. I know I shall do it, but the risks are very great. The last twenty-five miles will be in deep sand, a regular succession of hills, steep and without a drop of water. Emaum Ghur is their fighting cock, and before three weeks pass my hope is to take off his spurs," he finishes with his usual saltiness.

So the old soldier, perfectly alive to the danger, set out from Rohri on the day after Christmas, taking with him three hundred men, two twenty-pounders drawn by camels, two hundred troopers of the Sind Horse, fifteen days of food and water for four days.

" Oh ! the baggage ! the baggage ! It is enough to drive one mad. We have 1,500 camels with their confounded long necks, each occupying fifteen feet ! Fancy these long devils in a defile : four miles and a quarter of them ! Then there are the donkeys and ponies, and led horses and bullocks innumerable. I think our baggage would reach from this to Pekin : yet all the Indians exclaim, ' Never seen a force with so little baggage ! ' but I have done nothing except appeal to the good sense of the officers and reducing my own baggage. It is said no Indian General ever marched with less than sixteen camels for his own share, generally with several hundreds . . . I have four camels and one for my office papers, stationery, etc., which could not be carried in my small portmanteau, for I have but one and a pair of canteens, with two camp tables, a bed, and a private soldier's tent."

The march began on the night of January 5th, 1843, and we read : " Wonderful was the scene as the sun rose and discovered to the General his three hundred Irishmen taking their first ride on camel back, and dotted over the sandy plain more like a fleet of herring boats than a smart British regiment " (Bruce). And General McMurdo, afterwards to become Charles's son-in-law, but now a young lieutenant in the 22nd, gives a comical account of how the camels refused to be a party to secrecy. As the column moved off, acute differences arose between them and the couples of soldiers bestriding them. Their bellowings and the cries and curses of the men rose to an uproar which was carried away here and there into the distance as some of the camels bolted.

One suspects that Charles, always alive to the ludicrous, must have grinned sardonically even in the midst of his wrath.

No less than twenty-five miles was accomplished that first day, the little army travelling obliquely over a succession of monstrous corniced waves of sand. At night with the cold desert wind blowing, they rested in the hollows between the waves, which rose at times to a hundred feet in height.

The second day brought them to Doom, which, in spite of its ominous name, had water, jungle and some trees. "Air delightful," comments Charles, but forage was so scarce that one hundred and fifty horsemen were perforce sent back. The third day brought them to Luk, "A better name than Doom," thinks Charles; "our march to-morrow begins with a very steep sandhill, and very deep, so I turned out the 22nd soldiers this evening and they run the guns up it with cheers in five minutes, though from top to bottom is not less than four hundred yards. What fellows British soldiers are! All laughing and joking and such strength!"

For eight days under an incandescent sky, through burning sand and utter solitude except for the little sand rats popping in and out of their holes, the column trudged, dragging the guns. The sun beat down on them, and the desert wind moaned, blowing off the tops of the dunes so they appeared to be smoking.

On the morning of the 12th January they reached Imam Garh, the mysterious fortress.

Like statues, the staff stood motionless, looking right down on the fort cupped below. This fort, with its eight round towers, this hard-earned prize glittering in the thin desert air, which magnified every detail sharply defined in the sunlight.

Is it possible Charles was experiencing that fatal flatness, that

" what is the use of it after all ? " that assails us when we achieve what we have striven for.

The place was so still. Complete silence. Complete solitude. Doors and gates standing strangely open.

EVACUATED

Two thousand men had marched out a few hours before. On the towers the cannon loaded with priming freshly laid.

That bright-haired young lieutenant McMurdo must have caught something of his Chief's gift of expression, for he wrote : ' The complete silence strained the nerves somewhat, and I longed to order a bugle sound to break the enchantment. Our own soldiers even appeared to me under a spell, as the camels with noiseless step carried them past, their faces all turned with a curious sameness of expression in the fixed stare at the strange apparition beneath them."

Evacuated though it was, Charles determined to blow up the fortress. " The existence fosters a false confidence in all the other Ameers, and its sudden destruction will tell on them with sudden effect."

Thus with a deafening explosion the fortress, never seen before by European eyes, was shattered to atoms !

Charles watches sternly.

" The sight was grand and hellish. . . . Volumes of smoke, fire and embers flying were a throne fit for the devil. I do not like this work of destruction, but reason tells me two things. First, it will prevent bloodshed, and it is better to destroy temples built by man than temples built by the Almighty ; second, that castle was built for oppression and in future its ruins will shelter the slave instead of the tyrant. McPherson dreamed all night of the explosion. I dreamed of my beloved mother ; her beauteous face smiled upon me. Am I going to meet her very soon ? Well, we shall all meet again, unless this dreadful work of war sends me to hell, which is not improbable." He must crack his joke, but after all these years it seems his mother is still the theatre of his actions.

And now the trying march back, and lacking all previous incentive and excitement of coming battle. No laughter now. Charles remembers it is the anniversary of Corunna.

" Luk. A dreadfully fatiguing march . . . ten very high sand-hills, and the soldiers not pulling well. Paddy is not persevering in disagreeable things, and certainly there is no pleasure in drag-ging two twenty-four lb. howitzers over steep sandhills," and Charles, realising that the Madras Sappers were not doing their best, suddenly slipped off his camel, and in a rage snatched a tool from the nearest man and attacked the work with a fury of language and energy.

" Our eyes are full of sand, ears full of sand, noses full, mouths full, and teeth grinding sand ! Enough between our clothes and skins to scour the latter into gold-beater's leaf ; one might as well wear a sandpaper shirt. Our shoes are in holes from dry-ness, and we walk as if we had supplied their place with sand-boxes ; our meat is all sand, and on an average every man's teeth have been ground down the eighth of an inch according to his appetite. It is lucky indeed we are so well scoured with sand, for there is not a clean shirt in camp."

This is typical Charles, but all those who know Upper Sind . . . or perhaps our own Desert Rats . . . " will testify there is not the exaggeration one might suppose ".

The old warrior had not regarded the blowing up of Imam Garh as an act of war on his part, for though it belonged to a nephew of Rustam, the former aged Rais, yet Ali Murad, now Rais, had agreed with Charles to the expedition. On his return Charles found that Outram was still believing that war could be averted. Charles found this sentimentality : " In his indigna-tion against Ali Murad he every day puts such a fresh coat of whitewash on the others that they will soon be spotless ! " he writes. Outram persuaded Charles to stretch the period for negotiations into February. Charles must have felt this stretched elastic to snapping point. Reluctantly he agreed, for in addition to his uneasy disinclination for wanton aggression there were the bitter attacks in the Anglo-Indian Press upon Lord Ellenborough

and himself to consider. So to distract himself during this time
of growing suspense he takes up the cause of the camels. Not
only was he tormented by their sufferings, but he knew too what
a part they must play in any coming campaign.

"These poor patient creatures", he writes, "are cruelly
loaded, and when they sink under the weight are beaten, and
their nostrils torn to pieces by pulling and working to make them
rise. Three days ago fifteen died on the road under cruel treatment, no one denies the fact: the Government's order, reinforced by mine, limits a camel's load to 350 lb. and this is the
maximum. Yet I have seized and weighed the loads of many
camels on the march which have passed 8,000 lb. A camel is
different to a horse in nature . . . he never recovers being knocked
up, but grows weaker and weaker till he dies. . . . When struck
with a heavy cutting whip by the most rigorous and merciless
arm he never flinches, nor springs, but keeps his solemn and
majestic walk, with his nose in the air, as if not touched. Poor
patient brutes. I pity them much and hope to save them and
ourselves from the cursed fools who overload them and who will
cripple my operations: we lose about five camels a day now.
In the desert the camel has no rival: his great splay feet never
sink in the sand, the heat never worries him: he defies thirst
beyond all other beasts, and eats all that is to be had, nor does
he require a great deal. All he asks is not to be overloaded and
nature has pointed this out so clearly to him that the beast who
shows no sign of pain or complaint when whipped makes most
piteous moanings and growlings when too much is put on him:
they are his remonstrances, which the two-legged beasts will not
listen to, and the poor camels are killed by brutes."

Charles was so angered at seeing great brutality to a camel
that he struck at its driver with his clenched fist, and as Red
Rover leaped forward his master's hand was severely hurt. This
was the injury that caused him to go into battle ten days later
"holding half my reins with great torture in the broken hand.
Had it knocked my friend down it would have been some comfort, but his head was like an anvil. These chaps will for a bet

butt with their heads like rams, running full speed, sometimes two or three courses before one is stunned."

Right into February Outram was still believing the Baluchis had no thought of fighting. They were arming because they dreaded Charles, just as Charles was armed because he dreaded them, he argued. " Have little doubt that all their vaunting will end in smoke."

But Charles, so long pent up, exploded. " I will stand no more blarney at which the Ameers will beat any Irishman that ever drunk whiskey."

Now what is to be said ?

Charles Napier has become a legendary figure. Round him controversy has raged, more exaggerated both for and against him than his place in history seems to warrant. There are many who have seen him as a brave but blood-thirsty tyrant seeking aggrandisement, glory, even money at the expense of a helpless lot of rulers quarrelling amongst themselves. A man willing to quarrel with Outram, whom he himself had dubbed the Bayard of India, because the latter disagreed with his policy, and a man who from the outset had criticised openly, without mercy, the Directors of the East India Company, for their policy in the country, their parsimony to his cherished soldiers.

But there are others who find in Charles the perfect knight whose blood indeed thrilled to battle, but who yet was moved to compassion for the oppressed and suffering. A disciplinarian, and yet the joking friend of the common soldier. An adminis- trator of vision. The lover of children and all animals. The man of honour, abstemious and austere in an age of gross drunkenness and display, a man ready to work for the common good till he dropped.

Somewhere between these two Charles may be found. He has a temper. He swears violently. He admits to both. He can be ruthless in wrath, but gentle and courteous to an enemy in distress. Years before he had resolved never to disgrace his father's memory. " Were he alive he would be satisfied," Charles says of himself at this time.

Never let it be forgotten that the British prestige had been violently shaken by the disaster in Afghanistan. The British had to withdraw altogether from the Indus or strengthen their position. This was a necessity.

On February 13th, 1833, Outram himself was attacked in the Residency at Hyderabad. Fighting his way out, eagerly he now joined Charles.

The hour had struck.

On February 16 Charles sits writing the letters which might be his last. Among them is one, of course, to John Kennedy, his old friend of Cephalonian days. " God bless you. To fall will be to leave many that I love, but to go to many loved, to my home." Was he thinking again of " my beloved mother, her beauteous face smiled upon me. Am I going to see her very soon ? . . ." But in his journal he writes : " My troops are in high spirits, so am I. Not to be anxious about attacking such immensely superior numbers is impossible, but it is a delightful anxiety. Three hours I have to get some sleep, and at nine o'clock to-morrow my gallant soldiers shall be launched against the brave Baloochies. It is my first battle as a Commander, it may be my last ! At sixty that makes little difference, but as my feelings are it shall be do or die . . . God bless my wife and precious girls. My hope is to live or die worthy of them : no Cabul for me to make them blush."

Why paint the lily ? For this writer to describe the battle of Miani would be to offer a milk pudding to one who can feast on caviare. Inaccuracies they say are to be found in Sir William's gorgeous pages. Let the historian find them out and correct them by the more sober prose of Dr. Rice Holmes and others, but the general reader will prefer to be swept away on the tide of William's brilliant account.

" Thick as standing corn and gorgeous as a field of flowers were the Beloochies in their many coloured garments and turbans. They filled the broad deep bed of the Fullaillee ; they were clustered on both banks, and covered the plain beyond. Guarding their heads with large dark shields, they shook their sharp swords, gleaming in the sun, and their shouts rolled like peals of thunder as with frantic might and gestures they dashed against the front of the 22nd. But, with shrieks as wild and fierce, and hearts as big and strong, the British soldiers met them with the queen of weapons, and laid their foremost warriors wallowing in blood. . . ."

When the 22nd recoiled as the Baluchis came surging up the steep banks of the dry channel, there was the old General amongst them roaring on his men till he was almost speechless, while his bugler Delaney, who was running at his stirrup, kept sounding out the "Advance" without waiting for orders.

Charles was untouched in spite of the risks he took. He was obliged to ride between two lines of fire not twenty yards apart. His hair was singed by the fire of his own men, his face peppered, which made him very angry ! In agony, holding his reins in his broken hand, again and again he is in the very press of the fight, saved more than once by officer or soldier. When Lieutenant Marston goes down between a Baluchi soldier and Red Rover, and the Baluchi goes down between his sword and the bayonet of a private, and Charles is again involved in the press, the whole of the 22nd shouts out his name, cheering in wildest excitement.

The battle continues in closest contact for three hours before the Baluchis at last show signs of weakening. Soon afterwards Jacob's Horse and the Bengal Cavalry capture guns and standards. Charles is ready to drop from the fatigue of one constant cheer, and encouraging the soldiers for three mortal hours, but——

The battle of Miani is won.

Then rose up a mighty cheer led by his own 22nd. How proud they were of him ! How they loved him ! How they were ready to follow him to the ends of the earth.

"Who will not fight with Charlie ? "

What does Charles write himself ?

"Meeanee. Feb. 17. We have fought a hard battle and won the victory. The enemy has lost more than 5,000 and we nearly 300, of whom nineteen are officers : one third of the number engaged. I am too tired to write more."

And to John Kennedy the following day :

" We beat them John at Meeanee.   The battle was terrible."

At midnight, when his men slept, the old warrior rode out quite alone over the battlefield.   The dead lay in heaps, piled one on top of another.   The soldiers had bayoneted all that had life on those heaps as they passed.   Writing afterwards to his brother Henry, Charles said: " They would not take quarter, and turned on us from behind when passed.   Even if they had accepted quarter I could do nothing, our men would not give it.   We were in the midst of masses, and to let a mass of those faithless chaps in amongst us would have been too nervous an experiment.   I doubt whether a man of us had courage to leave one of them behind :   to disarm them was impossible :   their shields cannot be broken, and a broken sword in their hands is little the worse :   but the ground was strewed with arms.   I own to you, Henry, being shocked at myself, but when I saw their masses, each strong enough to have smashed us, I saw no safety but in butchery :   it was we or they who must die.   I urged no man to refuse quarter, and tried to save one or two in vain."

Now the glare of the moonlight was falling on those dead faces, the desert wind lifted locks soaked and matted with blood and sweat.   As Charles's horse picked its way among that dreadful stiffening multitude, with its strewn arms, we know him well enough to guess at that compassionate element in him disrupting his thankfulness, his pride of victory !   Two thousand brave Baluchis fallen, and of his own precious little army sixty-two officers and men killed ... Captain Tew, Major Teasdale and others ...   Long would he remember their gallantry, as long he had remembered Charles Stanhope at Corunna, and months later covering that same road, could not see its stones for tears.

" The blood is on the Ameers, not on me," said Charles.

Often had his mother quoted French, often he quoted it himself.   At that solemn hour as finally he rolled himself in his cloak, and lay down there amongst the dying and the dead, did the night wind as it whistled through the camel bush whisper : " *Qui s'excuse, s'accuse* " ?

We shall never know.

But feelings at midnight differ from those of the following morning.

"The 22nd gave me three cheers after the fight, and one during it. Her Majesty has no honour to give that equals that, if indeed she gives me any. I do not want any, none at least but what awaits a victory from history. I shall be glad though of a medal with the officers and soldiers : sharing with them all will be an honour of more value to me than any other that can be given."

Charles's despatch describing the battle was "the first in modern English history that recognised the valour of non-commissioned officers and privates by name". Drummer Martin Delaney, Private James O'Neil, Havildar Thackur Ram, Subadar Eman Beet, Trooper Motee Sing and many others, off went their names to London.

Let those who accuse him for glorifying his own deeds remember that.

The morning after the battle from the Amirs came their ambassadors asking for terms.

"Life and nothing more. And I want your decision before twelve o'clock as I shall by that time have buried my dead, and given my soldiers their breakfast."

That was Charles.

But when the broken but royally dressed Amirs came to lay their jewelled swords at his feet, giving themselves up as prisoners of war with promises to surrender the great fortress of Hyderabad, it was Charles, too, who received them with real courtesy, kindness and understanding as he returned to them their swords, as long ago he had had his returned to him in the Peninsular. It was Charles, too, who left these captive princes their Palace with its trees, its shady garden and water courses, whilst he the Conqueror stifled in a small tent with the burning wind sifting the sand against its canvas walls.

It was Charles, too, with his chivalry towards women, who allowed the Amirs to retain eight hundred fully armed palace

guards, fearing lest the Amirs might otherwise massacre their
women to prevent them falling into enemy hands.

In the Palace was treasure worth millions. It was Charles who
gave permission for the women to retain their ornaments. . . .
Not only these, but three-fourths of the whole treasure vanished !

Nevertheless, it must be conceded that the bulk of the prize
money for Sind came from property at Hyderabad and Charles's
share was £70,000. There were some discreditable incidents,
Charles's prize agents afterwards admitting that much treasure
was seized from the Amir's residences. One supposes that
Charles and his officers were imbued by the military idea of the
day that all property in a town taken by storm belonged to the
soldiers. Some point out that Hyderabad had been amicably
surrendered by the Amirs, and this spoliation was therefore
unjustified. There the question must be left with the writer's
own suggestion that Charles, finding the Amirs were intriguing
already with Sher Mahomed, the powerful Amir who had not surrendered with the others, may have considered this notion justified.

Incredibly Outram had still declared the Amirs had no hostile
intentions, and that if he could write a letter affairs could still
be peaceably arranged. Perhaps Charles was sickened by the
carnage that had taken place at Miani. He gave way. One can
detect a note of weariness in his " Write them what you like and
I will sign it ".

But what happened ? Sher Mahomed, the only real fighter
amongst the Amirs, retreated on Mirpur, and after a few days
restarted the war at the head of twenty-five thousand men !

Charles's little army numbered only twenty-five hundred men
all told, but he sends up and down the Indus for every available
man and gun and boat, and on the 22nd reinforcements and
supplies arrive. Then the battle of Hyderabad, near the little
village of Dubba, takes place. As at Miani, Charles was in the
thick of the fight and had the narrowest escapes, but Dubba was
to be a very different affair from Miani. Charles describes his
men as " cool as cucumbers ", whilst at Miani the struggle had
been desperate. " All would have been lost had the 22nd and

the 25th given way, and I had to lead them, to rally them, to risk all to keep them to their work." Then, too, at Dubba quarter was given, and the battle lacked the ghastly ferocity of Miani where Charles, seeking to save an exhausted but unyielding Chief, got that terrible reply : " This day, General, the shambles have it all to themselves."

And a week later Charles is writing in his journal :

" Nineteen long letters from Lord Ellenborough. He has made me Governor of Scinde with additional pay, and he has ordered a triumphant column with our name."

There sounds triumph. Years of frustration on half pay blotted out. The desire accomplished was indeed sweet to his soul . . . but he goes on : " I wish he would let me go back to my wife and girls, it would be more to me than pay and glory and honours. . . . Well, all the glory that can be desired is mine, and I care so little for it, that the moment I can all shall be resigned to live quietly with my wife and girls : no honour or riches repays me for absence from them. . . . Otherwise this sort of life is agreeable, as it may enable me to do good to these poor people. Oh, if I can do one good thing to serve them when so much blood has been shed in accursed war I shall be happy . . . May I never see another shot fired. Horrid, horrid war ! Yet how it wins upon and hardens one when in command. No young man can resist the temptation I defy him, but thirty and sixty are different."

He once wrote : " The young see unreal pictures before them, and the old see real pictures behind them."

Charles had written : " I have every reason to believe that not another shot will be fired," but Sher Mahomed had yet to be captured. He had fled with his family to Umerkot. This great sandstone fort, birthplace of Akbar, the Mogul Emperor, with its ramparts, round towers and bastions, had a large garrison and eleven mounted guns. It was set lonely in the desert, its crenelated walls with their loop-holes rising sheer out of white sand so loose that horses and donkeys passing beneath sank above their fetlocks in it.

Charles himself remained at Mirpur. He sent on the Scinde Horse and a camel battery in pursuit of the " Lion ", as he persisted in calling him. In the meantime snows were melting in the Himalayas and the Indus—that passionate river—was rising very rapidly before its time. By the capricious spreading of its waters it might ally itself with the enemy, by cutting off Charles's forces from Hyderabad. So bitterly, with no other choice, he ordered a retreat. No sooner was this done, than his officer farthest in advance and only a mere twenty miles from Umerkot learned that it had been evacuated just as Imam Garh had been.

Then it was a young officer named Brown made his ride to tell his Chief the great news.

It was April, the Sind sun scorching down from a shimmering white-hot sky, the desert shimmering beneath it. Brown rode through that blistering, withering heat hour after hour, particles of sand stirred by the galloping hoofs of his horse stinging face and hands like wasps. Forty miles he covered by noon to take the great news to his Chief, and that same afternoon, mounted on one of Charles's own horses—was it on Flibberty, or Mosaic, never on the precious Red Rover, one feels sure?—did that young Brown ride the forty miles back again. Surely he must have shared the sentiments of that young officer who later was to exclaim : " When I see that old man incessantly on his horse, how can I be idle who am young and strong ? By God, I would go into a loaded cannon's mouth if he ordered me to."

And on April 14th, only ten days after the battle of Hyderabad, the weary troops entered into Umerkot.

The marches had been long and pitiless and on one a touching incident occurred, which shines like a star after the butchery of Miani. The fury of the sun was at its height, the desert a furnace. Sepoys espied the approach of one of their own water-carriers, and beside themselves they set upon him, tearing at the *mussack* with its spurting seams, with cries of " Water ! water ! " . . . But then came straggling up a few men of the 22nd, conspicuous in their red coatees with white calicoes twisted over their caps. They were even more exhausted than themselves. The sepoys, seeing their piteous condition, their features whitened by sand, their cracked lips, their swollen tongues, assisted them to drink. Moreover, when all were able to move on, these same compassionate sepoys carried the muskets of their companions in arms, patting and encouraging them forward till the poor fellows could drag their feet no longer through the burning clogging sand, and fell. Then it was found that all had been wounded . . . one indeed had been shot through both legs. . . . Nevertheless, they had forced themselves to stagger and falter on in spite of loss of blood and pain of wounds, thinking there was to be another fight, and desiring, in the words of Charles, that " their last moments might be given to their country on another field of battle ".

Strange is Humanity, perhaps finding satisfaction only when " going all out ".

CHAPTER 13

ADMINISTRATION

1844–1846

"THIS completes the Conquest of Scinde," Charles had said. "Every place is in my possession, and thank God I have done with war ! never again am I likely to see a shot fired in anger. Now I shall work at Scinde as in Cephalonia, to do good, to create, to improve, to end destruction and raise up order."

But he had yet to capture Sher Mahomed, who had got clean away. His brother had been defeated by Jacob, and now Charles was anxiously awaiting news from the latter. The heat was violent. "As whirlwinds in the south pass through : so it cometh from the desert from a terrible land. A grievous vision is declared unto me," so might Charles have said with Isaiah.

The sun scorched down from a white-hot sky, the desert with its dust of mica reflected it back, metal taking the skin off flesh if inadvertently touched. Incredible climate ! Troops marched only at night, resting during the day in double tents, wet cloths twisted round their heads, yet even so they died in numbers of heat apoplexy. Charles himself was wasted to skin and bone from fever and dysentry. "So ill as to think I was." The heat increased. His mattress was laid under the table for further protection from the pitiless sun. The words "I am too old," are wrung from him.

Nevertheless, on June 15th, fever drumming and throbbing in him, this dauntless old man sits in his tent writing at the battered camp table. We see him in "trousers and shirt" and probably he still wore his sun helmet for further protection from the sun striking on the tent like the slap of a hand. At his feet, taking up an unconscionable amount of the limited space of the tent, lies his charger stretched out, his nostrils distended and quivering, waves of heat emanating from his distressed body. The General's anxiety must have been almost unbearable. He could hear the booming of Jacob's guns on that quivering bright air. His movements as his hand endeavoured to write on the paper gritty with sand must have been even jerkier and more spasmodic than ever.

"I cannot go to the east, it is too hot. My Europeans could not stand it; our livers are on the simmer now and will soon boil. The natives cannot stand it, and I have been obliged to take Red Rover into my tent, poor beast, where he lies down exhausted and makes me very hot. I did not bring a thermometer. What use would it be to a lobster boiling alive?"

His anxiety was too great to allow him to continue letters or even journal. Getting up he came to the door of his tent, there to crash like a fallen tree from heat apoplexy. McMurdo, rushing in, got two doctors. They bled him, rolled wet towels round him and rubbed his emaciated body. Old Charles came to, as they tied up his arm, and swore angrily at not being allowed to sleep again. But at that moment a horseman galloped up telling Jacob had been victorious! That roused the old warrior as nothing else could have done. It saved him.

That day "forty-three others were struck, all Europeans and all dead within three hours except myself".

It has been said that Charles killed many by taking them out in the heat. His comment was: "I do not drink. That is the secret." He was taken back to Hyderabad.

With amazing determination he pulled himself together after the heat stroke. His wife and the daughters, whose advanced education he was still superintending, were soon to join him, but even with the thought of this long-looked-for happiness Charles was now a very sick man, an aged man, obliged for the first time in his life to goad himself to work.

His journal of July 30th, 1843, makes the heart ache of those who knew him. " I am very weak, and my legs have fallen away, yet they swell at night, and with a tired feeling hardly bearable though keeping to my room all day long. I have been overworked body and mind under this sun ; I am sinking . . . I am so done up that to mount my horse is an exertion . . . live or die I must remain till a successor arrive. He should come soon though, for more fighting is not in me, this last illness has floored me, and even my mind has lost energy ; yet it is good to die in harness. Oh that I was forty. At that age I could work like a horse ; now I work like an ass without its strength. Unless something happens a few months must close the scene."

But when his doctors insisted on his return to England he writes : " I must go through one more hot season, live or die. Sir Robert Peel approves of everything, so does Lord Ellenborough . . . and I will not sneak out of his service by quitting Scinde . . . no, not to save a dozen lives. Why should I more than other soldiers ? In three days my service will be of fifty years ! This does give me a claim to rest : but what want I with rest ? Bah ! Talk of that when I am eighty." Truly he felt " there was no discharge in that war ".

He had disarmed the Baluchis. How vivid is his thumbnail sketch. " The Beloochee scorns labour. You know him by his swell cut, his slow rolling lounge, his shield, matchlock and dagger : the spade don't suit his hand, but your gold watch does."

In a few weeks Charles, by leaving full military honours to the chiefs, had conciliated them, and over four hundred came trooping in to tender their submission, and to say their salaams. Chiefs on great golden slouching camels with noses high in the air, with peaked crimson saddles, gaudy cushions and swinging woven trappings of scarlet and black wool, and chiefs with their retainers, on wiry Baluchi skewbalds whose cocked sickle-like ears met in half-moons. Here they came.

" Take back your sword. You have used it with honour against me, and I esteem a brave enemy. But if forgetful of this voluntary submission you draw it again in opposition to my government, I will tear it from you and kill you as a dog." Thus Charles the Conqueror.

SIR CHARLES NAPIER, G.C.B., IN THE DRESS HE WORE AT THE CELEBRATED ASSEMBLY OF THE SCINDIAN CHIEFS

Appended to the original drawing is a certificate signed by many members of the Scinde Staff to say that it was exact, and no caricature. The dress is a dirty old flannel jacket, trousers of coarse white cloth, not over-clean, hunting cap, no braces. Added was the remark: "Correct, but the stockings are not shown down-at-heel as they ought to have been."

134

A portrait of Queen Victoria was draped across with a curtain, and Charles, announcing to the chiefs and noblemen that no servants and common people must cast their eye upon it, displayed it to them with great ceremony !

" Sahib," said one wondering Baluchi, " she did not beat me at Miani. You are everything now."

Charles was unversed in Indian ways, and no Indian officer of experience would recall such sayings, but Charles genuinely believed them, and they in turn, seeing how he believed it all, would naturally continue.

"I always joke and tell them what fine fellows they are," said he. He had once maintained " the great receipt for quieting a country is a good thrashing first, and great kindness after ".

" Now my fearful work of settling the country begins, and the heat is violent. I have to collect revenue, administer justice, arrange the troops, survey the country, project improvements, form civil officers, and appoint proper functionaries. I have to get a thorough hold of a conquered country, and establish a government, and have really hardly anyone to assist me : all is confusion, and the military movements are still going on."

Nevertheless this was exactly what he felt himself suited to do, even more so than fighting ! He set about his task with the utmost confidence. The sword of his spirit burnished once more.

He was determined to hang all murderers. A chief asked pardon for a retainer of his who had murdered his wife. " No ! I will hang him." " What, you will hang a man for only murdering his wife ? " " But she had done no wrong ! " " No ! he was angry ! " " Well, I'm angry," roared Charles. " Why should I not kill him ? "

And did.

Happily suttee was practically unknown in Sind, but Charles was determined to put down what there was. The Brahmins came to him protesting that all nations had religious customs which should be respected. Charles agreed. " Be it so. This burning of widows is your custom ; prepare the funeral pile. But my nation also has a custom. When men burn women alive we hang them, and confiscate all their property. My carpenters shall therefore erect gibbets on which to hang all concerned when the widow is consumed. Let us all act according to our national customs."

Comments such as these, and his dictum that " an officer of irregular horse should never quit the saddle when he is on duty : he should eat, drink and sleep in the saddle ", illustrate Charles's character more than anything this writer could say about him. Did not Plutarch write : " It is not always in the most distinguished achievements that men's virtues or vices may be best discerned, but very often an action of small note, a short saying, or a jest, shall distinguish a person's real character more than the greatest sieges or the most important battles."

One of his first acts had been to ensure that the administration should be carried out by the military rather than the " Civil-villains " as he delighted to call them. He had always considered it derogatory that India should be governed by the East India Trading Company. "They are always in a false position as merchants ruling a vast and distant empire solely for their private advantage." He goes on to point out that a worthy Governor-General's aim is the welfare of the one hundred and twenty million people under his charge, while the merchant will be taking profit from these millions.

His plan had its disadvantages, however, for many of his young officers, however well meaning, knew as little of the country and its language as Charles did himself. Charles did his best to learn Hindustani, but unfortunately the old fellow always fell asleep after a few minutes, and his Munshi was too polite to wake him up.

An amusing tale is told in this connection. The General had given a lengthy and elaborate talk on manœuvres to some chiefs. Calling up a young lieutenant he bade him translate this. Salaaming to the chiefs the young man said, " Listen, you folks. The Great Man says there will be a fine bit of fun." " Have you explained all I said ? " demanded Charles sternly.

" Everything, sir." " A most comprehensive language that Hindustani," observed Charles dryly, as he rode away, for he knew there is a time to wink as well as to see.

His hero, the Duke of Wellington, had said that one of the greatest dangers from every new acquisition of territory in India was " the throwing out of employment and of means of subsistence all who had previously managed the revenue, commanded or served in the armies, or plundered the country ".

So Charles, whilst retaining the revenue collectors in their office, deprived them of judicial powers, but at the same time gave them a large salary, warning them that they held their office only with good behaviour. " Both legal and popular justice have their evils, but assuredly the people's justice is a thousand times nearer God's justice."

Certainly his justice was rough. He confessed as much himself, declaring that the poor people who came to him were such liars it was impossible to get at the truth ! " My plan is a most unjust one," declared this singular man. " For against all evidence I decide in favour of the poor : and argue against the argument of the government people as long as I can. When borne down by proofs as irrefragible, like Alexander I cut the knot and give an atrocious verdict against all clearest proofs ! Punish the Government servants first, and enquire about the right and wrong when there is time."

A very staunch admirer of his remarked : " All these comings and goings caused a good deal of commotion in the feel of the country."

There are divergent views of what Charles did and did not do in the pacification of Sind. The mixture of good and evil, of compassion and severity, wisdom and ignorance, is hard to disentangle. Suffice it to say that it would be ridiculous to condemn him as we should now condemn any man who proposed such action for carrying out necessary reform ; consideration must be taken for the circumstances at the time of action. Charles lived in his time, and in those days, ideas of right and wrong were not so " nice " as in the present day. In the writer's view the wonder is that the old soldier was as ahead of his day as he undoubtedly was. Dr. Rice Holmes, no partial critic, writes: " These errors did not seriously detract from the general excellence of the administration. Indeed the marvel is that a governor who started in ignorance of the language and manners of his people, and who moreover, was liable at any moment to be summoned from his desk to the field of battle, should have been able to construct from the foundation stone, so solid a fabric of government even for those who were keenest to detect blemishes in matters of detail, were unanimous in admitting that for confusion, corruption and tyranny he had substituted system, integrity and impartial law."

John Lawrence himself wrote: " I believe he did in Scinde wonderfully well; perhaps as well, if not better, than anyone under similar difficulties could have done. But to suppose that a man ignorant of the manners, habits and language of a people, with untrained men under him, could really have governed a country as he thinks he did Scinde, seems to me an impossibility."

It should be understood that he had three separate interests for whom to legislate. In his own words, the money-seeking Hindus " who go about all eyes and with fingers supple as his conscience robbing everybody by subtilty as the Beloochies robs them by force. To him conquest must be a feast and a blessing of grace. The Scindee, strong and handsome, is indolent from combined effect of heat and slavery, but he had the natural qualities, and, his bondage being of recent date, he may be recalled and fit for independence. To him also the conquest is a blessing and it shall be my business to make it a feast.

" The Beloochie, though fierce and habituated to acquire property by violence is shrewd and has a strong though savage sense of dignity and honour according to the customs of his race . . . he fought desperately for the Ameers because to fight and plunder was his vocation, but neither he nor his chief, nor the Ameers fought from national feeling. The Beloochie loves his race, his tribe, not the general community which he regards as a spoil, as a prey."

Mistakes in plenty. Charles disapproved of excessive taxation, and abolished the inland duties and Bombay custom rules and duties with unfortunate results, for cheap Manchester goods poured in in shiploads, and the old city of Tatta, which spun such exquisite silken scarves and worked one thousand looms, was soon to have a mere half-dozen employed. (But are we so much more successful to-day in our imports of cherries and tomatoes and so on?)

Then Colonel Steuart, a great admirer of Charles, tells us how he gave the town of Jherruk with considerable property over to one Mahomet Khan to induce him to stay after he had made salaams following the battle of Miani. Now Mahomet Khan was extremely fond of horses, and bought the finest available . . . a sure way to Charles's heart. . . . However, he became so unpopular that the tribes from the surrounding hills descended upon him, and he was then found to have crucified one of his servants.

But in spite of this and that things did get done.

Always had it been one of Charles's ambitions to make Karachi one of the greatest commercial cities of the East. "Kurrachee was my hobby long before I came to Scinde, and now that I know the place I am more sanguine than ever. Suez, Bombay, and Kurrachee will hit Calcutta."

The harbour was so shallow it was always difficult, and during the monsoon, impossible, for vessels to make the port. Charles built a lighthouse, and started on the mole which was eventually to run two miles out to sea, and still bears his name. It enabled troops, stores, and merchandise to land, independent of tides. His next effort was to link up Karachi with the Indus by the remains of an old water course, as the city was not built on any of the many mouths of the river. Hyderabad, though only five hundred miles away, was completely separate. The news of the battle of Miani had had to travel all the way down to Bombay and then back to Karachi, taking nine days in all !

Swimming-baths were now built for the troops, and a piece of useless land converted into gardens, growing vegetables for

139

the soldiers without charge, so that their scurvy quickly became a thing of the past. (The old name " The Government Gardens " has now been changed to Gandhi Gardens !) Always was the welfare of his soldiers in his mind. Before leaving Hyderabad roomy barracks had been built, twenty-five feet in height with double roofs and upper ventilation. At Karachi new barracks had been begun, but on the old bad pattern, so Charles insisted at all events on verandas, and later he built excellent barracks for the Horse Artillery. These things cost money and there was a great outcry at the Governor's extravagance.

" How strangely people confuse things," snorted Charles. " Scarcely one can be met who discriminates between economy and extravagance. People of generally good sense cannot see that a hundred thousand pounds may be expended with a view to the most rigid economy, while the not spending it would be most extravagant and impoverishing to a country. No European barracks should be less than 30 feet high, the number of men painted on the door, and the officer in command held responsible for this being observed. The heat of this country is tremendous, and if men have not thick walls and lofty rooms sickness is inevitable. Such barracks are expensive no doubt : so are sick soldiers, so are dead soldiers. But the difference is that the first is over and done with : the second goes on increasing like compound interest, and quickly outstrips the capital."

Sir George Arthur, the Governor of Bombay, was upset by Charles's incessant demands. " Have you no conscience ? " he wrote. " What a question to ask a Governor," Charles writes back with vigour. " No, to be sure I have not. Did you ever know a Governor who had ? He would, if discovered, be stuffed and sent to the museum. However, so far as I am personally concerned drying would be unnecessary : Scinde has done that."

It was in the October following the battle of Miani that a terrible pestilence visited Sind, adding to old Charles's difficulties. No one escaped. The army could not stir, public works and agriculture came to a standstill. Possibly Charles was right in supposing it to be due to the unusually high inundation that year. When asked what measures the medical men recommended to prevent a recurrence, he writes : " Nothing in the power of Government can prevent it whilst the Indus overflows its banks, and rain falls, malaria will prevail in Scinde." But what is interesting, showing he saw ahead of his times, is that he pointed out that hollows containing stagnant water should be filled up, and ponds be turned into tanks with masonry sides, and by his harping again and again on the necessity of building good barracks.

Then the old fellow himself fell ill. The army was now in such a state that at last there was no one to make out a report, and the gates of Hyderabad were fastened because there was no one to relieve guard. " Gwallior was on the point of declaring war ; the Sikhs were in arms . . . while the air was thick with rumours of preparations by the Afghans for a religious war. The Hill tribes, too, were like banditti listening for the sound of carriage wheels, the Scindiana and the Beloochies between a growl and a bite and Ali Murad turning traitor."

" Remember Meannee, Hyderabad ! " exhorted Charles. " If your Highness offers the slightest insult to the British Government I will consider you as the enemy, and your destruction will be inevitable."

Like General Foch he might have said : " My right has been rolled up ; my left has been driven back ; my centre has been smashed. I have ordered an advance."

For while troubles were threatening him on all sides, and he dauntlessly pushing forward his plans of construction, he was being bitterly assailed by enemies at home. He had originally said : " I cannot enter upon our right to be here at all. That is Lord Auckland's affair. I had no concern with its justice, its propriety, or anything but to see it maintained." But now the Directors of the East India Company, and the Press both in India and at home, were stinging him with the fury of wild bees. Every motive was queried and criticised. There was malignant misrepresentation. The thanks of Parliament had been so long delayed that a year all but a few days had elapsed since the battles of Miani and Hyderabad had been fought . . . " and," says Butler, " the greater part of the army thanked was in its grave ". True the Duke had said, " I have never known any instance of an officer who has shown in a higher degree that he possesses all the qualifications and qualities necessary to enable him to conduct great operations," " and his praise ", wrote Charles, " is after all the highest honour a soldier can receive. The hundred gun ship has taken the little cock boat in tow, and it will follow for ever over the ocean of time."

But the speech of Lord Howick, in the House of Lords, infuriated him. " How dare he say I forced a war to gain glory. I deny the infamous motive he charges me with. Does he believe that I have no fear of God ? Does he imagine that I was preparing by wholesale murder to meet the Almighty ? "

In truth Lord Howick had not said precisely that, but very nearly so, and Charles's indignation can be understood.

It is no new thing to see the curs yapping at the heels of a great man. We see it now. We see it then. Of course it would have been more dignified for Charles to ignore these attacks. Of course it would ! But with his temperament, augmented by old wounds, and exposure to a terrible climate, he could not. One recalls that irascible old professor who, when reproved by one of his pupils for so losing his temper, stormed : " Young Man, I control more temper in one day than you do in a month."

Charles had made himself unpopular by criticising the parsimony of the East India Company. Scathingly he had written that there were no Catholic priests provided for his men. " The Mussulman and the Hindus have their teachers. The Christians have none." Then it was not only his criticism of the Company's administration, but there was a political poison abroad. The Whig policy under Lord Auckland had been disastrous. To some it was gall and wormwood to see this successful Tory Administration after the deplorable events in Afghanistan. Though Charles had spent his early days under Whig influences, later he had never been able to forget how the Whigs had discredited Wellington, quoting in their Press the French figures and accounts of action in the Peninsula, rather than those of the British. "A Tory well chastened and taught to be like other men is well enough, but a Whig has all the Tory faults, and his own beside. . . . I do not know why the Almighty should afflict us with bugs, and Whigs, but he does so," he fulminated.

Then Outram was making considerable mischief with the Directors at home. He was showing to the Secret Committee of the East India Company the notes he had made of his interviews with the Amirs immediately before the battles of Miani and Hyderabad. The Directors formed the opinion that Charles had declared war to satisfy his own military ambition. (Did Outram really forget that he himself had written to his mother a few days before Miani: " Sir Charles Napier is fortunately so good and kind-hearted a man that he would never drive the Ameers to extremity as long as he could prevent bloodshed " ?) William, Charles's brother, had requested Outram to contradict the gross aspersions of an Indian newspaper, accusing Charles of starting a war to gain the prize money. Outram refused to do so, disclaiming responsibility. William, so passionately jealous of his brother's good name, wrote many bitter things in consequence, and Charles, egged on by William, broke off the friendship. In fact the "Bayard of India" was soon to be described as the "Knight *sans peur de reproche*" . . . and later worse.

For Charles himself was being decried in the Press as " the sordid shameless leader in Scinde. The Autocrat in Scinde. The unscrupulous murderer of the soldiers of the 78th and 26th Regiments. The Liar at the head of the Scinde Government ", and such pretty phrases. Scarce wonder he wrote in his vigorous way: "Don't ever expect me to be in good humour until I am in my coffin, unless I kill an editor which would make me fat, sleek and in good humour."

" *Cet animal est très méchant, Quand on l'attaque il se défend.*"
Now Charles describes his journals as " having all the rubbish

as it comes up ", and the writer of this book having just opened
a page at haphazard finds this :

"We are dropping down the Indus, the water like glass,
the beautiful moon high and brilliant, the stars glittering around
her ; the steamer is at her evening station, and the serenity of
the soft scene only disturbed by a hum of voices, heard though
by me slightly, being in a towed boat, and listening rather to
the chirp of the cicala coming over the still waters : yet the
Indus is here more than a mile wide ; I will go up and look at
this calm and beautiful night, on this grand stream, and think
on my wife, my children and my death.   This sort of thought is
not disagreeable : life has not been pleasant to me, and I feel no
dread at leaving it.   What is life that we should love it, and
fear to lose it ?   It is not from discontent I speak thus, being in
spirits and cheerful enough, and generally enjoying life as much
as others.   No, I am reasoning, thinking, as I sit in this beautiful
moonlit, tranquil night, looking at the Creator through all this
majesty and grandeur."

The man who wrote that is likely to be sorely wounded by the
too often unjust and lying attacks made upon him.   At the
ending of the year 1844 he wrote : " This last has been a glorious
year for me so far as mundane glory is concerned . . . and yet
it is like the faint smile which comes at times in the midst of
sorrow."

It is pleasant to think that in these days of strife the old General
had his family round him, for in truth he was the most domestic
of beings.   " Would to God I could travel like an Arab with
all my folk round me, pitching my tent anywhere, and everywhere at home," he had once written.

Those fervent young creatures, Susan and Emily, with their
Mediterranean blood, must have brought with them exquisite
if poignant memories.   Susan Sarah, called after Charles's
"beauteous mother", Lady Sarah, and Emily Cephalonia
evoking visions and memories of the lovely island.

Neither Susan nor Emily found their second stepmother
congenial company, after their first.   But all young people

SIR CHARLES NAPIER

From an engraving by Smart

delighted in Charles, as he in them. There must have been many interludes of jokes, of laughter, and happiness at Karachi. They rode together, and it is unlikely that Charles, who thought nothing of a non-stop ride from Tatta to Karachi, 72 miles, with the thermometer at 110°, would confine his lively girls to a rocking-horse canter along the sea-shore, nor that they, judging from their after lives, would consent to such a thing ! Emily we know was thrown one day, and picked up senseless on one of their headlong rides. Yes. They were happy together. " But I think that these little daughters were a great anxiety to grandpapa, and he very cleverly married them off, so *very young* to his two aides-de-camps," remarked an old old lady (the daughter of one of them) to the writer of this book.

For that is just what Charles did do. Susan was to marry the loyal and fiery McMurdo, that bright-haired, very blue-eyed young man whom even Charles considered " too zealous and fool-hardy in battle ". And the following year young Emily was married off to her cousin William Napier, at the age of sixteen and a half. A sort of " Happy Family " it must have been, for Charles's favourite nephew John, brother of William, had already married Minnie, a stepdaughter of Charles's ! So there they were, those three gallant young soldiers, John, and William Napier, and Montagu McMurdo, his " Three Trumps ", as old Charles loved to describe them.

" How life floats on, and approaches the great fall. I am in the rapids now. I hear their roar. Both my beloved daughters are now married . . . two good fine soldiers have them, and my mind is easy for their future . . . they are both good, and I trust religious, without which there is no good, and no power to sustain the blight of this life which strikes us all more or less."

CHAPTER 14

HILL EXPEDITION

1847

"I AM covered with boils which have given me great pain for three weeks, and kept me in bed for ten days." These were probably what we now call " Sind Sores ", but Charles was to suffer a severer blow than sores. " Pretty news ! Those East Indian Directors have recalled Lord Ellenborough. This is the reward of zeal, ability, honesty and the peace of India."

The removal of Lord Ellenborough enraged Charles. Although he had not personally met the Governor-General he had received constant encouragement, praise and approval since his arrival in India. Both men were at one in their detestation of the East India Company's policy.

Lord Ellenborough's successor was his brother-in-law Sir Henry Hardinge, an old friend of Charles's since Corunna and Busaco days. But as Charles wrote : " No man can supply Lord Ellenborough's place to me. Hardinge must hurt me ; common sense tells me he must have his own plans or he would be a fool, which he is not. . . . Lord Ellenborough left everything in my hands. This I can no longer expect, and plans will come for me to execute."

Truly he had once written : " I do hate a master."

It was in the cold weather following this disagreeable news that Charles set out on his hill campaign. It will be realised by now that his actions were often unpredictable, and this plan of pursuing Beja Khan and the tribesmen into their fastnesses of the Cutchi Hills was as original—and more risky—an adventure than the blowing up of the fort of Imam Ghar two years before. His staff, devoted as they were to him, were dubious, except the loyal headstrong young McMurdo, now his son-in-law.

These hill tribesmen, the Bugtis, Dombkis and Jakranis, were perpetually giving trouble, spilling down on the plains killing men, carrying off women and cattle, burning and looting, and then off and away on their small Baluchi mares. These fiery little animals had been trained to go for long periods without water: their food was slung under their bellies, and at times they were fed on raw meat! When the forays were over they were galloped back over the hard sand to vanish into a grim labyrinth of cliffs with their ravines and chasms, which rose sheer from the desert. Altogether this expedition promised to be just the kind of adventure to appeal to Charles, though it seems he did have some qualms at the outset. For this strange man was superstitious. On December 8th he wrote: " My spirits are bad. Things do not please me. Strange events occur of a dark nature. . . . My horse fell, and how I escaped is strange, for he rolled over me. . . . I never quitted the saddle, and one foot was fast in the stirrup, yet I got free because my boot came off. Red Rover stood still, but he my favourite horse fell ! Again I went to see the Sir C. Napier steamer. I fell down the hold. . . . These things affect me. Am I to fall or fail ? in the raid against the robbers. If to fall, well, I am not afraid : but am I to fail ? "

The Cutchi Hills were three hundred miles or more to the north, and Charles's spirits seem to have risen again as he exchanged the enervating sea level for the air of northern Sind, which at that time of year is like sparkling champagne. " I am feeling as strong as Red Rover," he exults.

Here is a letter written to his sister. In its vivid enjoyment and appreciation of beauty it recalls the letters from Cephalonia to his mother Lady Sarah.

" My march is a picturesque one. At this moment behind me is my Mogul guard . . . [Why Mogul ? One suspects his appreciation of the picturesque word here !] some two hundred cavalry. With their splendid Asiatic dress, and the sun's horizontal rays glancing with coruscations of light along their bright sword blades. Behind them are three hundred infantry . . . the old bronzed soldiers of the Thirteenth Regiment . . . the defenders of Jellabad, veterans of battle. So are the cavalry for they charged at Meannee and at Hyderabad where their scarlet turbans were seen sweeping through the smoke . . . by their colour seeming to announce their bloody work they were at. On these picturesque horsemen the sun is gleaming, whilst the Lukkee hills are casting long shades, and the Kurta range reflects from its crowning rock the broad beautiful lights. Below me are hundreds of loaded camels with guards and drivers, rude grotesque people, all winding slowly among the hills. Such is royal life, for it is grand and kingly to ride through the lands that we have conquered with the men who fought. Yet what is it all?"

And as in answer to this arrowy recollection that " Vanity all is vanity " two days later he is patiently trying to disentangle the truth from cultivators and humble fisher folk: " The poor people came to me with earnest prayers: they never come without cause; but are such liars, and so bad at explaining, that were their language understood by me it would be hard to reach facts. Yet knowing well . . . that no set of poor wretches ever complain without a foundation, here will I stay till the truth comes out, and relief be given."

And stay he did, to explain later: " The Collector has, without my knowledge, raised the taxes 40% on the very poorest class of the population. He is an amiable man, and so religious he would not cough on a Sunday, yet he has done such an act of cruelty as is enough to raise an insurrection. This discovery of oppression is alone sufficient to repay the trouble of my journey."

It was here at Sehwan that Charles treads the ground that Alexander the Great trod. He sees the conqueror's great tower, though doubts whether he built it. For the enormous brick building has circular arches, and with his memories of Greece Charles maintains the Greeks were ignorant of the circular in architecture.

He moves on, " discovering fresh villainies every day. There is a poll tax on Hindoos and Scindees, none on Beloochees. This must be removed, but cautiously; for the Beloochees are so close to the mountains that I dare not take them roughly by the neck, as my desire is: everything must give way to the preservation of peace "—a very unusual sentiment for Charles !

Fever is again in his blood, but " While life lasts let me be in harness, and die with my sword by my side " is his wish.

It was nearly Christmas when they reached Sukkur—Sukkur with its dense forests of babul and palms on either side of the river, its tall minaret, and the tree-clad island in the middle of the stream. . . . Sukkur immediately opposite the Hindu town of Rohri with its little huddle of tombs from the victims of suttee. Colonel Steuart, who was a great admirer of Charles, recalls in his reminiscences that they used to see the smoke rising from the pyres in Rohri where the Hindus burned their dead, and when a sound like a pistol shot rang across the water, it was popularly supposed to be the brain of the dead exploding within the skull !

Charles gave a great dinner on Christmas day, and " the officers made me speak. ' Gentlemen, I give you the great man who found India in gloom, and left it in sunshine.' "

It was true enough. Lord Ellenborough had restored British prestige after the shame brought upon us by Lord Auckland's policy, and now the late Governor-General's health was drunk with thunderous applause. By a curious coincidence, such as Charles delighted in, when the old General returned to his tent he found awaiting him a most friendly and flattering letter from Lord Ellenborough himself, together with a sword with " straight Damascus blade ".

He had told Lord Ellenborough that since his departure India had seemed like an empty house. " I did not tell him it was infected with bugs, but daresay he knew that well enough, and Hardinge will soon find it out."

Yes. Rather a difficult and outspoken person was Charles. It was from Sukkur that he had gone forth to Imam Garh, and from Sukkur he was now to set forth to an even more inaccessible spot, this time in savage mountains through the desert which lay between them and the river Indus. There were said to be some eighteen thousand tribesmen, and Charles's idea was to drive them into some cleft of these indescribable hills from which there would be no escape, much as elephants are driven into a keddah.

"All history tells us that neither barbarous nor civilised warriors of different tribes or nations long agree when compressed," he remarked. Had not his hero the Duke said that "when numbers of men get together there's a d——d deal of jostling ".

"Accident has given me the 16th of January (Corunna) for crossing the frontier," Charles notes with satisfaction ; and again : " This time, two years ago, I marched against the Ameers, and a comet appeared. Three days ago another comet appeared. Does this argue the same success ? How these coincidences strike the mind. God's will be done whether evinced by signs or no ; my business is to do my duty." Charles liked comets. He was wont to say, " Comets are souls of good post horses who still ply their trade charged with carrying angels' despatches."

"January 17. Shapoor. Came here last night, very tired, after more than seventy miles ride, but wrote my despatches before lying down."

The expedition was to take no less than three months of pitiless marches, often in deep sand under cloudless skies, or across scorching rocks which breathed out heat as from an oven : in ever present danger from the ferocious tribesmen who, armed with matchlocks, shields and swords, took and gave no quarter : in shortage of water and provisions, in extremes of heat and cold : in gorges and ravines black in shadow and sinister as in a lunar landscape, before the " Devil's Great Brother ", as the tribesmen called Charles, brought it to a successful, though only temporary, conclusion. But the reader of these pages will realise that a factual narrative has never been their aim. It is not so much what happened as what was in the mind of the man who caused these happenings. Otherwise it would be to consider

SIR CHARLES NAPIER PURSUING THE ROBBER TRIBES

this book as an inanimate affair of cloth, print and paper, ignoring the meaning it attempts to give.

All must be astonished at the unbreakable spirit of its leader. The newspapers from the first declared it to be a " wild goose chase ", or less politely " An insane old man about to lose all his troops and men ". Charles was conscious all the time of the undercurrent of doubt and apprehension in his camp, even amongst his staff, bar that vivid young McMurdo who stood against the stream. The old General kept his council locked, for his time was occupied by opposing all sorts of petty attacks from headquarters, and the Bombay Press. He feared to let his plans be known in case Buist, his arch-enemy of the Press, should warn the enemy ! He writes : " I am a hedgehog fighting about nothing, yet obliged to fight or be trampled upon."

There were many difficulties to occupy him. There was the scarcity of wells, and the fact that these were guarded by the enemy's forts. (He had brought many leather water-bags and apparatus for digging.) There was the nauseous sulphur in the water. (" When they say ' No water ', I say ' Dig '. When they growl ' Water bad ', I say ' Boil '. I will go on bad or good.") There was the desertion of the camelmen : " The rascally camelmen to the tune of 500 have refused to bring up provisions. Am fairly put to my trumps, half rations for a week, and in two days we shall have none. I will use the camel corps, and dismount half the cavalry if need be. I will eat Red Rover sooner than flinch before the tribe : My people murmur but they only make my feet go deeper in the ground.

" . . . Dammit, why do soldiers want to eat ? It's as bad for war as being married, yet somehow we can't get on without women and sleep. . . . Moses was a proper clever fellow ! How he managed to get bread I know not."

The old General is hours in the saddle ruminating on his plans, " chewing the cud " as he calls it, passing all things in review. How best to make use of Ali Murad and Wulli Chandi, who are with him. (Ali is honest enough but a barbarian is a barbarian). How to protect the women and the children of the tribesmen, whom the tribesmen may all massacre when cornered. For the compassionate strain in Charles is inseparable from the military element, interfering with his outlook. He had avoided this slaughter once already : " I would not fall on him [Beja] wishing to give time for the women and children to escape into the hill. Thus I lost my blow for their sakes. These poor creatures, however, never believe we spare a life : some children we found here have regularly asked each day, ' When are we to be killed ? ' The poor little things thought the good food given to them daily and which they enjoyed exceedingly, was preparatory to their being killed, and of course eaten by the Kaffirs. I have them close to my tent, and have found two of their own women to look after them. They are merry as grigs."

How like him !

And when Charles is out of the saddle this extraordinary man is not only writing out his despatches in that flowing hand of his, but to clear his mind is setting forth his thoughts in his journal on a vast variety of subjects. Here are pages on religion, philosophy, politics and military matters together with notes, such as that sulphur and iron are present in quantities in these rocky hills, and that sea shells abound in the sand, and that his orderly Ali Bey had brought him a handful of manna. " This is a miracle. It is on the bushes, it is food. It comes from God. Down from Heaven." And that the desert sand itself is full of life : " I dropped a bit of butter, and in a moment a little aldermanic animal was on it, one two three, it is covered. These creatures feed birds, birds feed men, and men die to feed vegetables which are again eaten ! the world is one self-consuming, self-creating animal."

Charles even describes in detail a " disagreeable dinner " with old Hunter, when they compared the relative value of sepoy and British troops. " How little my company could reason on human nature. I could not persuade them that in courage one nation is equal to another. Oh no ! Because Europeans are the strongest they must be the bravest. That I deny . . . the sepoys of India are like other soldiers with some difference of religion and customs. As a recruit he is vaunting and eager to fight, so are Europeans; as a veteran he is cool and daring and so are Europeans: both are vain of being soldiers, both will run away at times, and both will fight desperately when well drilled."

Then the old General is disturbed at the love of ease he notes in some of his officers. "There are boys in this camp who require and have more luxuries than myself who am sixty-three and Governor of Scinde. The want of beer and wine is an absolute misfortune to them. These men or boys are unfit for war, the success of which is endurance, and not only that but a pride and glory in privation. . . . A young officer always rides now, and heaps his comforts on the horse keeper who runs at his horse's tail. Such men may be very good fellows, but they are incapable of leading men."

Nevertheless, the old martinet was loved . . . nay worshipped. Here is a revealing comment in his journal.

"A blow-up for talking under arms, and they gave me three cheers in return."

He rowed his " dear boys " John and William Napier, and McMurdo who still loved the bright eyes of danger no less than the bright eyes of his Susan ! "My heart was wrath with McMurdo pursuing the robber like a recruit," " McMurdo has a good military head, but he is too fond of single combat." Indeed, McMurdo's name seems like dancing flame whenever it appears in Charles's journal, so full of life and zest of life is he.

"I tried to prevent the boys going out, but they went off at a gallop, and did not, or would not hear my voice," complains Charles. "Where was no honour or glory or object, and the services might have lost two noble soldiers, leaving miserable widows behind . . . yet their high spirit must be admired," the old fire-eater adds, relenting.

To us, still stunned by Pearl Harbour, Belsen and Hiroshima, the chivalrous warfare of those days seems fantastic. On the occasion of the above incident Charles had written: " Before the cavalry could get there John and McMurdo were fighting an expert horseman. McMurdo first closed with him in single combat for twenty minutes, but then being exhausted (he had just ridden over 70 miles) said : ' John, you may try him. I am quite tired.' They were then all at full speed careering in flight. John had not stricken while the match was fair, but when McMurdo spoke, he rode at the Belooch who was then flying, but soon turned and aimed with his matchlock at John, and he only a yard behind, instantly fired his pistol but missed. McMurdo, thinking it was the matchlock and expecting to see John fall, furious at what he thought unfair, dashed forward, pistol in hand. ' You don't mean to kill,' cried out John. ' Yes, by the Lord,' was the answer, and the next moment the Belooch warrior fell while in the act of drawing a second sword. McMurdo, seeking only a second sword fight, had become angry at the matchlock being used as he thought unfairly, and was now angry with himself for using his pistol, and both he and John were also sorry for the man's death. Yet all was right on both sides. The rules of chivalry allow a man to use whatever weapon he carries."

John had not interfered during the sword fight, continues his uncle : " One admires this high tone of honour, but these robbers are assassins : push the principle further, and I ought not to bring more men than the enemy have to oppose me. These single fights must and shall be stopped . . . yet their high thoughtless spirit must be admired : and also the way they behaved to the Belooch, who expected to be supported by his people, and would have given no quarter."

Fantastic.

As we turn the pages of Charles's journal so intense is the illusion cast upon us we think we too can see, we too can feel, what these men saw and felt. It is our life no less than theirs of which we are reading. The strange Gustave Doré landscape is all about us. The desert spreads defenceless beneath the dazzle of the sky, and rearing from the sand are those sinister cliffs into whose draughty black ravines and gorges the sun can only strike at noon. Here the fire of matchlocks reverberates deafeningly and smoke and din ascend to a mere riband of sky overhead.

We are annihilated by Charles's words to one whose name is in asterisks only. He had been offered command, but showed, to put it mildly, no zeal ! Now Charles rated " zeal " even above courage. Courage could come, but " lack of zeal is a floorer ".

" I see you have no confidence, and a man shall command who has," says Charles witheringly. " Get your corps ready." In his journal he adds : " I sent John Napier, who has zeal, spirit and head : very likely nothing may be found, but I will have my own way. . . . I do not form them [his opinions] on light ground, so to-night Jack marches, resolved to do all he can to succeed : it will give him the habit of command in a night march."

And the following day he adds : " Jack has come back . . . he has brought in two thousand head of cattle . . . we now have taken six thousand cattle and a vast quantity of grain. I am a good robber at all events."

No wonder the Duke of Wellington expressed a desire to read this journal and all correspondence too. " But there are many queer rough things, your Grace," put in William Napier hastily. " So much the better," retorted the Duke. " That is what I want."

Yes, rough things. But there is beauty too and truth. It was not for nothing that Sir Robert Peel said to Edward Coleridge : " You are acquainted with the Napier family. To whom do you award the palm in literature ? " Taken by surprise, Coleridge answered that he had never regarded Sir Charles as a writer, but as the most heroic and generous of soldiers. " Well," returned Sir Robert, " I can assure you that I am inclined to raise him up above his brother, not only I but all those who have read his letters . . . and articles are immensely struck by their mastery, clearness and vigour of expression and feel with me he is as good with his pen as he has long proved himself with his sword."

155

Not a few soldiers will agree with this brief entry. "Energy fails. I know not if others think so, but I feel it and no mistake. I do not tire over matters of importance but of the petty details and correspondence about trifles . . . and cavils from Bombay."

On one occasion there was a march of fifty-six miles through deep loose sand in which the exhausted horses sank. Charles had been in the saddle thirty-six hours, the last two in a violent storm which he describes thus. "Horses and men were filled with electricity in the sandstorm we encountered; the sand adhered to the horses' eyes and nearly blinded them : the officers' hair stood up, and as there was little wind we concluded the sand was raised by an electric influence. None of us had ever before witnessed a sandstorm so extraordinary : the feelings were affected by it, and everybody much distressed," and similarly : "On one night march every man's bayonet had a bright flame at the point."

What a picture !

On February 17th his thoughts turn back to Miani. "The second anniversary of Meannee, and I am again in the field. Am I doomed to war and blood ? " Sadly he recalls : "What heaps of dead were round me. How many friends were dying. The shrieks from the hospital tent where men were suffering amputation. Peace be with all, for all behaved nobly, those who died and those who survived that terrible conflict."

This was the Charles who thus laments for his "brother Major's" death at Corunna two years after the battle. "Stanhope ! Stanhope ! Where are ye ? Every turn of the road, every stone brings you back before my eyes, and often prevents my seeing them. . . ."

The Charles who wrote years after the battle of Miani :

"God knows I was very miserable when I rode over the fields, and saw the heaps of the slain : and then all my own soldiers stark and stiff as we laid them in a row for burial next day."

The arduous days go on, hours in the saddle over burning sand, and loose stones which wear the horses' hooves and shoes. Chatting with the soldiers. "On the march I usually got into a jaw with the soldiers ", but when they lay down to sleep at night their old General was still up writing despatches, and replying to carpings and cavillings.

" I have been on horseback from four o'clock in the morning until two of the afternoon, and without food. It is not every man of sixty-three who can do that and work after," he remarks casually. But while this great bodily and mental activity continues we come across a rather touching entry.

" Being a little tired with riding and incessant thought from daybreak on 15th till daybreak on the 16th I fell asleep on my horse, and was awakened by him stopping : then I found that the advance guard, with which I was, saw lights not far off, but when we looked for the cavalry and guns they were lost. This was very awkward for we were but fifty men in a desert, close to a numerous enemy. . . ."

It was McMurdo who rode off to reconnoitre, reporting Baluchis were firing in the plain below. Charles writes : " I drew up our handful of troopers in whose pluck it must be confessed I had not much confidence, but thought they would stick by the sahibs of the staff . . . and at that instant our errant guns and main body came round another hillock of sand ! to my no small satisfaction for fifty tired men and horses were not in a state to give battle to many hundreds of good swordsmen quite fresh."

On another occasion the following words were wrung from the old man, whose strength was diminishing : " How I long for rest of mind to get up and feel there is no work, and there will be no neglect of duty. How every moment the traces feel slack, the whip of conscience cuts to the bone, and convulsive efforts follow."

But the end was in sight.

Beja had devoted himself to Mahomet, had dressed in black and had divided his property and was resolved to die a Gazi sword in hand, but on March 6th he and Doonkee Islam Khan, Bhoogtee Darian Kahn, Jackranee Hussein Khan and another all came to the tent of Charles with the Koran on their head, and fear in their hearts.

157

Delay and anxiety, but on the 9th Charles writes in his journal : " Beja Khan has been captured. The campaign is ended."

" I ought to have hanged Beja," he adds, " but when a man surrenders at discretion, my own dear brother, Satan himself could not hang him unless for some peculiarly atrocious act brought home personally and recently. Had they killed their women and children every man should have been bayoneted."

So now there remains but one thing to be told.

Beja had been trapped within the great gloomy cliffs at Truckee as Charles had planned. Charles blocked the southern pass whilst a column under Beatson pushed in at the northern entrance. Somehow a sergeant and ten men of the 13th got on the wrong side of a small ravine, and came to the foot of a rocky platform crowned by the enemy, and where the ravine in which they were suddenly deepened to a frightful chasm. The sergeant did see his officer and the main body gesticulating. He thought they were encouraging them to go on.

They began to climb.

Then as the little party, exhausted and breathless, gained the summit they were met by a matchlock volley from a low breastwork, and a charge of some seventy Baluchis sword in hand ! There on that dizzy and narrow ledge, precipices yawning below them, the little band of eleven men fought the unequal fight. Six out of the eleven fell at once, five others, four wounded, were pushed over the edge. . . .

" Such are British soldiers. Where mortal men can stand in fight they will. Every man had a medal ; two of them had three on their breasts. They died gloriously but uselessly on that sad cliff in the Cutchee Hills," lamented Charles, and later he was to add in passionate anger : " Those glorious men who fell at the Northern entrance of Truckee have not had justice, but they shall by God ! "

And William, dipping his pen in gall, wrote down in his History :

" These were the deeds Lord Ripon forgot, but the names of these gallant men are recorded in the History of Scinde Administration, and their enemies more susceptible of generous emotion, thus testified to their heroism. Among the tribes, when a warrior dies with noted bravery a red or green string is tied round the wrist of the corpse, the red being of most honour: here, before casting the bodies of the slain down from the platform they tied red string on both wrists."

CHAPTER 15

SIKH WAR
1847–1848

WAR with the Sikhs seemed now inevitable. Charles, always on the alert, sent to Headquarters a memorandum showing how, if Multan were used as a base, he himself might utilise his army in Sind to divert the Punjab army : seize Multan, and from there co-operate with the Commander-in-Chief. This sent, Charles waited for six months ! No instructions were received by him. The word " frustration " was not in use, but one can imagine the old soldier fretting, consumed with impatience as day after day the monsoon days passed with their low dark clouds sliding in endless procession from the Indian Ocean over the parched desert. Not a drop of rain falling, though the air was loaded with moisture giving prickly heat, Sind sores, and irritability of mind. Flies buzzing : a tearing wind blowing. Precious days slipping. No orders. He had knocked on a door which remained closed. He began to prepare on his own account. He was told to stop.

The war did break out, in December, and on the 24th of that month at long last Charles at Karachi did receive his orders. He was to assemble fifteen thousand men at Rohri with all possible speed.

Rohri ? Rohri ? How the old war-horse must have pricked his ears. Sukkur-Bukkur Rohri, as the Indians pronounce it, all in one word ! That starting point of his successful Sind campaign, and of his recent hill campaign. At last ! At last ! Charles rushed on his preparations. Much of his force had to come from Bombay. He writes : " I only heard of the war on the 24th : this is the 26th, and already my siege train has advanced 100 miles towards Roree : that is not bad, and I give myself a month to assemble all at Roree, 400 miles off . . . i.e. 26 marches which are regulated by water. Hardinge promised me six weeks' notice ! But my work is to remedy mishaps : it is half the glory of war to rise over the waves like a ship."

"Ready aye ready" was on his coat of arms. On "July XXVII James King of Scottes had granted a border of ffleures de lises about the coatte of armes, sik as is on our royal banner, & also ane bundell of lances above his helmet with the words Readdy ay Readdy that all his after commers may bruick the saimne as a pledge, & taiken of our guide will & kyndnes for his true worthiness ".

Charles was " ready ".

Sure enough the old warrior by February 6th had arrived at Rohri at "head of 15,000 men with 86 pieces of cannon, and three hundred yards of flying bridges consisting of pontoons, native boats with rafts and plankings, the whole ready to march, carriage and everything complete and such a spirit in the troops as cannot be surpassed ".

Then to his consternation orders to halt his army ! He was to come on alone, and fast as possible, to Lahore to meet the Governor-General and the Commander-in-Chief.

He travelled across enemy country with extreme speed by camel, with God knows what bewilderment in his heart. On arrival he found the battle of Sobraon had been fought. With it the first Sikh war was ended. His masterly preparations, his forced marches were not needed.

Now he was merely to take part in a Council of War.

Those who do not know what it is to be possessed by conviction, to be driven by one's nature to extreme exertion of mind and body as though by whips, have found it amusing that Charles had to blink away tears at the collapse of all his plans.

The Governor-General greeted his old comrade warmly and the troops gave him an ovation.

In spite of his disappointment Charles writes : " I cannot

enter into the cause of being ordered up here, but it is very honourable, and in all things Hardinge has behaved towards me with extraordinary personal kindness and in the most flattering manner "; and of the Commander-in-Chief he writes : " Gough is a glorious old fellow, brave as ten lions, each with two sets of teeth, and two tails "; but he does add : " I am afraid to say what I think. First it would look like a desire to censure Hardinge whom I love, for he is a noble fellow : second, it would look as though my wish to get Gough's place, which would be false : he also is a noble fellow, but he owes Hardinge a debt of which he is not aware. Then it would appear boastful, but until at Lahore I had no idea of how much could have been done. Meanwhile India has lost much blood and money, and the *tragedy must be reenacted in a year or two.*"

Thus he asserts his belief—to be justified. . . . Nevertheless Charles never took credit to himself for being a military genius. " I am not of great ability, working diligently but without any of that astounding power of mind like Napoleon or the Duke," he maintained.

He had said he could not " enter into the cause of being ordered up here " and spoken of Hardinge's personal kindness. A letter written three years later to his brother throws some light on this. It appears at Lahore he had offered to take the command till danger was past. He only told this to his staff. But Hardinge himself might have mentioned it to others. " I never mentioned it ", but some journalist had got hold of the talk, and was now putting abroad he had wished to be Governor of the Punjaub. " I did it from a sense of duty, thinking there was great danger, and seeing there was no one able for it, about him, for I have no opinion of Lawrence. Happily for me Hardinge refused. . . . Hardinge was right, for I should not have lived a month."

Now he was worn and weak from fever and dysentery. There was nothing to keep him in Lahore. It was natural he should wish to get back where at least he was of use. After that hurried useless journey of 1,800 miles with a " burning tent and a camel's back for comfort", after those months of futile preparation, when he eventually arrived back in Karachi, Havelock wrote : "It is impossible to conceive without seeing it, a frame so attenuated and shattered yet still tenanted by a living soul, as this old soldier. . . ."

But his cup was not yet full. Two months later, cholera. For two months it had raged amongst the natives, and in one night it suddenly sprang on the Europeans. Charles had with him not only his wife and two daughters, and their babies, but also his very dear nephew John, his wife and their little daughter Minnie. And another child was very shortly to be born. He still remembered the hideous scenes on the decks of the *Zenobia*, but this was to be worse. From the 14th of June till the 19th cholera struck like a fiend. "Had it lasted three days more our whole staff must have been destroyed, cooks, butchers, bakers, all died or fled and the country is said to be strewn with carcasses."

He fought like a tiger to save his men.

Immediately he separated the troops and started seven different hospitals. Some of these hospitals were two miles apart, but twice a day did this gallant old fellow, sick as he was, visit each hospital, speaking words of encouragement and comfort to the dying, urging the reluctant doctors to give their patients plenty of cold water to drink, " . . . seeing death was inevitable I thought it cruel to add intense thirst . . . the summer is hot beyond anything we have had since we occupied Scinde ". His daughter writes : " Papa is working himself to death. Ever since this dreadful cholera broke out he has been twice a day round the hospitals ; but he has done so much good for it cheers the poor men so seeing him among them." " Merciful God ! " cries Charles, " but this cholera tries the nerves of the heart. In this small place where we are but a handful of Europeans and natives, seven thousand have died. I have lost eight hundred soldiers, and we are the portion most cared for—having hospitals, able doctors, every comfort, every attendance. One and all cried out as they died, ' Oh that it were in battle ! ' A dying Beloochi said to me, ' Oh, General, if we were dying in battle with you we should be happy, but to die thus ! ' "

There were three carts with four horses plying constantly to carry away dead bodies ; heaped, with their legs stiffly sticking out.

Seven thousand persons died in the town (more than a third) and 50,000 outside. But by June 30th, though 120 died in the town that very day, Charles could write : " Cholera fast abating, thank God."

And then on July 7th the little daughter of his much-loved nephew John died.

Worse. " The following day John was struck as we were sitting down to dinner, and at ten he no longer existed. I have seen many die, but not one in such dreadful agonies."

And the following day Charles's step-daughter Minnie, John's unhappy widow, gave birth to another daughter.

What wonder that old Charles writes to his brother : " My heart is almost broken, William. The day before yesterday John and I laid this little child in its grave ; to-day I shall lay him there . . . he who from his infancy I had saved and cherished and so loved. . . ." One of his " three trumps ", John, William Napier and Montagu McMurdo.

Meanwhile his relations with the Court of Directors were becoming more and more strained. They had transferred to him the bitterness they held for Lord Ellenborough. Certainly Charles had criticised the Company in no uncertain way from the first. He had arranged the Government of Sind entirely on his own without reference to the Directors.

There were misrepresentations in Press and Parliament not helped by his outspoken anger. The battle between William and Outram raged, and all life was soured for Charles by his own ill health. His John dead : perpetual thwarting and frustration of his plans, and a deep sense of injustice that he had received no recognition whatever of his services in the Sikh war. " Letters calling me up from Roree to his headquarters because things were in danger, and he thought I was the man to pull them through. I am not so vain as to think there was no other ; but they thought so, and the army thought so, and I have the Governor General's letters saying so. The Government at home have of course copies, for the letters were official."

Yet when Ministers at home thanked all officers by name who had taken part in the campaign, from the Governor-General down to a Captain, Charles, in spite of his warnings, his preparations, his forced marches, was not even mentioned. Some may say that, though deserving all credit for his readiness, his army had no actual share in the campaign, and this was a misfortune rather than a grievance. But coming on the top of much else Charles found it one of many injustices.

Then : " Why did not the Horse Guards make my poor boy a major for the Hill campaign ? I scarcely got thanks from them, and my staff got nothing but hard work ! I care not for myself, but I do care for those boys who worked so hard at their duty, giving up all the pleasures of youth . . . they are deserving of acknowledgments, and that they have not had."

The fact of the matter was the tragic death of John had, as he himself says, " Broken my nerves to pieces."

His health was wretched, and his preoccupations innumerable. He was carrying a burden of work and responsibilities under intolerable conditions. Government House was still unfinished and Charles and his wife had to sleep in the same room as John's widow and baby. " Our bedroom is our parlour. We sleep in the hall, and as the doors are only blinds we might all be in the same room." And this with a new-born child ! No wonder poor Charles wrote " this is a serious interruption of the constant pressure of work ".

What with the Directors striving to halve his prize money. . . . " Well my girls are safe without prize money, and that is all I care for." . . . What with slanders in the Press, and sluices on the canals ; what with the two war steamers to trade between Karachi and Shikapur, and persuading the merchants to co-operate . . . " A great step towards the Commerce of Central Asia has thus been made. A camel reaches Shikapur in five weeks, a steamer in sixteen, days, a camel must be guarded, and may be robbed, a steamer is safe, and only one man delivers the whole merchandise, whereas each camel requires a man to lead, and another to guard, meaning thirty men for a ' kafila ' to be kept and paid for three months." . . . What with " grain so abundant and sold at half price, and taxes all paid in kind, and crime has everywhere ceased with the cheapness of food. Had prices kept up we should have filled the treasury, but poor people's bellies would have been empty. I thank God that the bellies are full, the treasury low : every shilling taken before the just expense of government in any country is a robbery." . . . Yes, what with all these preoccupations, we are reminded of a conjurer striving to keep up too many of his bright balls in the air at the same time . . . and all the while Charles is thinking : " I am wasting life in this climate of death. . . . I no longer feel myself of much use. Hardinge is good and honourable but we are very different in our ideas and character. . . . In Ellenborough's time, for all I did, or proposed to do, down came an answer affirmative or negative direct and decisive with reason and cause in every line. Now I get no answer for months, and then comes a weak letter . . . full of kindness though towards me. . . ."

Meanwhile Susan is having fever, so too her husband who does not seem to be able to recover from the shock of his brother's death. Emily too is ill. " Emily is twenty," writes her father. " Her illness makes me very miserable. So good, so cheerful, so clever, all a daughter and a mother should be at her young age. . . . Great God grant that she be spared." Then McMurdo, in a fury of loyalty, had rushed off to Bombay to horsewhip Dr. Buist the journalist, for slandering Charles. When the old man finds this out he is greatly troubled. " Montagu is so fiery. When his blood is up he would probably have gone farther than mere beating, and even taken life."

When Charles's wife is taken seriously ill it is too much for Charles. He had once said a soldier should not have wife and daughters. His hat should cover his family. He decides to resign. The whole family, eight in all, prepared for departure.

No wonder Charles writes : " Here I am like a man smothered with women and children, like a duck with onions," but he goes on more cheerfully : " You will soon see my dear little Charlie. He is a broad-shouldered beautiful boy. Whether he means to grow up so I cannot say : but he is a very stout chap now, and I wish him out of India. . . . Would that my next four months were well over, and I clear of this grand India with all its glories and wants, and bad government. . . ."

His last weeks were stormy. Half humorously Charles writes to his brother Henry :

" Here am I now held up as a betrayer of confidential papers ! I hope they will stop short of sending me to Sodom and Gomorrah ! All else I have been accused of . . . robbery, murder, dethroning innocent princes, refusing beds to princesses in labour, lying through thick and thin . . ."

The incident of the bed is an example of the persistent and wilful calumny to which he was subjected by some of the newspapers.

The *Bombay Times* had published : " The Ameer's wife was in labour. Sir C. Napier ordered the prize agents to drag the miserable truckle bed on which she was lying from under her to swell his prize money."

" The true story is this. One of the ladies pretended to be in labour and sent for a state bedstead, which was mounted with pure gold in large quantities : the prize agent sent her word she might have her choice of all others, but that one he could not give her. The trick to get that valuable gold bedstead having thus failed, the lady not choosing to take any other was not confined at all in the fort, but long afterwards at her own residence," wrote Charles. " In short the devil had never found such a complete job out of hand as himself," he added a little bitterly, and jokes to his brother : " Before you get this I shall be at Malta or with the ghosts in the Red Sea. I hope not the last as I am so like Moses that Pharaoh would shout, ' We have him at last,' and fall on me tooth and nail."

He embarked with his family at Karachi on October the 1st.

Indians love a show, and as was to be expected an immense crowd had gathered.

There were tears in the General's eyes behind his spectacles as he shook hands with his friends. Sir Dermot Daly wrote: "The hearts of those around were too full to cheer, no one spoke, but many instinctively uncovered their heads. It was not till the vessel moved that the cheers burst out."

In his diary he had written: "I will go home, and patiently await the blow of nature which I believe is not far distant—I have conquered Scinde, but have not yet conquered myself."

CHAPTER 16

THE DUKE AND DIRECTORS
1848–1849

DREADING the damp cold of an English winter, because of the agonising pain it would induce in his facial wound, Charles spent the next few months at Nice with his brother George, who had just returned from Cape Colony. There in the sunlight, amidst the dusty palms and mimosa, the two old brothers had much to talk about.

There was the tragic death of John Napier, and his little child, but Charles had always cherished John as a son, and surely he would tell the father of John's zeal and dash throughout the Sind campaign, and subsequent hill warfare, not forgetting the young soldier's exploit in bringing in that two thousand head of cattle when rations were so low.

George himself was now none too well. He confided he, the intrepid rider, was now unable to sit on a horse, owing to some internal inflammation. This as it turned out was to have vital consequences for them both.

The affection between all the Napier family was like a strong and beautiful tree. They thought Charles in particular could do no wrong. For months past William had, with that far too passionate pen of his, been waging war on Charles's behalf, thereby doing him much harm, let it be said. Now in May he wrote, urging Charles to come home by Havre instead of Boulogne to meet Lord Frederick Fitz Clarence, and have a grand reception at Portsmouth. Charles was always destroyed by seasickness. He writes in reply that he dislikes making a gaby of himself, and this would mean ten hours of it instead of two.

However, if McMurdo and John Kennedy really thought the reception a good answer to his enemies, he would get " over my repugnance to this display—if not I will hold my course by Folkestone to the advantage of my stomach.   God bless you ! I cannot describe my delight at seeing you again."

A day or two later he wrote from Paris : " I have just heard of you being made K.C.B. and I am in great spirits at it.   I sat half an hour with Soult yesterday, who twice desired me to say how much he regarded you.   He paid me the highest compliment ' as he had studied all my operations in CHINA ! and entirely approved of them ' ! ! !   This was flattering ! ! ! Depend upon it when a French soul is damned it puts on a greatcoat and compliments the devil on a fine climate tho' ' *un peu froid*'."   But in spite of his jokes Charles adds he is glad of the respite caused by delay of the packet, as " this infernal pain seems never to leave my guts for any time ".   Already the ulcers which were to kill him were gnawing into his liver.

On his arrival at home he found himself to be a lion : public dinners, complimentary receptions.   The dinners he disliked. But what happiness to meet the Duke again, to hear those warmest congratulations from one naturally bleak in manner ; pleasure, too, to encounter for the first time his old chief Lord Ellenborough, whom in spite of such volumes of intimate correspondence he had never yet met.   Then Charles held a great admiration for Sir Robert Peel, and after a banquet the latter had exclaimed : " Were I to begin life again to be a soldier, I would enlist under you in preference to any other General."

All this was balm.   Charles might say—and did—that he welcomed it only because it was " wormwood " to the twenty-four Directors of " Leadenhead Street " ... but we know better ! For he had been subjected too long to continued abuse and misrepresentation in the Press.   There were private anonymous letters, and even forged papers from persons of importance.   A note of insult purported to be from the editors of *The Times*, but when sent up for verification was found to be a forgery.   All this seems to us incredible.   It is hard therefore for us to realise

how Charles and William had been stung to almost madness, as
cattle are stung by dung-flies. Charles once wrote : " Neither
George nor Henry are the least revengeful, but William and
myself are when resistance is continued." They were. So we
find Charles calling Outram " a d——d impudent rascal ", and
when Sir James Weir Hogg is unable to answer Charles's attack
on him for slander, and remains silent, Charles's curt comment
is, " The hog grunts no more."

But a letter from Bolwell " flatters him more than all the
dinners from clubs in London ".

Now James Bolwell was a radical shoemaker, who at the time
of Charles's command in the north had had great influence over
the Chartists, and in spite of his views had been always zealous
in the prevention of violence.

Charles writes, pacified : " I have all the reward I wish for or
desire, and all that to my ideas any public servant ought to
receive. This I have received from Bolwell, from my own
family and friends and from many others, so that I have my
reward, and all the rest of the world may go to the devil for
aught I care. . . ."

Nevertheless, he *did* care for making war on his East Indian
enemies ! " I left my card on John Russell yesterday. The
messenger wanted me to go up to him, but I did not. I said,
' I merely called in case he wished to see me, and to leave my
direction here, but I had nothing to say to his Lordship.' ' I
am sure his Lordship will see *you*, Sir Charles.' ' But I don't
want to see his Lordship,' and so I walked out."

In September Charles took a house and settled at Cheltenham.
" On October the 5th they give us a public feed. I have been in
a whirlpool since I came, visits, changes of lodgings, and dinners :
how I hate these effusions of fish, and folly ! " And then his
tetchiness turns to what was always uppermost in his mind . . .
the soldiers ! " Every old soldier in Cheltenham comes to tell
me how little way his pension goes in these times ! Poor old
fellows, it vexes me to see them so hard run for small comforts,
and I am glad I came here, if it were only for the chats with them

of old fights and hardships. They like this, but complain bitterly that old officers take no notice of them."

This is the lovable, affectionate Charles, tender to his soldiers and children and all animals, the Charles who on the anniversary of Miani writes : " Red Rover and I must have a long chat, and Flibberty Gibbert also ; tho' Flibberty was off that day in reserve in case Red Rover should be killed." A Charles completely unknown to those who attacked him so virulently.

By and by he is writing : " Winter is dreadful here. It is as bad as London and drives me mad." The pain the cold caused him was so extreme he writes he would sooner " be broke on the wheel ". Meanwhile the libels, anonymous and otherwise, continued, and one gathers Charles's state of mind from this letter of Montagu McMurdo.

3 Tavistock Place,

Cheltenham, Oct. 22, '48.

"My dear Sir William,

" I entirely agree with you on the necessity of preventing anything like a duel taking place between the General, and any of his opponents, and I am convinced that nothing would be so conducive to the ruin of the General's cause in the eyes of the whole world . . . and consequently more satisfactory to his enemies . . . than the circumstances of his fighting a duel . . . no matter how justified he might personally be in going out ! His age, his position, and the present state of public opinion rejects such an alternative ; and I promise you that I will, peremptorily, and at all risks interfere. I am,

Yours sincerely,

M. McMurdo."

Turning over these old letters saddens. How little, how very little these injustices, these suspicions, these hatreds matter to-day ! But they still live on in that dashing, flowing characteristic writing, even though the writer and those of whom he writes are dust. We feel even now from their brittle pages, the atmosphere of anger, of suspense, of waiting for letters to appear in *The Times* and other papers, in which not only Charles and William lived, but in which his wife and Montagu McMurdo, the whole family, must also have been surrounded. What a waste of life ! . . . But in these almost daily letters there *is* fun too, and anecdotes which may still interest, and tend to give a truer picture of the man.

" They are ruining my Camel Corps," writes Charles. " Edward Campbell made me laugh. Their regiment have got for their mess Cubbadhar Moll, the elephant that ought to carry the lanthorn. They regularly overload old Cubbadhar Moll, who lets them, and when they have done he takes as much off as he thinks ought not to be on, and slips away. They dare not put an ounce back after this hint. Delightful beast ! How entirely he comprehends the spirit of my camel corps.*

" Hunter told me a curious thing. He was showing a huge sword which cut off his own arm at Burtpur. He was leading his men in the assault, and was met on the ramparts by a giant in complete armour who was flourishing his sword, and instantly advanced upon Hunter who held his sword up. The Giant, at one dextrous blow, sent Hunter's sword with (to use his own words) ' a whirr into the air '. Hunter held up his scabbard, which he took in his right hand, to parry the coming blow that cut through the scabbard, and cut his left arm off below the elbow, leaving merely a bit of skin uncut . . . he fell on his bottom and held his left arm in his right hand, and when an officer tied his sash above the wound to stop the hæmorrhage and the surgeon coming up put the two ends of the arm together, and it was tied in that position, and united ! . . . Hunter cannot use it, and sometimes it flies about as if he were shaking his fist at you, only with rather a circular motion till he catches it with his right hand, to do which is not always easy, poor fellow. He told me that the soldiers took a long time to kill the Giant ; his armour was so strong that they could not get their bayonets into

---

* Charles's Camel Corps was led by an elephant bearing a large flag by day and a lantern by night. " Moses, that great soldier of the desert, was in my mind," he wrote.

him, and he laid about him like mad. The sword is a beautiful one . . . this shape . . . [and here is a clever sketch] . . . sharp on both edges, and of damascus steel with watermarks."

In these almost daily letters, whether they be of abuse of his enemies, anecdotes, or plan of campaigns, all breathe forth Charles's passionate affection for his brother, William concern for his health, gratitude for the public battles he was waging on behalf of himself . . . though many may think how much better had he stayed his pen, and not further enflamed and excited Charles !

" God bless you, dear brother. No one loves or admires you more or as much as your affec. C. J. Napier," writes Charles.

It should never be forgotten that Charles, as well as William, lived in constant pain. The bullet was too near William's spine to be removed, and ever since those Peninsula days he was apt to suffer tortures. Then Charles tells us how he himself had often to get up in the night and light a candle, or he should go mad. " The light seems to relieve, but I live in terror lest it should come on violently." " I would sooner be broke on the wheel." If we remember, too, that even now he was suffering from the liver trouble which was to kill him, we make allowances for his fury at attacks far better ignored.

But now the almost daily letters passing between Charles and William talk less of their own annoyances, and show a growing concern over affairs in India. The outlook was indeed threatening. " The Indian news speaks tolerably plain language," says Charles. " Gough has gone ahead, as usual, and will get into a scrape."

England herself was growing mistrustful of Gough—Gough so brave, so reckless. In August Charles had danced with rage at England's cry, " Give us another Outram ! " but now it was Charles himself they were crying for, not Outram.

" They will find me a very good prophet when I said at Lahore, You may *now* conquer the whole Punjaub without further bloodshed, in a year or two it will cost plenty. . . . I dread the next dispatch . . . there are at this moment the elements of disaster. . . ."

" Our Sepoys have been rather shaky in their fidelity of late. Did you know the Sikhs collected a great number of beautiful wives and it was by their agency they seduced our Sepoys. The girls are all there still, and perhaps the treason too."

There must have been chatter in clubs and papers about the possibility of Charles superseding Gough, because as far back as August he had written this to William: " I am worried by the expression ' Paralleled ' by Wellington alone because there can be no parallel between us. How can a man who has won two battles against barbarians be on a parallel with one whose long life has been a chain of victories against the greatest generals of the world? I might bear a parallel with Hardinge . . . and not having false modesty in me I think I am as good as Hardinge and better than the others. Why, William, I no more consider myself as a first-class General than I consider myself as equal to Napoleon."

The clamour against Gough increased. Men were now looking to Charles, and his friends insisted he would have to return to India. Charles himself was positive the Directors would never consent unless in the face of real disaster.

Eventually the Duke of Wellington did advise the Directors to appoint Charles Commander-in-Chief. Not unnaturally they refused, for had he not abused them consistently for years? The Duke then suggested George. Unwillingly the Directors agreed to this, but George was unable to sit on a horse, and like Charles his opinion was a Commander-in-Chief should " live in the saddle ", and in any case under no circumstances would he have accepted a post which he felt could only be worthily filled by Charles.

Then the Duke sent for Charles to Apsley House, and Charles in a letter to William thus describes his visit:

" I saw the Duke this morning. ' How do? Very glad to see you.' N.: ' Very well, thanks, your Grace '. D.: ' Sorry I sent for you up from Cheltenham. I thought I could employ you, but can't . . . that quarrel with Hogg, that quarrel upset everything. Sorry I gave you the trouble to come. Well, I am very glad to see you. I shall keep you in my eye all the same . . . another time perhaps' ! N. : 'I don't think I could go to India, my Lord Duke.' D. : ' Why, aren't you well ? ' N. : 'Yes, quite well, but I have too many enemies there.' Duke, laughing very much : ' Poo . . . Poo . . . Poo . . . Enemies don't care for enemies. Poo. Poo. Well, good-bye. Very glad to see you,' and again he shook hands and walked with me to the door, and so we parted. Lord Ellenborough will be in town to-morrow, and I shall get him to tell the Duke my opinion, and that I won't go out as Commander-in-Chief without extra-ordinary powers."

The Directors breathed again. Sir William Gomm was told to hold himself in readiness, but late in February came news of the battle of Chillianwallah, and now the nation's shout for Charles to supersede Gough was deafening.

Still Charles held back. Innately generous, he angered at the unjust outcry against a fine and noble soldier. We are told that Charles was shocked that while hysterical crowds were following him about, his old comrade of the Peninsula could hardly have shown himself in the streets of London without risk of his life. As Balzac said, " How terrible is the vengeance of a sheep."

There must have been some busybody who urged Charles to take a step to meet the Directors. For a letter is written off to William : " I've not the least idea what he means by a ' step '. The only foot I should ever take with the Directors would be anything but conciliatory ! "

He had met with antagonism because he had dared to tell the truth. Just as his mother, when a girl of fifteen, had told George the Third that a German woman was not the best person to govern England, so with like bluntness Charles had told the Directors that their policy incited the soldiers to mutiny, and that their civil system was one of Indian spoliation !

Truly he was not easy to deal with.

But John Kennedy was doing what he could.

" Your triumph is complete. The world knows your opinion of the Directors. But no obstacle to your being offered command, because that is a triumph the more whether you accept it or not."

"I told him I disagreed," writes Charles to William. "Tell me your opinion. If you join Kennedy I give way."

Finally the old Duke's words : "*If you don't go I must.*"

Charles turned again to William for advice, and just as William had told him ten years before that it was his duty to go to India, so he told him now.

The Directors objected to Charles joining the Supreme Council as his predecessors had always done. One can picture the nervousness which Lord John Russell would feel in communicating their decision to the old warrior whose help they were calling upon.

Charles listened to his halting words in growing fury, then springing to his feet, and clenching his fist before the Prime Minister's eyes, he shouted : "Look here, Lord John. If they can't find a precedent for going out without a seat, I will, by God, find one for a Commander-in-Chief not going out when offered the situation." "They will, I am sure, find one," replied Lord John, whom one pictures backing uncomfortably away ! "My Lord, I do not care whether they do or not, but to India I will not go without a seat in Council," exploded Charles.

Again the Directors had to yield with as good a grace as could be mustered. Moreover, there was the inevitable banquet to be given to a Commander-in-Chief on departure. Charles, seated between the Chairman and the Duke, would be speaking.

He did.

"I go to India by the Command of her Majesty, and by the recommendation of the Duke of Wellington : and I believe I go also with the approbation of my countrymen." A pause. Then he added, every word a dig : "Least said soonest mended."

This was bad enough, but now the Directors had to sit back in their chairs, and listen to the Duke of Wellington declare : "I have frequently enjoyed your hospitality on occasions of festivals, which you have given on the appointment of Governor-Generals, Governors and Commanders-in-Chief, but I have never attended with so much satisfaction as on the present occasion," following this up with the warmest and most enthusiastic eulogy of Charles.

Now began the frenzied time of preparation for departure. Comical in some ways, though behind it all one senses the strain and press on a man of Charles's temperament and age. There is nothing to show it, but probably the faithful Fanny did not find her husband easy to live with these next few weeks, nor McMurdo, nor John Kennedy. Charles's carriage was mobbed in the streets. Letters poured in, interrupting his preparations ; letters asking for special patronage for young men of whom he had never heard. One lady desired her son to be on the staff, and moreover " assured to have him guaranteed from all casualties ". Another had a son very clever breeding horses. It was " momentous that John should be your A.D.C. The military bearing being suitable for the staff of a Commander-in-Chief." Best of all was a secretary offering his services, as Sir Charles Napier " would be too illiterate to write his own despatches ".

The folly of man is immeasurable.

The spare old man with his profusion of long grey hair, his challenging eye had only to appear in the streets to receive an ovation. Such was the unseemly hysteria of the time. The print shops were full of his portraits. Everywhere, too, was displayed a cartoon of four Directors of the East India Company as bearers of a palanquin, trotting towards India House, whilst in the palanquin Charles, the object of their venom, reclined, smiling disdainfully.

It was a cruel age.

Then there came Thackeray's amazingly outspoken comment : " The Tale of Koompanee Jehan." It is unlikely that the reader of to-day will be familiar with its wit, and it is too long to quote in full. But after describing John Company's years of injustice, not only to the peoples of India but also to their own servants, in a manner which would have delighted Aunt Hester Johnson, after saying an army had been utterly destroyed because the Queen Mother chose to give the command to an officer out of

THE MODERN CINCINNATUS: A PROPHECY OF 1849

whom age and illness had squeezed out all the valour, Thackeray comes down to the battle of Chillianwallah. . . . "The Indian soldiers said, ' Why is this old man to be left to jeopardise the lives of warriors, and bring our country to sorrow? If the Queen Mother will appoint chiefs for the armies of India over the heads of those who are brave and more experienced, let her give us men that are fit to lead us ' ; " then the account goes on :

" Now there was, when the news came to the city of Lundoon that Goof Bahawder had been beaten upon the banks of the Chenab, a warrior who, though rather old, and savage as a bear whose head is sore, was allowed by all mankind to be such a Roostum as had never been known since the days of Wellington. His name was Napeer Singh. He with 2,000 men had destroyed 30,000 of the enemy ; he despised luxury ; he had a beak like an eagle and a beard like a Cashmere goat. When he went into a campaign he took with him but a piece of soap and a pair of towels ; he dined off a hunch of bread and a cup of water. ' A warrior,' said he, ' should not care for wine or luxury, for fine turbans or embroidered shulwars ; his talwar should be bright, and never mind whether his papooshes are shiny.' Napeer Singh was a lion indeed ; and his mother was a lion of lions.

" But this lion, though the bravest of animals, was the most quarrelsome that ever lashed a tail and roared in a jungle. After gaining several victories he became so insolent and contemptuous in his behaviour towards King Koompanee Jehan, whom he insulted, whom he assailed, whom he called an old woman, that the offended monarch was glad when General Napeer Singh's time of service was out. . . . But when the news of Goof's discomforture came to Lundoon, and the Hall of Lead, and the Queen of Feringhistan, all the Ingleez began to quake in their shoes. ' Wallah ! Wallah ! ' they cried, ' we have been made to swallow abominations ! Our beraks have been captured from our standard-bearers ; our guns have been seized ; our horsemen have fled, because Goof Bahadin knew not how to lead them into battle. How shall we restore the honour of our arms ? What General is that capable of resisting these terrible Sikhs and their sirdars ? '

" The voice of all the nation answered, ' There is but one chief, and his name is Napeer Singh ! ' The twenty vizeers in the Hall of Lead, remembering the treatment which they had received from that General, and still smarting uneasily on their seats from the kicks which he had administered, cried out, ' No ; we will not have that brawling samsoon . . . take any man but him. If Goof Bahawder will not do, take Goom Bahawder. We will not have Napeer Singh, nor eat the pie of humility any more.'

" The people still roared out ' Nobody can help us but Napeer Singh.'

" Now Napeer Singh was as sulky as the twenty-four vizeers. ' I go,' said he, ' to serve a monarch who has been grossly un-grateful, and whose nose I have tweaked in Durbar ? ' Never, Never.

" But an old General, nearly a hundred years old, very old, brave and wise, the great Wellington, came to Napeer Singh and said : ' O Khan. In these times of danger men must forget their quarrels and serve their country. If you will not go to the Indus, I will go . . . one of us must.'

" They were two lions, two Roostums, two hook-beaked eagles of war ; they rushed into each other's arms, and touched each other's beaks. ' O father ! ' Napeer Singh said, ' I will go ! ' and he went forth, and he bought a piece of soap, and he got two towels, and he took down from the wall his bright and invincible tulwar. . . . And when the Ingleez heard of this elmzshedeh or good news, they all rejoiced exceedingly : and the Queen of the Ingleez clapped her hands for joy. And as for Napeer Singh he took his two towels and his piece of soap and his scimitar, and he went away to the ship which was to carry him to the sea."

It is doubtful whether Charles relished his revenge. He had a too imaginative generosity of spirit. He was profoundly disturbed at what lay ahead of him as we realise from his endless letters to William. Then there were the worries of preparation, the dinners, the Queen's command to dine at Osborne at only a few hours' notice. Charles's speech might sparkle, but the shabbiness of his clothes was a byword. He realised he had only an old drab waistcoat to wear. " Oh, I daresay Nicholas [his valet] has a fine waistcoat; I'll borrow his," which he did.

In a long letter to William, dated March 20th, he begins : " I will not go down to you for the parting gives me such pain." He is puzzled and worried by the news from India. This is a touching letter, the writing very hurried, and less legible than usual. There is apprehension as to what he will have to do. " My work will be more difficult . . . you are among the few who know how little value popularity is when trials are at hand unless powerfully supported by realities, unless I can do some *acts* which show the troops that these expectations are not idle, I shall certainly lose my moral position as it is certain I now possess it, and that if unimpaired is my strongest point. The Conquest of Scinde has sent me out to India, but for that I could not have held my own even, and Outram would have been the grand fellow in the newspapers, not *me*. To be sure I don't value their praise but I may as well die with an honest character as with an infamous one, which but for your pen I think I should have had !—' Your violence ' as it was called ! Christ was violent when he whipped the rascals out of the Temple ! I wanted to say much more about India to you as I shadow out my course the better for writing, but it is impossible. I cannot get an hour's quiet, and so the thread of my thoughts is all broke, and at every second line this is not possible to write, and so God bless you, my dear William."

There seems a shadow of age, a premonition of failure. And what must Fanny, his wife, have felt at parting with this husband of hers, so worn, so old, so tortured constantly with his wounds, turning his face again to the climate which had already nearly killed him.

We do not know.

CHAPTER 17

COMMANDER-IN-CHIEF
1849–1850

HARASSED, keyed up, uncertain whether he was right in answering this call to India, Charles said his good-byes. Good-bye to William. How ailing, yet still noble and handsome as some bearded Greek god with those sculptured curls springing from his brow ! Good-bye to his wife, good-bye to Susan and Emily and all the little grandchildren he so loved, and who so loved him. Turning his back on the longed-for rest and domestic life Charles set out once again.

He left England on the 24th of March, the anniversary of his great victory at Dubba. That must have heartened him. The old man remembered how McMurdo, with wound still bleeding, had galloped around to find a village they could call the battle instead of Dubba, which meant greased leather ! But that was six years ago, and the fiery lad was now the father of three children, and expecting a fourth in the following month. McMurdo had other things to think of than the naming of a battle !

At Ceylon, like a douche of cold water dashed in his face, Charles was to learn the war was over !

History had repeated itself. Just as he had pressed on to Sukkur with his army in 1846, only to find he was not needed. Now the same.

He had come to India fully expecting it would be his glorious lot to finish a great war. Gough had finished it after all.

Charles writes to William that Gough had come off with flying colours and that he rejoiced. " For I like that noble old

fellow Gough more than ever," and later he added in his honest
way : " I am glad, at least I pray, to be glad at having no more
battles."

To add to the general confusion of plans and upset his valet
Nicholas (he who had lent his waistcoat for dining with the
Queen), falling in Ceylon, had broken his leg and died.   Charles
was sincerely attached to this man, and as a small surface burn
may hurt more than a deep one, we imagine how this was the
last straw.   Charles writes : " His loss has cut down my spirits
more than I can describe."   He buried Nicholas at Calcutta,
raised a tomb over him and himself went on up to Simla, old and
upset.

The situation was detestable to one of his imaginative generous spirit.   Gough had pulled off his battle and so reinstated
himself as it were.   But the fact remained Charles had been
sent out, not to relieve him, but to supersede him.   Charles's
orders, signed by the Duke, were to assume the command without loss of time.   Such were the commands of her Majesty.
Yet unaccountably the Duke had also written to Gough he was
to lay down his command at his convenience !   The rumour
was Gough did not intend to return till October.   What on earth
was Charles to do ?

Distastefully he took the plunge, and assumed command.
Gough himself said he was right, but one of his friends disagreed, and no doubt Charles winced at that !   " I like that
noble old fellow Gough more than ever.   I told him my wish
was that he would order me home : it would be a kindness, and
saying I told the truth " ; and : " Again let me express my
delight with old Gough : he is so good, so honest, so noble
minded.   I do rejoice in the promotion that has made this
brave and high-minded veteran so happy and content, and all
which has passed is forgotten."

That was all very well, but it left Charles to exchange the
expected exhilaration of leading an army in the field, for the
pedestrian life of a Commander-in-Chief in peace, for which he
knew he was not suited.   He longed to escape.   As far back as

1846 he had written : " I do not want to be Commander-in-Chief : it is an empty name. Mischief will be vigorous, and I shall be weak, encountering it with handcuffs on my wrists, and chains on my ankles."

Dalhousie was nearly thirty years younger than Charles. The Directors, though temporarily silenced by the nation's clamour for Charles, had of course given him a bad name to the Governor-General, so the two men met rather like dogs circling round each other with stiff legs and feet, though tails are wagging. But Lord Dalhousie wrote to Lord Ellenborough : " I have no anticipation or suspicion that Sir Charles has any intention or wish to be more than Commander-in-Chief . . . on the contrary I have every belief we shall pull excellently well together : if he has any such intention, by God, I shall soon stop that."

Charles describes to William how at the first meeting in Simla Dalhousie jokingly exclaimed, " I have been warned, Sir Charles, not to let you encroach on my authority, and I will take d——d care that you don't."

Unexpectedly, the two men got on famously at first. " I like Lord D. so much," declares Charles, driving his quill across the paper with zest, to William. " That it goes against the grain to find fault or criticise, fault here is none." While Dalhousie writes even more enthusiastically : " Sir Charles's manner is peculiarly young and gay . . . he is full of anecdote . . . full of fun and cleverness. I never had a more agreeable inmate in my house. I was sorry when he housed himself. In all our views of public questions we vary little, and I venture to believe that, working cordially together, as we shall do, much real good may be affected by us."

From *Punch* downwards, Charles's eccentric appearance in his enormous pith helmet, his coat of native leather, his big Blucher boots, had been the subject of many jokes. But ignoring these peculiarities Dalhousie speaks with admiration of the brilliance and beauty of those beaming eyes, and describes his Commander-in-Chief's grey hair combed straight back, with his whiskers and beard resting on his breast and descending to his belt. "What a life he has led, what climates he has braved, how riddled and chopped to pieces with balls and bayonets, and sabre wounds he is."

All seemed set fair.

On arrival Charles had been given a dinner at the Military Club in Calcutta. There he was overheard to say " that there had been an editor of a newspaper at the review. I care little what they write about me. I don't intend to take in any papers

SIR CHARLES NAPIER, COMMANDER-IN-CHIEF IN INDIA, REVIEWING THE TROOPS AT BARRACKPORE IN MAY, 1849—*From a Contemporary Sketch.*

during the short time I shall stay in India, and so they may say what they like."

It was true he had been subjected to unjust and malignant criticism both in the English and Bombay Press, but now turning over the papers of the day, the writer finds change had taken place. The Press seems to regard their new Commander-in-Chief, who has come to pull the country out of a mess, with a kind of proprietary affection and pride even though tinged with sarcasm at times.

The *Bengal Hurkura*, after describing the arrival, added that

he was received altogether with as little ceremony and display
" as even he could reasonably desire. Of the crowds who
would, under more favourable circumstances, have awaited his
landing, many perhaps were kept at home by the threatening state
of the weather . . . the advent of *Shaitan ka Bhaee*, the Devil's
brother, being appropriately heralded by whirlwind and
storm ! . . ."

At his first appearance as Commander-in-Chief Charles made
a sincere and highly characteristic speech which was well received. " Let me give you a bit of advice . . . that is, don't
drink. I know young men don't think much about advice from
old men. They put their tongue in their cheek, and think they
know a good deal better than the old cove who is giving them
advice. But let me tell you that you've come to a country
where, if you drink, you're dead men. If you be sober and
steady you will get on well, but if you drink, you're done for.
You will either be invalided or die. . . ."

Then in a speech which rang through the Military Club he
spoke of the glorious sepoys who have so often fought side by
side with their European officers, striving with them even unto
their death. . . . " I feel proud whenever I see the native
soldier bearing the same medals on his breast which I wear,
though his perhaps are better deserved. . . .

Certainly the *Bengal Hurkura* had been a trifle sarcastic !
" Sir Charles Napier left Calcutta yesterday under salute . . .
in his eternal solah hat, a tusser coat, and a pair of white un-
mentionables which appeared to have done duty on the previous
day ; while betwixt his finger and thumb he held a nosegay
whose freshness had gone, and fragrance had flown, but which
nevertheless he ever and anon gave to his nose and took't away
again. He arrived at the Chandpaul Chaut with the Deputy
Governor (who was in full uniform). . . . The military
Secretary of his Excellency followed in a separate boat dressed
as negligently as Sir Charles, and with a more fantastic head-
dress ; for it bore the shape of an ordinary hat on an enormous
scale (Sir Charles is cut after the jockey fashion) and something

that looked for all the world like a bathing towel . . . placed over it so that the borders in front overhung the wearer's face like a nun's veil, and kept flapping against his eyes continually."

The *Delhi Gazette* was more critical. "A guard of honour suited to His Excellency's exalted rank was in attendance, and everything arranged to do honour to the distinguished visitor. The gallant officer, however, despised such ' pomps and vanities ' and sent the guard to the right about. . . . After inspecting the troops and presenting colours to the 41st N.I. Sir Charles departed for Agra, no doubt very disgusted at having been treated with marked civility and attention. What the native opinion of these eccentricities may be we will not venture to enquire, nor do we suppose Sir Charles cares two straws about it, but in a country where the observance of pomp and splendour is looked upon as indispensable on all state occasions, and where a man is known by the magnificence of his train, we should consider the observance of a little form as not only prudent but necessary."

This view, however, was one which Charles vehemently denied. He had written : " Old Indians say there is no respect for you in India without magnificence and show. A greater fallacy does not exist. Trumpery and humbug are the enemies in India, as they were and are of the Indian Princes." And a little later this same paper was to write : " Sir Charles appears to have been in great spirits and won the heart of everybody by his urbanity and kind manner ; while at the station he clung firmly to his bit of soap and one towel principle " ; he in fact remained at the Dak bungalow refusing all luxuries in private houses, and when warned of the probability of thieves replied : " My dear Sir. We are quite safe. We have nothing." The Commander-in-Chief was as happy as a small boy getting himself into a great mess, going into every hole and corner of the magazine. They brought him a basin of water, but with it no soap. "Have you no soap ? " he asked the officiating Commissioner in surprise.

Now this was a young man, and his answer illustrates the happy terms on which our old hero was with his youngsters.

"I am sorry to say I have not. There is none here but Company's soap, and I am sure your Excellency would not care for that," returned the youngster gravely.

"Oh," Charles's eyes twinkled through his spectacles. "Let's have the Company's soap."

At Agra he reviewed the Brigade. Afterwards, he rode the 2nd European Regiment to their barracks, inspected them and the hospital, tasted the bread served to the soldiers, held out a half-eaten crust—"No wonder you have half your regiment in hospital"—abused the Commissariat contractor, and said he would like to hang every contractor in India. He then bade good morning to the officers accompanying him, and apologised for having kept them in full dress so long. "The impression that the Commander-in-Chief (so often accused of harsh brusquerie) has left on Military men at Agra is very favourable. If he was well pleased with them they were equally well pleased with him," said the *Agra Messenger*. At Peshawar we read: "The review went off beautifully. Twice the whole cavalry Brigade charged, and each time Sir Charles, with his whole staff, Sir Colin, and his staff too, kept at their head." Wonderful old man! He enjoyed that like a boy, one guesses. "At the conclusion he called all mounted officers round him, and said, 'I say now, as I say everywhere, I am not making this tour to praise, but to find out faults, and to-day I have watched everything most narrowly, and I must say I could not detect a single error. The discipline and appearance of the Force reflects the highest credit on Sir Colin Campbell and the Corps.'"

It was from Peshawar that he wrote to his sister:

"Got up at four o'clock and rode my elephant till daylight: then mounted my beautiful white arab Mosaic and galloped him fourteen miles to the disparagement of some of my retinue half my age who were knocked up; a hearty breakfast after at seven, and from that time to five o'clock write! write! write! and my horse is now waiting for me to review two regiments."

It has seemed worth while to quote from these old newspapers, not only to show that Charles was wrong in suspecting the enmity of *all* editors, but also to show he was certainly enjoying life at times in 1850, though from his letters to William one would not suspect it.

CHAPTER 18

COMMANDER-IN-CHIEF
1849–1850

DALHOUSIE wrote in 1850 that "the discipline of the Army, from top to bottom, officers and men alike, is scandalous", and Charles on his arrival had quickly decided he must carry out drastic reforms. Unfortunately this meant working with the Military Board, or would it be more correct to say against the Military Board?

Dining with Lord Dalhousie he once flung out:

"My Lord. It's no use; I might as well resign my authority at once as go on the present system. The whole authority is engrossed by the Military Board." "Not at all, Sir Charles. In all things your authority would be respected and appealed to." "You are mistaken! The only person I have any authority over in India are the apothecaries, and I could not give a dose of medicine to one of them without first obtaining leave of the Military Board to expend a certain quantity of their d——d medical store."

Nevertheless, Charles's eye for difficulties was as bad as Nelson's, and reforms began. He would not tolerate that offences should be passed over because the officer is a "good fellow" or a "poor fellow". Charles writes on the subject of courts martial: "I am refusing leave of absence to idlers, and doing all sorts of vile things, and shall soon be the most unpopular Commander-in-Chief that ever was in India. I have smashed a dozen blackguards." He does not add that, with his devotion to duty, in the course of eighteen months he attended no fewer than two hundred courts martial, giving each his closest personal attention just as he had done years before in his Northern Command. There was a lad whom he broke by confirming the court-martial sentence. His mother, a widow, interceded for her son. Charles did not change the sentence, but in pity, from his own purse sent her money to buy a new commission. Accepting it, she showed her gratitude by boasting it had been given by the Commander-in-Chief as hush money !

Then Charles criticised the regimental messes. This was bound to be resented. To Sir Colin Campbell he wrote off impetuously : " I am resolved on a great attempt ; I expect to fail, still I will try to reduce the expense and drinking of messes. . . .

" 1. To begin with myself and abolish all wine at my own table except sherry and claret . . . no hock, no champagne. I did not do this at Kurrachee ; I did all I could to keep down extravagance, but I did not show the example : now I will.

" 2. I mean to dine at no mess where expensive wines are drunk, saying that I cannot accept of a style of hospitality which I cannot afford to return at my own table.

" 3. I mean rigidly to examine the accounts of messes at the half-yearly inspections. The damning sin of the magnificent armies in India (Queen's and Company's) is an outrageous and vulgar luxury. I say ' vulgar ' because we soldiers (like the frog in the fable) burst ourselves in trying to live like men of 20,000 a year in landed property ! We, who in private life could hardly buy a pint of beer, must drink the most costly wines ! This is, I think, gross vulgarity ! snobbish ! and I know you think so too ; for you had the 98th all right in that point. This I hold to be my duty to the parents of hundreds of these boys. . . . Give me your opinion freely, and if we can save a parcel of youngsters from ruin we shall not sleep the worse."

But it was impossible that men of such different character as Charles and Lord Dalhousie should continue to work very long without differences arising between them.

" He is quick, and catches up small things," Charles admits, " but has no great general views, and his mind cannot grasp them . . . his quickness makes him lose time in small matters, which he should leave to his shoes, and not trouble his head with. . . ."

Very soon Charles's letters to brother William have shadows of coming events cast across their pages. " I have a great deal to say to you, but I have really no time even to dress myself. The mass of detail is so great and I find it necessary to go into things that I ought to leave to others. Kennedy works as hard as I do, and saves me much, or I should limp badly through my work. . . ." After generous praise also of his Adjutant-General with whom he is delighted " because he has a profound know-ledge of the individual conduct of every officer ", the letter continues : " I send you my report and for the love of God don't tell, for there is long correspondence going on about it, and were it known that I had given you a copy it would do great injury. I have shown it to several officers here for the purpose of learning their opinion, but in confidence, and because I was bound from their position to take their opinion ere I could make up my own on particular points. But were it known to the Duke that I had sent a copy home, I know he would be savage as the devil . . . now his support I cannot afford to lose, and if thrown into the scale against me I should have no chance of carrying a single point. . . . I rely on your and Fanny's secrecy. I have no time to tell you the whys and wherefores, but you know how one is harassed when dealing with fools and knaves, and weakness worse than all. I would not send you the report were it not that I never think my military ideas proof till they have been seen by you. God bless you, and let us meet once more. I long to get away for reasons which I can tell you another time. . . ."

Letter after letter went off to William. Might it have been better had Charles not written so copiously ? Apart from the danger of leakage, which he clearly suspected himself, for in how many letters he implores caution ! " This is only for you. For God's sake be secret." " Tell no one of what I have said to you in this letter." " I am afraid to write lest my letter fall into bad hands." "All I tell you in privacy." "Say not a word, it will make my difficulties ten-fold." . . .

Apart from these indiscretions there was the physical exertion of so much writing in letters, and journals, in a day which at one time was of fifteen hours. Even more important still, to a writer of such telling and vivid phrases, must have been the temptation to heighten the effect by exaggeration. Yes. It is impossible not to wish the old warrior had stayed his hand . . . even though the writing of these pages of complaint and sus- picion was no doubt a safety valve. Perhaps the Duke of Wellington had suspected this weakness in Charles, for he had once said to him : " If a man defends himself he must not expect the Government to defend him. I don't want to dictate to you, but I never wrote a word of anything even to my own family. I never made any confidence, and I advise you to do the same."

He had said that to Charles when he was in Sind, and he had repeated it to him when he came out to India this last time !

Charles was up against the Directors of the East India Com- pany, up against the Military Board. It must be admitted he was intolerant and abusive. But the fact remains, the bar- racks were a disgrace. Not only the health, but the lives of thousands of soldiers are due to this old man's persistence in improving and building better barracks for them. Charles's name should shine in gold over every Indian barracks, for what he achieved for his soldiers.

At the Colaba Barracks in Bombay he had found that in the men's sleeping room he walked upon planks laid on the water covering the floor ! Things were no better in Sind. " The heat of the country is tremendous, and if men have not thick walls and lofty rooms sickness is inevitable. Such barracks are expensive no doubt : so are sick soldiers, so are dead soldiers. But the difference of these expenses is that the first is over and done with : the second goes on increasing like compound interest, and quickly outstrips the capital," he had written with indignation.

It is, of course, difficult for those who have not experienced the heat of Upper Sind for four months of the year to imagine it. The natives say there is only one place hotter. They have a saying " Sukkur-Bukkur ko jao ", e.g. " Go to Hell ". Colonel Steuart, when serving under Charles, wrote thus of Sukkur :

" The summer heat in this part of Scinde was so great that the wind during the day, and part of the night, was as if blowing from a furnace. This made it imperative for me to reside as near my office as possible. Having tried covered carriages to go this short distance, I found it impossible to do so without risk of sunstroke. I therefore had to use a felt hat, over which I put a wet towel, and used to ride a swift pony as hard as I could go. The effect of the heat on my clerks was at times truly alarming . . . on one occasion two of them (Eurasians) had to be confined in strait jackets from sunstroke."

" Make the rooms high and narrow," was Charles's insistent cry to the Military Board, " for that not only gives pure air, but debars overcrowding."

And yet in spite of his storming, troops were occupying rooms of ten, or in some cases even only eight feet high, the Board calculating how many men a room could hold by floor space, not by cubic feet of air. " Every man should have 1,000 cubic feet of air," Charles insisted, as the minimum.

Inspecting barracks at two healthy hill stations to discover why men were so ill as to be unfit for service, and the barracks forced to be abandoned, what did he find ? Each man was getting 400 cubic feet of air instead of the minimum of 1,000 ! Up went the roof, down came all the overhanging trees. One can almost hear the oaths that accompanied these operations ! The 60th from Peshawar, who were in very bad health, were ordered to march and take up their quarters there ! Gloomily and apprehensively they moved in to find, instead of two regiments crowded into one barrack, they themselves were to occupy both wings.

There was no more sickness.

Charles wrote : " There is not room for the soldiers in the

Barracks at Agra, nor in those at Dinapore : the answer to this is a mere acknowledgement of my letter, and the soldiers are left to get sick ! This little goose [Dalhousie] is quite unfit for his place : he works at small details, and leaves the great things to take care of themselves ! "

But it was not only over barracks that there was turmoil. Charles was setting men by the ears in his efforts to raise the moral tone of the officers and rank and file. Some of his decisions are certainly eccentric, as with recollections perhaps of school days at Celbridge he ordered an officer to write out all the articles of war as a punishment for being late at church. " How the devil can I make soldiers attend by sending a civil message to a rascal a thousand miles off with ' Pray Sir do me the favour not to get drunk at midday : do think how wrong it is, at least if not wrong not quite right ! ' . . . By the Lord Harry it won't do. Oak trees cannot be chopped down with pen knives, and so I must and do use the hatchet now and then."

This had its comic side, and the Governor-General himself was amused, reporting the eccentric ways of his Commander-in-Chief to Sir John Hobhouse, the President of the Board of Control. But a very serious affair was to bring down on Charles's head many abusive and anonymous letters. A trooper had actually called his Colonel a coward. At the court martial he was sentenced to transportation. As has been said, Charles attended courts martial in person. Believing the man to have spoken in a fit of drunken rage he revised the sentence. The man returned to his regiment, whereupon the Colonel committed suicide.

Charles felt very strongly that the regiment thought their name had been dragged in the mire at Chillianwallah, so that their " spirit was broken ". In a few words to restore their self-respect, he said he had " full confidence in them ". According to him they " went mad with joy " and there were shouts heard in the barrack all day after he had spoken. On another occasion at Karachi an officer had blown out his brains after being severely reprimanded by Charles for "gross neglect of his sick men". "I gave it well as he most richly deserved," he had said on that occasion.

There is a certain callousness here which seems foreign to his nature, but it must be remembered that the care and love for his soldiers was not some vague sentimentality leading nowhere. It was the tendency and desire of the whole man towards a certain goal. For it he laboured ceaselessly with all his heart, with all his strength. Rightly or wrongly Charles did not reproach himself for either suicide. It must be remembered that in those days there was none of that glib psychological talk to which we are now accustomed. Charles from childhood had been embued with the sense of *noblesse oblige* : that an officer could let his men down in sickness or on the field was unspeakable.

He writes : "It is lucky for me, my dearest Caroline, that I am not so sensitive, for between Lord D.'s reprimand, the Duke's opinion, the attacks on me about the suicide (with which I have no more to do than you have, except that a mad man fixes on anything to hang his acts) I should 'fret my guts to fiddle strings' . . . But being right is a wonderful tonic, and one laughs at what can do one no harm, I am now so used to ill usage, that I only think 'can it spoil dinner? sleep? breakfast? or reduce my pay? No!' Then Government, Court, Duke and Governor-General may all go to the devil!"

It is startling, even painful, to hear Charles alluding to the Duke in this fashion. Can this be that young soldier at Bussaco, who when the Duke enquired his name as he was borne bleeding past him, waved his hat and tried to mumble through his shattered jaws, "I could not die at a better moment"? Could it be that elder man who had vowed after the Duke's praise, "The hundred-gun ship has taken the little cock-boat in tow, and it will follow for ever over the ocean of time"?

What use to blink the facts. At times it is hard to recognise the eloquent expression of the young in the ravaged face of the old, after life has done with us.

The fact of the matter was, Charles was now deeply involved in the affair which was to cause his eventual resignation. It is not edifying to watch a Governor-General and a Commander-in-Chief villifying each other, and dragging into their quarrel the almost legendary figure of the Duke of Wellington. The affair is so involved, the accounts on both sides so contradictory, that the truth is now impossible to disentangle.

For instance, Napier Bruce asserts in his life of Charles that Lord Dalhousie was the last person to quote the Duke's opinion against Charles, for he himself had said the Duke was an old twaddler, his mind was fast going, and it would be a good thing when he left the Horse Guards, but Dr. Rice Holmes declares that Napier Bruce offers no evidence for this statement, and that, on the contrary, after reading some memorandum by the Duke, Lord Dalhousie commented, " All he says is in my poor judgement very true and very good."

This is no place to go into the rights of the Wazirabad affair, but to avoid a great danger Charles had taken an unauthorised step, but then had not the Duke himself written : " On a station so distant and of such magnitude and political importance, you must necessarily act in a great measure from your own discretion " (and mark you, the Governor-General was himself at sea) but " the moment I did so ", writes Sir Charles in his memoirs, " I was reprimanded, and the Duke thinks Lord Dalhousie right . . . at least he says so in public, but privately I am told he says, ' This reprimand was shameful.' "

In a nutshell, when Lord Dalhousie was at sea for his health Charles took upon himself to suspend a regulation on the cutting of pay before the Supreme Council could meet. His reason being, he feared mutiny. To quote again from Napier Bruce, his grandson : " He had no suspicion that his conduct would not meet with general approbation. Lord Dalhousie had written to him, approving of the policy he had up to that time adopted in the treatment of mutiny. . . ." Charles had further consulted the instructions prepared for him by the Duke of Wellington about the distant station, quoted above.

He was separated from the Supreme Council by 1,200 miles. The whole sum did not amount to £10 a regiment.

Afterwards, Charles wrote : " Had an idea crossed my mind that Lord Dalhousie would regard this as a desperate effort to usurp his supreme civil power, willingly would I have paid the sepoys myself to save bloodshed. . . . But the *principle* ! That is the gravamen of the question. Yes, the *principle* must be considered. It is precisely that which let a Spanish king burn to death in the midst of his courtiers, because the official extinguisher of fires was not present."

One suspects that Charles's vivid mastery of phrase, his knowledge of history, and his great general ability were no help to him. They infuriated his enemies less gifted, exactly as at the present time another great man infuriates those of fustian words and woolly thoughts.

The Duke did censure Charles.

It was a staggering blow, a blow perhaps from which Charles never recovered. Charles . . . indeed all three brothers had worn the Duke as a plume as it were, since those Peninsula days when they were boy soldiers together . . . the Napiers who always got hit. . . . How often the Duke had singled them out . . . and only a few months back that terse remark, " If you don't go, I must."

The Duke said he saw no evidence of the danger to justify the step. Charles was never allowed to see the memorandum. (The Duke himself only saw just those pages which Dalhousie chose to put before him according to William.)

It is painful to think of Charles's state of mind. He tried to reassure himself. " I knew the Duke would turn upon me. His habit of supporting authority has grown too strong for a sense of justice ", but this does not ring true somehow. Wiser his remark, " I think, till I get clear of India, the less my family talk of the matter the better."

For he sent in his resignation. It was accepted with the same words he had himself used to the Directors in what different circumstances ! " The least said, soonest mended."

He had long wished to escape from that " vast orderly room, for that is India to the Commander-in-Chief ", but now one can only faintly guess at the hurt astounded feeling of the old soldier, as the staff on which he depended broke in his hand ; the sense of being let down before Lord Dalhousie, whom he had come to despise.

His panache was indeed stripped from him.

Bitterly disappointed over the progress of his mole : " The Mole in Kurrachee is more to me than all the wars I made in Scinde." His camel corps, his barracks : " I have just heard this day the Board have beaten me, and my new barracks are to be reduced from 30 feet to 24. This upsets the whole affair at once, and the soldier must die." It would have comforted him to know that in years to come, Florence Nightingale was to make his cause her own. What wonder Charles wrote to his sister that last Christmas : " I must wish you a happy Christmas, as happy as old people can expect ; the difference between old and young in this sort of happiness being that the young see unreal pictures before them, the old see real pictures behind them. You wish you had children, and think of all the pleasure of having them about you ; I see all the cares which you are ignorant of . . . the parting from them, for ever perhaps : aye, and the being with them, and it may be the more to bear for that. Well, I think of all the good and not the evil, and so enjoy life : I am as a sentry : sometimes it rains, sometimes thunders, but also sometimes the sun shines, and I wait patiently without a wish to quit my post, till the hour of relief comes : and with it ? God knows what. I do not."

That is very different from his usual certainty of a hereafter.

He was then on his last journey down the Indus before leaving India, but before that there had been some cheap and unworthy sneers at the Governor-General. He was the Laird of Cockpen ; he was " weak as water, vain as a pretty woman, or an ugly man ".

And Dalhousie himself was abusive. Bitterly, too, he wrote : " For six months at the risk of discontent and mutiny, *both of which occurred*, I have been doing my duty to the Company by getting rid of all extra allowance. By this order, the Commander-in-Chief has thrown down all I have been doing, yet I cannot reverse the order for the feeling is too feverish to admit of the Govt. disallowing an order for extra allowance to the Army in the Punjab, issued by its own Commander-in-Chief."

After all these years, does it matter so very much who was right and who was wrong ? The toys have long been shut away in their boxes. Let us only remember both these men suffered from acute physical pain, and both were acting according to the behests of their characters.

It may be remembered that many many years before, when George III, yielding to his mother's and Lord Bute's importunity, jilted Lady Sarah, she, after expressing natural vexation at being made " to look like a fool ", almost in the same breath grieves over the sickness and subsequent death of her squirrel. So now Charles, true son of that mother, breaks off from the anger in his diary to write : " I am most in grief at parting with my beautiful Arab Mosaic. He is my last, and is such a coaxing, playful animal, that it is hateful to sell him, and then my fat little pony Rajah. . . . How fond we do get of our beasts. . . ."

A lovable man.

CHAPTER 19

CHARLES LEAVES INDIA

1851

CHARLES left Simla on November 16th. It must have seemed to him that the river of his life was losing itself in sand. He writes in his journal: "After seventeen months of hard work, no thanks, and much abuse." Then he pulls himself up. "I am not half grateful enough to that Mysterious Power which has ruled my destiny. I cannot be satisfied that I am really grateful to God. I say so in prayer, and even feel so, but also feel that I ought to be a thousand times more so. . . . Ambition, vanity, anger, all struggle with what is right, and dissatisfy my heart with my own conduct. Well-doing is the remedy. I am angry with myself for not despising my enemies, and forgiving them: being right in what I have done, why should I feel angry with these enemies? Yet I do feel so, and spiteful withal, which is wrong."

But sore as he was feeling, the old warrior was not to quit India after all without a tremendous flourish of trumpets.

He stopped at Miani and Hyderabad to take a last look at his battlefields. O men of Miani!

And then, though with that miraculous telephony of the East all Sind knew that their conqueror was now out of favour, here came hundreds of Sirdars, hundreds of miles, each with their train of followers, to do him honour. On they came like a tumultuous sea, "Before you leave us for ever," they shouted.

Astounded, Charles caught hold of Rathborn, the Collector, demanding to know if he had had any part in this demonstration.

"If it is not spontaneous it would be to me disgusting, instead of the most gratifying honour."

"Sir Charles, upon my honour I have no more to do with it than you have, or any Englishman."

Then must Charles have surrendered himself to the intoxication of the hour.

What a picture ! At that season an edgy wind blows from the North, the sky is a blue diamond. Glittering clouds of dust must have been stirred by the hordes of mounted Sirdars, dust whirling to the very tops of the babul trees, dimming the blue of the sky. And the Sirdars themselves, riding short in their stirrups, wheeling and whirling their excited little horses, controlling them perfectly with those savage native bits which would have broken the jaws of any English horse. Shouting, laughing, talking, these Sirdars, like barbarian children, streamed alongside of Charles all the way to Kotri where his steamer, the *Comet*, again awaited him. These the same men who had fought against him, now salaaming, now shaking him by the hand, now talking so fast no interpreter could translate—once they had declared his kismet was a cubit longer than any other man alive, and how eagerly they presented to this Commander-in-Chief whom they knew to be out of favour (and Indians are sensitive to such things), they presented to him a magnificent sword. But not so magnificent as they had desired ! For the Chief Sirdar had headed the list with a sum of £3,000 to purchase it. It was the English Collector who insisted the total subscription was not to exceed £300.

Would Charles have been human did his heart not swell with pride ? Dalhousie ne'er had such a reception, and what of those who had accused him of " robbery, murder, dethroning innocent princes, refusing beds to princesses in labour, lying through thick and thin " ?

One can picture the old man struggling with mingled pride and emotion ; and when at last the wiry figure, so thin, so sharp, disengaged itself from the jostling crowds to go on deck, a loud cheer rose from the Baluchi battalion, to which the Sirdars themselves, and their followers, added their own strange attempt at cheering.

The paddle wheels churned up the water so thick with silt. The space between the steamer and the shore widened. There on that scarped bank the skewbald horses, the sun winking on silver encrusted bridles and flashing swords, the variegated colours of the crowds! Clouds of rising dust, rising excitement, yells of affection and delight. . . . What an answer to those yapping curs who had maligned him in Press, and in letter by name, and anonymously.

So Charles felt.

Bombay, too, was a triumph from beginning to end.

On the Apollo Bunder the Highland Regiment had received him.

"Men!" said Charles vehemently, "I have not had the pleasure of seeing you since you suffered so fearfully at Sukkur. I have never had an opportunity of telling you publicly, and to your faces, that an infamous falsehood was propagated respecting your march to Sukkur, by the lying papers of India. I tell you men, on your parade, that is an infamous, a damnable—a worse than damnable—lie . . . but the low lying papers of India never broke my heart, and they never will, and they may all go to the d—— !"

It was turning away from the pier after this outburst that Charles spied amongst the crowd a horse artillery man. Almost instantly, with that royal memory of his, Charles was grasping him by the hand. "Delaney, I am delighted to see you! How is your wife, and your dear little boy? How have you been since we met last? To what troop do you belong?"

Replying as fast as he could to this volley Delaney exclaimed: "Sir, I thought my heart would have leaped into my mouth when I saw you land!"

Charles cried delightedly to those about him: "Gentlemen! This fine fellow belonged to His Majesty's 22nd, and was my bugler at Meeanee, and when I had roared myself hoarse, and almost speechless, sounded many and many a cheering blast, such as a sound-hearted soldier in the hour of danger knows how to send forth to his comrades in arms."

The Delaney incident was reported by the *Bombay Times*, who added : " If only Sir Charles realised how much more pleasure the newspapers found describing those things which redound to his favour than to dwell on the opposite, he might think differently of them."

A great banquet awaited him at the Byculla Club, attended by all classes of Europeans and natives. On arrival Charles was shaking hands enthusiastically with all those of his old friends who could push through the crowds to get at him. He had complained of " no thanks and abuse ". But where was this ? Sir William Yardley, the Judge, was presiding ; the Chief Justice was there ; Pringle, Charles's successor in Sind, and many others. In that great seventy-five-foot dining-room, sparkling with lights, the tables were set out in a U, and when the dinner was over, into the new wide veranda with the race course dimly seen behind, ladies, Emily amongst them, came slipping in to hear the speeches.

One cannot help wondering how Charles was dressed ! The writer hopes in full uniform and medals . . . but when he had dined at the Military Club in Calcutta we read in the local paper : " Sir Charles arrived at ten minutes to eight. When I saw the jockey cap coming out of the carriage, I fully expected the tails of the ' blue Frock ' to follow, but I was glad to see otherwise."

Sir William's speech was extremely laudatory, concluding, " should our country ever again be assailed by her enemies may she always have the sword of a Napier to defend her, and my life on it she will not require the pen of a Napier to record his victories ".

Charles had prepared no speech, intending merely to rise and say a few words of thanks. But the enthusiasm carried him away. He spoke at length, concluding with these moving words : " This very day, fifty-seven years ago, I received my first commission as a boy, and girded on this sword, which was my father's sword, which for these long years has hung at my side :

I received that commission as a boy : your kindness has made me finish my career, rejoicing as a man."

His father's sword. Fifty-seven years.

Were the old man's bright eyes dim behind his spectacles ?

But more and more speeches were to follow. The applause was deafening, Charles had to speak again and again. He was in excellent form. Perhaps the toast that pleased him most was to " the lady who makes him happy and calls him hers ".

The embarkation ceremony was characteristic. Who but Charles would have come " galloping down the line " on horse-back. Perhaps it was the " Irishman's canter " up the drive home.

There were good-byes, shaking of hands, even the kissing of some ladies (he dearly loved a pretty cheek), all amidst the warmest cheers. The salute, and even louder cheers.

The *Bombay Gazeteer* wrote : " Immediately after the boat had passed the Honourable Company's ship the *Hastings,* a salute was fired from her guns, and several of the merchant ships followed her example. All the shipping in the harbour was decorated, and beflagged for the ' demonstration of respect and esteem for the distinguished General '."

There was plenty to think about on the voyage home. Above all, one suspects that Charles was dwelling on his meeting with the Duke. It has been said that men might worship the Duke, but they did not love him. But old Charles had always loved him, and in spite of his hurt, still loved him, and would love him to the end.

Then his last act before laying down his office as Commander-in-Chief had been bold, bold for any man, but particularly bold for one leaving under a cloud as he was. He had written a General Order condemning the extravagance and reckless expense of the Army in India. " To drink unpaid for champagne, unpaid for beer, and to ride unpaid for horses is to be a cheat and not a gentleman." His enemies would probably say he had done this out of pique, but this was no new idea of his. The writer has already quoted a letter of his to Colin Campbell, and in 1845 he had also written : " They think to be gentlemanly they should drink a certain quantity of wine, and as much beer as they can hold : that they should be insolent to black servants and have all comfort and great order."

Now he had spoken out in the plainest and most forthright terms.

His brother William received the following letter :

" DEAR SIR WILLIAM,

" We are, I may say, all with the exception of some few old East India Madrass officials, of opinion that Sir Charles Napier's Farewell Address to the Indian Army is the most important and ablest document ever published. I doubt whether the Duke would have the courage to issue so truthful a document. . . ."

This certainly is a mistake, for had the Duke not once declared that the demoralisation and misconduct of the British Army had surpassed anything he had ever seen. Right or wrong, no lack of courage there ! This had caused intense anger and bitterness at the time. Now the Duke, with his glittering military career, had been the most influential, the most outstanding personality in Europe, the idol of the day. Even such a man as Goethe had eagerly asked Eckermann if he had seen Wellington passing through Weimar on his way to Russia, declaring if so he had " beheld a hero ". Nevertheless, there was a frostiness in Wellington's character, a bleakness in his justice. He was the very opposite of Charles with his bonhomie. The Army might revere and admire Wellington beyond all men, but he did not inspire love except in a few of his staff. It was just possible that Charles, in his General Order, might rouse less bitterness than the Duke had done on occasions.

The Times, which incidentally had written critically enough of Charles, now had a long and approving article on the subject :

" We need not dwell on the energetic and straightforward style of the military moralist. Suffice it to say that Sir Charles Napier denounces in the most uncompromising terms the slip-shod code of ethics . . . no debt need be paid but a gaming debt, and act like a rascal if you please, so you shoot any man who calls you one . . . there must be some person after all to give the tone to the military society of India. It cannot come from below : it must, therefore, come from above. If the Colonels commanding regiments, and the field officers do not discountenance habits of reckless expense, where is rebuke, where reform to begin but with the Commander-in-Chief ?

" The young officer, the boy let loose from school, is the victim of an atrocious system. He is plunged at once into the midst of an expensive circle . . . affiliated to an extravagant mess, compelled, almost out of false shame, to drink costly wines, and give return ' Champagne tiffins ' . . . short of being a wonder of fortitude and self-control he must needs be drawn into the vortex. He takes up advances at the nearest bank at high interest . . . he borrows money from his friends, from his acquaintances, from his inferiors, and finally makes his appearance before a Court of Requests in as shabby a position as the meanest insolvent that ever received judgment from a Commissioner in Portugal Street. It is against this state of things Sir Charles Napier protests in his final ' order ' . . . and who shall say he has acted unwisely." But that the Order was not merely fault-finding *The Times* makes clear : " There are tributes to courage and endurance on campaigns . . . but nothing can be more unfavourable to the development of a heroic character than an Indian office in time of profound peace. . . ."

The concluding paragraph so illustrates Charles's own view of " the Happy Warrior " it must be quoted in full :

" He refused to recognise all claims to respect in mere fighting qualities. An officer may be the best shot, and the hardest rider in the regiment : he may be perfectly prepared to halt coolly under the fire of a battery or to gallop into the midst of a Sikh square ; but all these soldier-like properties only elicit from the Commander-in-Chief that the possessor of them is an ' officer '. He is Major or Captain or Lieutenant So and So by virtue of his being of his commission. As to being an officer *and* a gentleman, that is quite another matter. Before admitting his claims to such a character Sir Charles Napier requires to know if his fire-eating friend has kept his word inviolate, has fulfilled his engagements, has *paid his debts*. If this be not so, were he as brave a man as ever led a storming party, the Indian Chief has nothing for him but words of scorn and rebuke. He is a ' swindler ' and a ' rogue ' and a ' rascal '."

By March Charles had reached London. There he met the Duke. There were no explanations on either side. The interview was short. Charles writes off to William : " I was never so kindly, so graciously received as just now by the Duke : I thought he would have embraced me ! Will your Grace let me put your name on my card for the levee on Wednesday : ' Oh yes. Yes ! and I will go there, and take care to tell the Queen you are there, and she will be glad to see you safe back, and so am I, and so is everybody.' "

But Charles stayed no longer in London than he could help. He was ill. He was old. The cold tried him. These dinners are charlatanry, quackery ! What have I and the public to say to each other ? Nothing ! What do I want ? To be let alone ! My wish is to be out of the world all together."

In spite of his friends he felt he had gone out to India like a rocket, to fall down a dead stick. " All in my weak power has been done to show London world my dislike of its company and attentions," he writes cantankerously, " being made a lion of when I came back from Corunna nearly killed me with jaundice : my return from Scinde gave me another jaundice : my return from India all but killed me. I can't get rid of pain."

There is no pleasing him it seems.

His wife's life cannot have been easy. Copying out endless letters to William and others, sharing indignation at calumny, watching growing weakness, rebutting accusations. Possibly only a woman can enter into these trying days of hers.

They wished to bring him in as a Member for Bath. He refused. It would have been pleasant to give rein to his feelings of Ripon, and " to munch Dalhousie's head ", but long ago the Duke had once written to him : " After you have seen one or two sessions in Parliament, and will have obtained a knowledge of the mode in which questions are discussed, and business done there, you will probably be as astonished as I have been, how England came by her greatness."

No.   Charles would go down to Oaklands and grow cabbages. Go he did.

Creep into thy narrow bed,
Creep, and let no more be said !
Vain thy onset ! all stands fast,
Thou thyself must break at last.

Let the long contention cease,
Geese are swans, and swans are geese !
Let them have it how they will !
Thou art tired : best be still !

They out-talked thee, hissed thee, tore thee,
Better men fared thus before thee ;
Fired their ringing shot and pass'd
Hotly charged . . . and broke at last.

Charge once more, then, and be dumb,
Let the Victors, when they come
When the forts of folly fall,
Find thy body by the wall.

MATTHEW ARNOLD.

CHAPTER 20

DEATH OF THE DUKE

1852

IN going to Oaklands Charles seems to enter another room of the House of Life, as it were. . . . A room from which, as he might have observed himself, he would only leave in a " very awkward shaped palanquin indeed ".

But that is not to suggest he was defeated, or that he was not taking the keenest interest in his life of a country gentleman.

As one muses on his life, so vigorous, so vibrant, one seems actually to share those scenes in which he had taken part. It is not only the dramatic hours, but trivialities standing out of the distance of years, much as the sun picks out the gilt weather-cock from a faraway steeple, or perhaps the glisten of a car's window moving along between the hedges of an unseen road. So from the Peninsula it is not only Charles's shocking wounds one remembers, but we are concerned too for Blanco : " A hundred miles with only three hours rest, and barely a bite to eat, did he carry me coming to the army. My fear was that it would kill him, but that was better than being too late for the action expected at Conduixa. Poor fellow, I kiss him, and coax him, but that does not make up for no oats."

Likewise Sind. Miani and its carnage, the irrepressible Mc-Murdo and his single combats too ; yes, but the smell of camels, the blistering glare, perhaps even that poor little child " who has just come to my tent with his arm all bloody, having been bitten off yesterday by a crocodile. The poor child bears it admirably. I have sent him to Kurrachee, poor little fellow.

He seems about ten years old, has no father nor mother. The world has gone hard with him, but I hope it will be better now, poor lad. He shall go to school, and if he learns English, he can earn his bread in a place where interpreters are few."

So now at Oaklands. It is without feelings of anti-climax we accompany Charles and his wife about the little estate she has found for him. She sees to the farm, but Charles rather thinks he will keep the drains in his own hands ! There is much unemployment, and with heart compassionate but anxious to avoid any feeling of charity, Charles takes on fifty men instead of the necessary four. But we may feel sure there were explosions of wrath and bad language at any scrimshanking ! He is angry, too, over the shooting of his Pyrenean sheepdog Pastor. A clergyman is brought forward to say the dog was dangerous, and Charles, affecting a tone of great solemnity, said : " The reverend gentleman entered my premises for the avowed purpose of converting my maidservants to his peculiar views. Pastor, my dog, thinking perhaps from his name that he was the rightful guardian of the maids, barked and advanced hostilely, as was his duty. Instantly the reverend gentleman extended his umbrella, bearing it like the seven-fold shield of Ajax, and fled for protection and consolation to the dairymaid. Poor Pastor remained victor without a blow struck, and now after his death, his defeated enemy reviles him : it is not generous."

This was typical of his sardonic humour. So, too, the entry : " I am again unwell and wish to be like the cockroaches, kept by a man to prove that insects have not our feelings ; he disembowels them, stuffs them with cotton and they run about, happy as princes . . ."

There is not much humour, however, in his feud with Outram and John Jacob ! He had publicly called Outram " a liar " and is expecting to be called out. That duelling has long been illegal and that he himself is over seventy years of age matters not a jot ! He does, however, express his fear that McMurdo, so loyal, so touchy in defence of his father-in-law, may meet Jacob at Sukkur. " For if so there will be a fight."

But in spite of these tempests and uproars there are still happy and vivid moments in his life.

All centres round the " little Ogre of Oaklands ", that broad-shouldered beautiful boy of Emily's he had wished to get out of India. The darling child ! Little Charley, called after him. The boy is to inherit Oaklands, and a little oak tree has been planted for him.

A few miles away lives his cousin Charles Napier, the Admiral, that same Charles who had cried out to him to dismount at Corunna and who had written so strange a letter to the First Lord of the Admiralty. " I'm having fun with Black Charles," declares Charles in his journal; " he told me to cut down some fine fir trees, saying they looked like poles for monkeys, but liking trees I told him I would buy monkeys for my poles. Then he ridiculed my new water tank, saying my fish would be queer ones : I said I would put him in, and he would be the queerest fish there : it is surrounded by cherry trees, and therefore I call it Pondecherry. . . ."

Being so near Portsmouth, Charles takes interest in sailors as well as his soldiers. " It makes me, when I go into Portsmouth, inclined to take the first soldier or sailor by the arm, and walk with him, certain of knowing how to talk to him of matters of which he is familiar, and which would interest him. If he is clean and smart I picture him as he would be in action, his mouth black with gunpowder from biting off the end of his cartridges, his hands also black and bloody, his eager animated eyes bent fiercely on the enemy, and prompt to do my bidding : firm of frame, armed for the work, and of ready courage to follow and support me in all ! Then it is I feel I can never do too much for them, and soldiers always know what their officers' feelings are towards them."

But these philosophical musings are now savagely torn apart, for Charles was to write in his journal : " My Emily has lost her little boy Charles. How proud I was of that child, bearing my own name, and I, like a fool, thinking he would inherit this little estate. . . . I doted on that little child. I would have given my life for him, and now he is gone. . . .

" I cannot kill his little oak, and yet it gives me sad thoughts. . . .

" I doted on that little child. I would have given my life for him, and now he is gone. . . ."

That most bitter cry wrung from him, Charles goes on: "There is a loss never out of my mind, but neither have I nor do I worry others with my grief. A fair time must be given to sorrow, and then the selfish feeling should be put down. This child is in heaven; what have I to grieve for on his part?"

The old man was as good as his word. A day or so later he is attending a grand dinner given to him by the Freemasons of Portsmouth. Later he is working himself into a rage reading Lord Grey's speech, when as Lord Howick he had stated that God held Charles's conduct as stained with wanton and unnecessary blood-spilling, and that if he were thanked by the House it would share in his damnation. But humour is constantly present in spite of sorrow and rage, and without pause from this Charles notes in his journal : " Pamela has been here ; when the devil tempted St. Dunstan in the form of a beautiful woman, he no more took hold of her nose with a pair of tongs than I would. Depend upon it he had a daughter by the she-devil, and Pamela is certainly a descendant of hers : for nothing else could be so agreeable, so pretty, so wonderful as she is."

Now this particular Pamela was the child of Charles's ill-fated cousin Lord Edward FitzGerald, who had married Pamela, the lovely daughter of Madame de Genlis and Philippe Egalité.

No wonder Charles was bewitched.

For old and worn as he was, that deep delight in children, in a pretty woman, in animals, in planting a garden, never failed him. It was as though Lady Sarah had tossed those traits of hers, like a garland, over a lion's neck.

Yes. He was good as his word. "The selfish feeling should be put down. The child is in heaven. What have I to grieve for on his part?"

So he busies himself with public affairs, squeaking his quill across the paper with a vigour quite astonishing in one of his state of health : " I am getting on with my book but I need not say how pain disheartens me." He writes a treatise on the defects of the Indian Government which by and by was to raise a storm. " Regimental officers are overwhelmed by work which should be done by adjutants, but much of it should not be done at all ! Every orderly room is now a little War Office." He continues to say the changes he would have made had he stayed on as Commander-in-Chief. He speaks of the great age of Lieut.-Colonels and Majors, averaging over sixty and worn out with climate and Indian life. He would have compelled commanders of regiments to give in diaries of the manœuvres they executed daily. " Distances are so great the Commander-in-Chief has no means of knowing what goes on without such diaries. . . . Very little has been done by me about drill because it appeared silly to nibble at such a gigantic job. Court of Directors, Governor or General, old officers, the Press and the Whig Government all against me and in league."

At times he felt he had ploughed in sand.

All this was of interest to soldiers, but now came the rousing letter on " The Defence of England by Corps of Volunteers and Militia ", to the Members of Parliament. For with the general peace of 1815 the local militia and the volunteers had melted away, and there was the possibility of French invasion. From Lord Hardinge Charles had learned there were no volunteers, no reserves, no adequate south coast defences, and only 7,000 men to meet the French if they landed. " If we are invaded the country will have nothing but their eyes to weep with : all will be devastation." The Duke himself was seriously concerned. He prayed " not to live to see such horrors ".

So Charles continued to wield his pen as furiously as he had wielded his service sword.

" But we have the Duke, you will say. Ay, fortunately, we have the Duke, and for that reason I write this letter . . . for my part I have no disposition to sit down unresistingly till a

French General of Brigade walks into my house, and cleans his boots by kicking me out of it."

Charles urges all to support the Duke, to call on their neighbours to arm. He stresses the importance of simplicity of dress, and drill, of constant practice at target and marching. Gamekeepers and labourers should be their comrades, urges this forerunner of the Home Guards. " Should you require to throw up a breast-work with the spades and pick-axes, they will be more handy than yourselves. . . ."

But in his journal he adds sadly : " But where the Duke is not attended to, speaking is hopeless, who will be heard ?" adding words once spoken by Sir John Moore : " I hope that all will not happen that may happen."

He was still indefatigable in writing his journal. Two hours after his carriage was overturned, both thrown, and his wife picked up senseless, he was describing the incident, and the very next day is off to the big dinner at Preston, given annually " to the old Peninsular pensioners who sit below the salt, the gentlemen who give the dinner above ". It is clear from the following he enjoyed himself :

" I found the 50th there, and was obliged to dine at my old mess : great speechifying of course. We sat down 200 gentlemen and 450 pensioners : rather a large dinner ! After the cloth was removed, all the medal men of the 50th Regt. were admitted to stand around and hear the speeches ; and in that immense room full on six hundred British soldiers were assembled, and not one without a medal on his breast, and some with two, with three, with four—all with wounds. The 50th men were, except myself, young. . . . The old 50th took the horses off, and dragged the carriage I was in a long way : then the old pensioners took up the shouting ; and when we reached the town the people took it up, and I entered Preston in such triumph I was ashamed. When the 22nd met me at Dugshai I did enjoy their greeting and shouting, because we had fought together, and men and officers knew that I led them honestly in fight, but here I am taken on trust like many a bad shilling."

He was pleased.

Old and too often suffering, yet now his blood must have warmed at the memory of that eagle youth through whose veins the blood had leaped so exultingly. Yes, his life was still plaited in with the glorious days of the Peninsula. Only a few months ago—on the anniversary of Miani to be exact—he had received a letter from an English clergyman actually written forty-three years before ! It was directed to Major Charles Napier at Corunna and asked after his wounds. It told him that his note, written from the battle to his mother Lady Sarah, had been safely received, having been forwarded by a French Captain " for the people in Paris were so kind to all prisoners ".

Now Charles had seen his own note years ago, for his mother had shown it to him on his return. But from whence had this forty-three year old letter now appeared ? Faded though its ink, it linked him right back to the youth he had once been, so eager, so gallant, so fired by the example of the ancient heroes in whose company he had lived since childish days . . . a youth he saw again in his impetuous son-in-law McMurdo.

Susan and McMurdo were on their way home from India. Unfortunately Outram and his wife were to travel on the same boat ! When McMurdo was asked to change ships, he refused, observing that he disliked brawling before ladies, but he would not suffer any offensive language about Sir Charles, so a guarantee must be given with the alternative of a duel.

It was not McMurdo who changed ships.

Trivialities, but serving to show how great a difference lies between 1850 and 1950.

And in 1852 the Duke of Wellington died.

It must have seemed to Charles that the bottom had dropped out of life.

The DUKE !

The constant companion to his imagination. The riband he had worn in his coat !

There is no mention of the Duke's death in Charles's journal

216

nor in existing letters. Not one word. William implies this
was due to pique. It may be so, but the writer of this book
finds it hard to believe that Charles's life-long hero worship had
evaporated at rebuke. William was vindictive. Charles was
not. It seems more likely that this unexpected silence was
because the event was too much. Charles was overwhelmed.
Surely that sentence, written some time later, gives the clue :
" I cannot get rid of his face as I saw it young in battle, and old
in peace."

It must be remembered that on the occasion of Lady Sarah's
death, his beloved mother, to whom he was constantly writing,
to whom he referred all his plans to the time of her death, there
was this same silence.

It was only six days before the Duke's death that Charles
had written from his bed : " Internal ulcers won't bear being
pooh-poohed. I have been lying in great pain, and been very
low, and in great danger."

Nevertheless, ill as he was, old Charles got up, went to London
and took his place as a pall-bearer at the funeral.

The body of the Duke had been brought up to London. The
Duke lay in his coffin in the Great Hall at Chelsea. Two
hundred thousand stricken people passed before it.

Here was death not on the battlefield, as he would have wished,
but in its most awful aspect. Pomp. Gloom. Grandeur.
Crape, and black trappings. The massive swaying funeral
hearse, with its quivering plumes. Complete negation of light,
of vigour, of hope.

The procession crawled through the packed streets to
St. Paul's, the stunned multitudes heard the tramp of boots
beating through the music of the massed bands, and the distant
boom of guns. But they themselves were stricken into silence.
There was something crushing, something ominous about that
silence.

Never again would they see the neat figure of the Beau with
his silver head, and beaked nose, constantly putting his fingers
to his hat, as every man had raised his own in homage.

They were awed as though feeling this was the end of an epoch.

This pomp ! This panoply ! Was Charles thinking what connection had it with the Duke who had stretched himself out on the field under his cloak with his men, who when asked his opinion of Napoleon replied briefly, " Wasn't a gentleman."

What connection had it with the Duke who, when some fussy old gentleman took his hat off and began to speak of his happiness in assisting the greatest soldier England ever had, over a crowded thoroughfare, barked, " Don't be a d——d fool."

What connection had this great creaking top-heavy funeral car with its quivering plumes, with the man who only a few mornings before, lying in his narrow camp-bed, had asked his valet :

" Do you know where the apothecary lives ? "

" Yes, Your Grace."

" Then send for him, and let him know that I should like to see him. I don't feel quite well, and I will lie still till he comes."

And twelve hours later expired.

Beneath the dome of St. Paul's the bier, and round it these grieving old men, warriors who had followed their Chief through battle.

Which were the memories blown like bright autumn leaves before Charles's eyes ?

Busaco ? He a stripling, his place by Wellington, the fire so severe all the staff had dismounted but himself, the one man in a red coat.

" No ! This is the uniform of my regiment, and in it I will stand or fall this day." So he had cried. The bullet that had smashed and shattered his face. The Duke as he was borne by. " Who was that ? " And Charles, waving his hat, just able to mutter, " I could not die at a better moment." Or was it those words written in the Duke's own hand, " The two glorious battles of Miani and Hyderabad." Or perhaps it was the old man laughing, " Pooh ! Pooh ! Don't like enemies. If you don't go, I must."

And then the Duke, who in spite of his censure had yet welcomed him back so warmly, so affectionately, saying, " Yes ! Yes ! " he would be at the levee. " I will go there and take care to tell the Queen that you are there, and she will be glad to see you safe back, and so am I, and so is everybody. . . ."

" I was never so kindly, so graciously received as just now by the Duke : I thought he would have embraced me . . ." Charles had written.

And now rousing him from these reveries the startling, the inexplicable stir and movement of the coffin as eerily it began to descend into the vault at his feet, drawn by some unseen agency.

" The Most High Mighty, the most noble Prince. Arthur, Duke of Wellington . . ."

What had Charles exclaimed years ago in Sind, when receiving high praise from the Duke ? " The hundred-gun ship has taken the little cock-boat in tow, and it will follow for ever over the ocean of time. . . ."

CHAPTER 21

DELANEY'S BUGLE

1853

HANGING about at the funeral had been chilly. Charles was concerned that "the poor old fellows" from Chelsea had not been cold, but the Adjutant-General was able to assure him that they "were very warmly clad, having two cloth waist-coats . . . cloth both back and front, and thick warm cloth coats and a great coat".

That Charles himself had caught a severe chill did not seem to matter so much.

Anyway, it had to be put resolutely behind him just as the death of the "ogre" and then the death of the Duke. *The Times* had said of the funeral: "They saw that eagle face, that bold strong eye, and felt there was still a mighty man of battle before them . . . the next in genius stood by the bier. . . ." And much remained to be done. For though Charles's letter on the "Defence of England by Corps of Volunteers and Militia" had been the last service he could do for his Chief it had still to be followed up: fresh blows to be driven on the head of the nail.

We find Charles writing such sentences as these:

"I know England, if prepared, can fight the world. I know also that, as she is she cannot resist 20,000 French troops thrown on her southern coast. . . . The Duke's death had added largely to our danger. Our people cannot get sailors . . . the French armies are working double tides to increase their navy, and finish the railroads leading to their ports. The people of Portsmouth swear a large body of men daily practise embarking and disembarking near Cherbourg. . . . I may have means to get away with my family and save my life, but what is to befall the poor? Murder, rape and arson! and this because our government do not at once place us as we ought to be, strong as a rock against waves. . . . We are doing something, but very little. I do not know that the Emperor means war. . . . I think not willingly, but if he does, and finds us unprepared, God help us, the results will be horrible . . . it will be suddenly and powerfully, not without a declaration of war, but as Frederick the Great said, ' Give me the money to make war, and I will buy a pretext for half a crown.' "

He writes to Lord Ellenborough in the same vein, constantly harping on the helplessness of the poor in case of attack. Practical as always, he is thinking out details which afterwards enabled McMurdo to do much to re-establish the volunteer movement. He goes into minute detail that when the Royal Marines were increased, there should be two large camps of instruction raised in which militia volunteers, marines and regulars should assemble. Forestalling criticism he declares: " I know the volunteers could not encamp permanently; but those near the camp could join in the first exercises, and those more remote could come the night before and sleep in standing tents kept for them, have next day's exercise, sleep a second night and march home the third day. Doing this even once in the year would teach the men what a field life is; it would teach them to pitch and strike a tent, and mess in squads, etc. In short, a corps after a night in camp would be twice the value next day." And he goes on to say that by such details a confident spirit would be raised that can do work " and is not produced by nonsensical boasting and singing—Britannia rules the waves! which would not be very strong after the first shot".

With his usual twist he goes on to say that his house and the Admiral's are too near the coast, and that Black Charles is selling his. " I shall not do that," says Charles. " But expecting an invasion, as I am too old to fight now, I mean to put on a red nightcap, and sit at my door with a flannel petticoat over my knees, a black draught in my hand, and my feet in hot water, awaiting the arrival of a French General of Brigade. ' *Je suis un pauvre ancien militaire, Monseur. Ayez pitié de moi,*' and Oaklands shall be called Frogmore in compliment."

With all this martial planning it must not be supposed that Charles's personal affairs were not running briskly along as the waters of the Rhône and Arve sweep along green and blue side by side though unmixed. He took keen pleasure in his little estate, and though interrupted by pain and illness yet there were visits from dear brother William, and Sir Colin Campbell, his " fellow criminal ", for Sir Colin had resigned his command in disgust because of the whole frontier policy of Government, and the interference of " politicals ". Then Charles was interested in the Peace Society, which he respected because of the sincerity of its members, though he adds : " But reason tells me to defend ourselves is the real way of keeping peace." The writer mentions this because too often Charles is regarded as an incorrigible fire-eater, which he was not, as the next quotation will show. Writing to Lord Ellenborough he says of the Burmah campaign : " We have made a war with Burmah for £90 10s. 6d. and it will cost far above a million . . . We provoke our neighbours, and I must say we have always been too ready to do that, being far too ready to meddle with other people's affairs." Words that may seem strange from his pen, but it is well to remember that Charles, on going out to India, had written : " What right had Lord Auckland to depose Dhost Mahomed ? It was a scheme of self-seeking merchants that caused the war, and we have caught a tartar . . . and Cabul retaken, what should follow ? Perhaps if a noble, generous, not a vindictive warfare be pursued by our troops, as I sincerely hope, it might be very practicable to retire immediately with honour from Afghanistan, leaving a friendly people behind us. The Afghans are a noble race, and although their mode of warfare is abhorrent to civilisation, a sanguinary inroad would be disgraceful to us, and would not give them more humane ideas."

It may be argued his ideas on Sind were very different.

But in spite of all these interests the candle was beginning to

burn low. In January he writes from London : " I have no
heart to keep up this journal. Long ago Solomon told the
world that all was vanity ; so we need not regret the approach
of its closing on us." He continues : " Here we see the young
running after courts and balls and parties which is natural as
they see no end to life . . . but the old here seem as eager as
the young. Well, it is a curious world, and the most difficult
thing I find to account for is myself." But the flame, sinking
though it is, gutters and flares up. He immediately after this
writes of an old Mrs. Power of 109 who " lately walked six or
seven miles at a stretch. We are making a great offer at Methu-
selah ! " And that spring he was corresponding with Lord
Ellenborough over the question who has the right to command
when naval and military are acting together. Charles asserted
that this was of the highest importance, giving an account of
his own experiences in 1813 when fighting the Americans.

Then, too, he was corresponding with Lord Hardinge, en-
closing an official letter to forward to the Secretary of State.
For he had just seen that the *Gazette* mentioned a number of
officers had received the C.B. for their good conduct in the
Kaffir war. Now Charles had long been hoping for this honour
for McMurdo, who had been head of the Quartermaster-General's
dept. in Sind for five years, who had prepared the march from
Sind to Bahawalpur, who had served at Miani and Hyderabad and
the Hill Campaign, been wounded, yet never quitted his duties.

This application failed. And what is more, Hardinge himself
presented Outram at Court.

To William, Charles writes :

" Is this consistent ? I feel indignant, for I, too, have a letter
from him about Outram pretty nearly to the same effect as that
written to you, one expressive of the greatest contempt and
disgust. Yet now he presents him at Court."

It was too much for the old man. Shortly after he took to
his bed. He turned to Oaklands as a sick dog turns to its kennel.
Still abed he travelled there, settling in in the large ground-
floor room he had had built for himself and his treasures.

He lay on his low Indian camp-bed, with its short screw-in ivory legs whose gold patterning was now growing dim. His eyes could rest on Baluchi spears and sabres and old matchlocks : on the Baluchi shield darkened, and stabbed by many bayonet thrusts. The faded colours from Miani and Hyderabad hung there, and there, too, were his four treasured swords.

There was his father's sword he had worn at his side since a lad.

He said : " I took up my sword at eleven years of age, and I now sheathe it at seventy-two with honour. I have never stained it by a dishonourable or a mean action, or by a desire to use it for my own aggrandisement. I have served my country zealously and honourably, but my chief aim has been to protect the poor soldier. I may have to reproach myself for some things, but not for my regard for the soldier's welfare : tell them so, Montagu, you who have followed me. Yet even in that I had to check myself, lest my bitter enemies should say I courted popularity with the soldiers. I only strove for their rights."

Times have changed. It is doubtful that any man would thus speak in these days ; but we know that Charles was sincere in doing so.

There, too, was the sword of honour presented after his American warfare ; the sword of honour presented by Lord Ellenborough ; and the sword of peace the Sirdars of Sind had given to him in excited affection and gratitude, after galloping and escorting him in clouds of white bright dust to the steamer at Kotri, which was to take him away from them for ever.

But alas ! these trophies could not keep his mind from constantly reverting to his detractors. Enough dirt had been thrown for some to stick. He begged Montagu McMurdo not to let his enemies pursue him after death. Familiar with the *Odyssey* as he was, did he think of that description of Odysseus whom the Trojans were besetting " as tawny mountain jackals surround a wounded stag that a hunter has hit with an arrow " ?

Sometimes the candle guttered up in a steadier blaze of light before death. Then he pretended he was getting better. But Dr. Scott knew him to be dying. And what were his wife's thoughts when Charles asked one day that Red Rover should be brought to his bedside?

And what were Charles's own thoughts as he heard the approaching hoof-falls of Red Rover? Red Rover, aged now, and who must be petted and chatted to, must be reminded of great days. . . . But the old charger was startled. He backed. Red Rover, always " so steady under fire ", backed. He would not approach his master.

He backed.

No more pretence now. Red Rover was led away, and Charles turned his head aside as the retreating sound of those still trim little hoofs died in the distance.

He begged that Red Rover should be cared for.

Unceasing pain was to follow, and confusion of thought. Thought not focussed, but wandering through veil after veil of memory as one lay superimposed upon the other. And always the brightest, the blue hills and woods and waters of Celbridge, and the sun-baked rocks of Cephalonia with its wild thyme and asphodel.

In the latter days of August, when the robin's plaintive treble is heard, and the first indefinable breath of autumn suggested, the family were assembled. And at five o'clock in the morning on August 29th, on his low camp bedstead, the wind blowing freely in upon him, our old hero died.

Then at the last Flame united Flame. For McMurdo, that impetuous, that passionate, that loyal McMurdo, snatched up the colours of the 22nd, waving them triumphantly, gloriously, so that he who had once said, " I never ask a soldier to do what I would not do myself," passed on, under the colours of Miani, " Where Generals had fought like privates."

And the echoes of Delaney's bugle sounded for him on the other side.

Sherborne, 1950.

APPENDIX

A FEW CHARACTERISTIC LETTERS

TO HIS FATHER

December, 1800.

Douglas, my brother aide-de-camp, told me yesterday evening that he had heard Sir James read to Lady Duff the letter he wrote to you advising you to get me leave of absence from the *Duke of York* on the plea that I was not fit for duty. I am sure you will not consent to do anything of the sort, which you must think, and which you may be certain I think, would be disgraceful and unbecoming the character of a British soldier. Sir James would not have done such a thing for himself, and could not have considered much when he proposed it.

[To prove his fitness to return to duty after his very serious accident in which the doctors feared he must lose his life, or at all events his leg, Charles, instead of taking the extended leave, mounted his cob and rode the 110 miles from Limerick to Dublin between sunrise and sunset.]

I dine with Sir James Duff to-day, so you see I must be very well. The doctors tell me that if the blood collected at the place where the bone was broken had not dispersed, my leg must be cut off. You must not, dear Father, tell this to Mother or anyone else.

LETTER TO HIS MOTHER

Cephalonia, 1823.

Lord Byron is here, and I like him very much. He is going to Greece, but it is hard to get there, harder to get back; and if the Turks catch him off goes his poetical nob ! He lives in his ship but comes ashore to my house . . . Lord Byron tells me he has touched up the Duke of Wellington in Don Juan. He means to write one hundred and fifty cantos, and he gets £2,000 a canto ! Good trade a poet's !

TO ENSIGN MURRAY

March 12, 1850.

When the Commander-in-Chief sees a man distinguish himself, and sees this with his own eyes, the said C.-in-C. must be the son of a bitch if he cannot break rules and show his regard. You have 8 officers on the staff, but none of the 6 ever saved 2 or 3 sepoys lives. You have, and I have appointed you to be Adjutant of the 13th Irregular Cavalry. . . . I wish I could do as much for the men that are with you. For with me officer and private soldier are all alike, but want of power is an undeniable excuse.

Yours truly,
C. NAPIER.

TO LORD ELLENBOROUGH

1843.

Your lordship's private letter, 20th ultimo, has given me very great pleasure. We were all longing for medals. There was not an officer or a soldier, from myself downwards, that would not have given up the hope of prize money, the decoration of the Bath, promotion, everything for the medal ! We rarely talk of the prize money; if it comes so much the better, if not we shall not break our hearts. I confess I did not feel as deeply as otherwise I should, and now shall, the high honour of the grand cross. I could not have met with satisfaction those who stood by me in battle, and received no honour save that which danger undauntedly met carries with it. Now all will be rewarded, and though my portion be larger so was my responsibility. While the officers and soldiers received nothing my ribbon sat uncomfortably on my shoulder ; *now I can meet Corporal Tim Kelly and Delaney without a blush.* And Lieut. Marston of the 25th N.I ! Casting himself between me and a big Beloochee, he received on his shoulder a blow intended for his general ; it cut nearly through the brass scales on Marston's shoulder ; the red ribbon will not grace mine more.

227

APPENDIX

TO PRIVATE JAMES NEARY

I have your letter. You tell me you give satisfaction to your officers, which is just what you ought to do; and I am glad to hear it, because of my regard for every one reared at Castletown; for I was reared there myself. However, as I and all belonging to me have left that part of the country for more than twenty years, I neither know who Mr. Tom Kelly is, nor who your father is; but I would go far any day to serve a Celbridge man; or any man from the Barony of Salt, in which Celbridge stands, that is to say, if such a man behaves himself like a good soldier and not a drunken vagabond like James J——, whom you knew very well if you are a Castletown man. Now, Mr. James Neary, as I am sure you are, and must be a remarkably sober man, as I am myself, or I should not have got on so well in the world as I have done: I say, as you are a remarkably sober man, I desire you to take this letter to your captain, and ask him to show it to your lieutenant-colonel, and ask the lieutenant-colonel, with my best compliments, to have you in his memory; and if you are a remarkably sober man, like I am, and in all ways fit to be a lance-corporal, I will be obliged to him for promoting you now, and hereafter. But if you are like James J——, then I sincerely hope he will give you a double allowance of punishment as you well deserve for taking up my time, which I am always ready to spare for a good soldier but not for a bad one. Now, if you behave well this letter will give you a fair start in life; and if you do behave well I hope soon to hear of your being a corporal. Mind what you are about, and believe me your well-wisher. Charles Napier, major-general, and governor of Scinde, because I have always been a remarkably sober man.

TO A YOUNG OFFICER

1844.

By reading you will be distinguished; without it abilities are of little use. A man may talk and write, but he cannot learn his profession without constant study to prepare, especially for the higher ranks, because he there wants the knowledge and experience of others improved by his own. But when in a post of responsibility he has no time to read; and if he comes to such a post with an empty skull, it is then too late to fill it, and he makes no figure.

Thus many people fail to distinguish themselves, and say they are unfortunate . . . which is untrue. Their own previous idleness unfitted them to profit by fortune.

TO LIEUT. (LATER LIEUT.-COL.) E. P. HARDING, 22ND REGT.

Oaklands,

October 28, '51.

MY DEAR HARDING,

My getting you the rank of Major is out of my power. I never asked for William's rank, nor even hinted at it ! It was a spontaneous act of the Duke's after-[illegible]. You are the man I am most anxious to serve, but how the devil I am to help you I do not know, for I will not ask for favours, as you know. . . .

LETTER WHEN COMMANDER-IN-CHIEF

SIR,

I have received your complaint, and your very sensible remarks on Mrs. Sergeant Rowe's letter. There is, as you say, nothing disgraceful in being a sergeant, any more than in being a tailor, which by your letter Sergeant Rowe appears to be. My opinion is that he who wears a uniform is of higher rank than he who makes it ; and the sergeant is, in my mind, much the highest rank of the two. All soldiers are gentlemen, whereas tailors are only tailors. But it seems Mrs. Rowe thinks otherwise, and prefers being a tailor's wife to being an officers wife. Now, in my view a lady has a right to hold her own opinion on these matters, and I am unable to give you any redress, because my commission as commander-in-chief gives me no power to make ladies apologise for being saucy ; it is an unfortunate habit they fall into at times, and more especially those who are good looking, which I suppose Mrs. Sergeant Rowe happens to be.

As to the sergeant having written this letter, that is neither here nor there ! Some husbands cannot help doing as they are ordered, and he may be innocent of malice. The only thing I can do, is to advise you to apply to your superior the collector and magistrate of Ferruckabad, who will represent the insult which has been put upon you as you state by Mrs. Sergeant Rowe ; and, if possible, Major Tucker will endeavour to persuade the lady to apologise for calling you an ass. More than giving you this advice I cannot do.

APPENDIX

Oaklands,
3 November, 1851.

. . . I got a letter from Mrs. Baghiscar, the widow of my Nicolas, saying she had got £10 sent home by my nephew George who was with poor Nicolas when he died. . . . I am very glad to hear of her, and if you will draw upon me at Cox and Co. for fifteen pounds and give it to her with the enclosed letter I will thank you. What age and sex are the two children? Can I put them to any school in Florence? If you can tell me of any way to assist them to earn their bread I will be obliged, for their father was a noble fellow. At the same time I cannot trust to the correctness of an Italian dame whose pleasure might rather take the line of ever increasing the number, than educating the children she has already, a straight line no doubt! Well, just tell me what I can do in any way, but the direct transmission of cash for her disposal, and if you can dispose of the £10 I send her, better than giving it to her, do so like a good fellow. . . .

INDEX

INDEX

Peace Society, 222
Peccavi, x
Peel, Sir Robert, 155, 170
Peninsula, 27, 28–52, 59, 53, 76, 115, 215–16
Philippe Egalité, 213
Pitt, 24–6
Plutarch's *Lives*, 19
Poona, 96–7
Poor Law, 72, 88, 91, 94
Pottinger, Colonel E., 105
Power, Mrs., 223
Press, attacks of, 120, 141, 143, 151, 167, 185–9
Prince Regent (George IV), 53
Pringle, succeeds Charles in Sind, 204
Prize money, 122, 127, 165
Punch, x, 184

Ranjit Singh, 103
Rathborn, Collector of Hyderabad, 201
Red Rover, 109, 121, 129, 132, 147, 172, 225
Red thread of honour, 159
Religion, thoughts on, 115, 144–5, 199, 201
Renaud, General, 35
Rice Holmes, Dr., 87, 138, 197
Richmond and Lennox, Duke of, 1, 6, 10, 11, 18–19, 26
Ripon, Earl of, x, 158
Robertson, Captain, 56
Rowarth, William, 91
Royal Marines, 221
Russell, Lord John, 171, 177
Rustam, 116

Sehwan, 148
Selwyn, George, 17
Sepoys, chivalry of, 129, 153, 175, 186
Sher Mahomed, 127–8, 131
Shorncliffe, 27, 53
Sikh War, 3, 160, 162, 175
Sind, 97–98, 101 et seq.; conquest of, 131; customs of, 136–7; heat of, 131–2, 194
Soap, 59, 180, 187–8
Sobraon, battle of, 161

Soldiers:
    devotion of, x, 35–6, 43, 124, 153, 161, 164, 203
    praise of, 118, 126, 130, 158
    solicitude for, 23, 25, 38, 53–5, 92, 111, 140, 163, 171, 188, 193–4, 199
    understanding of, 195, 212, 228
Soult, Marshal, 38, 170
Spur, silver, 37–8, 41–2
Stanhope, Charles, 27, 32, 37, 156
Steuart, Colonel, 139, 194
Stuart, Lady Susan, 13
Sukkur, Bukkur, Rohri, 108, 112, 117, 149, 160–1, 203
Suliots, 65–6
Sullivan, Tim, 22
Suttee, 135, 149

Talavera, 42
Tatta, 106, 139, 145
Thackeray, W. M., 178–80
Trevelyan, G. M., x
Tribesmen (hill), 146–7, 157
Truckee, 158
"Turban", the, 116

Umerkot, 128–9

Victoria, Queen, 94, 135
Volunteers, 21, 214

Walker, Colonel, 55
Walpole, Horace, 3, 12
Warren, Sir John, 58
Wellington, Duke of, x, 26, 44, 47–8, 51, 107, 137, 142, 150, 162, 170; summons Charles, 175–7; eulogy at banquet, 177; contradictory order of, 183, 192–3, 196–7; censure of Charles, 198, 205–6; touching reception of Charles, 208, 214–15; death and funeral of, 216–19
Westmorland, Earl of, 17
Whig policy, 142–3

Yardley, Sir William, 204
York, Duke of, 53

Zante, 83–4
Zenobia, S.S., 98–9

236